SOUTH
CAROLINA

American Historical Press
Sun Valley, California

SOUTH CAROLINA

An Illustrated History of

THE PALMETTO STATE

Mr. & Mrs Lawrence Starkey
320 Ferry Land g n w
Atlanta GA 303028
with best Wishes for Continued Happiness
Whitey Lander

ERNEST McPHERSON LANDER, JR.
& ARCHIE VERNON HUFF, JR.

Library of Congress Catalogue Card Number: 2007936588
EAN: 978-1-892724-56-4

Bibliography: p. 248
Includes Index

CONTENTS

PREFACE

The purpose of this volume is to give the reader a brief, illustrated history of South Carolina. For the text we have depended mainly on reliable secondary sources. For illustrations we have relied primarily on paintings, drawings, and portraits for the pre-Civil War years, except where historic buildings and sites were preserved long enough to be photographed.

The colonial years presented the greatest problems because authentic illustrative material for those years is scarce. There are few surviving portraits of early colonial South Carolinians and, to the best of our knowledge, only one late seventeenth century building has survived to the present. Most early colonial structures were built of wood and soon fell victim to decay, fire, or other destruction. Fortunately, preserved descriptions combined with recent archaeology have permitted artists to recreate some of these early structures with a reasonable degree of accuracy. As for backcountry people, their buildings and their way of life, authentic illustrations are indeed rare.

From the Revolutionary Era onward there is a considerable amount of illustrative material. Portraits of many prominent Revolutionary figures have been preserved, as well as many buildings. Of course, paintings and drawings of Revolutionary warfare are based largely on various artists' imaginations, sometimes many years after the events took place.

Beginning in the 1850s, *Harper's Weekly*, *Harper's Monthly*, *Frank Leslie's Illus-*trated *Newspaper*, and the *Illustrated London News* furnished fairly accurate pictures of Southern life and Civil War scenes based on drawings of artists on the spot. And with the advent of the Civil War a few photographers, practicing a new art, left an impressive record of wartime scenes and activities. Between that time and the end of the century, improved technology made photography increasingly popular. Professional photographers set up studios in cities and large towns ready to render their services for any occasion, whether a political rally or private wedding. Thus the wealth of photographs that have survived since the 1890s permits a more accurate picture of the last century than of the previous years.

In selecting numerous portraits, maps, drawings, and photos, first the historic value of the pictures and how well they would serve the text, was considered. Of necessity some photos of poor textual quality were chosen, especially in the early years of photography, because they were the best available on the subject at hand. Also, while recognizing the historical importance of Charleston and Columbia, we have sought to avoid overloading the text with scenes and personages from these two cities to the neglect of the rest of the state.

For many photos there is no accurate way to be sure of the exact date the picture was made. In such cases *circa* (about) is noted before the date.

This shrimp boat is at Shem Creek, in Mt. Pleasant. Shrimp fishing, an important business along the entire South Carolina coast, was started commercially near Charleston in 1924 by a Florida shrimper, Captain Regan. Photo by A. V. Huff, Jr.

Acknowledgments

In collecting illustrative materials I am indebted to many persons and depositories, both public and private. Without their generous cooperation in permitting duplication and use of their materials, it would have been impossible to produce this work. In a few cases I supplied photographs in my possession.

For significant contributions to the pictorial material herein I wish to thank Allen Stokes, South Caroliniana Library; Michael Kohl, Clemson University Library; Hurley Badders and Donna Roper, Pendleton District Historical and Recreational Commission; Gene Waddell and David Moltke-Hansen, South Carolina Historical Society; Kathryn Gaillard, Charleston Museum; Philip Racine, Wofford College; Horace F. Rudisill, Darlington County Historical Commission; Steve Richardson, Greenville County Library; Patricia Wilmot, Hartsville Historic Museum; Oliver Smalls, College of Charleston Library; Risher R. Fairey, Camden Archives; Martha Severens and Angela Mack, Carolina Art Association-Gibbes Museum of Art; Cherie Had, Dana L. Sawyer, and Ray Sigmon, S.C. Department of Parks, Recreation, and Tourism; Bruce Rippeteau and Darby Erd, S.C. Institute of Archeology and Anthropology; Henry W. Smith, S.C. Department of Agriculture; David Crosby, *Greenville News*; Catherine Horne and John R. Heiting, McKissick Museums; W.D. Workman, Jr., Columbia; Clayton Kleckley, Fort Jackson Museum; Kate W. Hood, Georgetown County Library; James L. Walker, Jr., S.C. Department of Highways and Public Transportation; Rodger Stroup, S.C. State Museum; James Childers, Security Federal Savings and Loan, Columbia; and Choice McCoin, Greenville.

Many other persons were helpful with information and pictures: Stephen Chryst, Anchor Bank of Myrtle Beach; G. Wayne King, Francis Marion College; Ronald Chepesiuk and Ann Evans, Winthrop College Library; Patricia Ryckman, Chester County Public Library; Penny Forrester, Pickens County Library; Donald P. Woodward, Hoechst Fibers Industries; Riley Stone, Donalds; Ralph Payne, Southern Bell; E.T. Crowson, Rock Hill; Russ Gantt, Easley; Sam McCuen, S.C. Department of Corrections; Walter Edgar, University of South Carolina; Percival Perry, Wake Forest University; Mrs. C.C. Cutts, Conway; Iva R. Welton, Bluffton; H.L. Sutherland and Mrs. W. Randolph Hawkins, Union; Jane Harrison, Abbeville; Robert Willingham, University of Georgia Libraries; Julie Zachowski, Beaufort County Library; Senator Strom Thurmond; Jerry L. Stafford, Santee Cooper; Janson L. Cox, Charles Towne Landing; Bruz Crowson, *Sumter Daily Item*; Bill Steiger and Robbie Goode, *Charleston News and Courier*; Lewis Moorhead, Anderson; Charles Hall, Museum of York County; Alice Skelton, Springs Industries; S. Elliott Puckette, Jr., Charleston; Bettylou R. Terry, S.C. State College; the late I. DeQuincy Newman, Columbia; Wilbur Meneray, Tulane University Library; Elaine Kirkland, Atlanta Historical Society; Robert F. Looney, Free Library of Philadelphia; T. Benton Young, Jr., Columbia; Rocco V. Lombardo, New York Public Library; J.M. Huff, State Development Board; Ed McAllister, Mt. Carmel; Donna Quaresima, Colonial Williamsburg Foundation; Joseph L. Young, Clemson University; James R. Lindler, Carlisle Associates, Columbia; Kirk Craig, Craig, Gaulden, and Davis, Greenville; Barbara Hodges, Ed Pinckney Associates, Hilton Head; and Jakie Lee of Lee, McCleskey, Miller, Hilton Head.

I also wish to thank Jim Martin, Clemson University photographer, and the staff of Clemson University Library for many services; the late Olivia Jackson McGee, Clemson, for paintings; Jim Mehserle, Clemson, for maps; and A.V. Huff, Furman University; Daniel W. Hollis, University of South Carolina; Robert T. King, University of South Carolina Press; David Moltke-Hansen; and my wife Sarah Shirley Lander for reading the manuscript and offering helpful suggestions. I am also indebted to the late Carl Julien for several fine photographs, some of which were reproduced in books published by the University of South Carolina Press.

Finally, errors are entirely my own.

This large beef herd could be found on the E.T. Gulledge farm in Wedgefield, Sumter County, in 1953. South Carolina beef cattle herds have increased 60 percent since 1940. Courtesy, Special Collections, Clemson University Library

Chapter I

Indians and the First Europeans

So far as we know, the Spanish were the first Europeans to set foot on South Carolina soil. In 1521 Lucas Vasquez de Ayllon sent an expedition from Hispaniola to explore the southeastern coast of North America. His mariners dropped anchor in the Winyah Bay area, traded with the hospitable Indians, and tricked a number of them into boarding the Spanish ships. The Spaniards thereupon abducted their guests and sailed away, beginning an unhappy relationship between whites and Indians in South Carolina that was to continue with little respite until the American Revolution.

Most Indian tribes within South Carolina during the colonial years have been classified as Iroquoian, Souian, or Muskogean on the basis of language. There were also a few Yuchian and Algonquian tribes and one tribe that remains unclassified, the Saludas.

The Iroquoians were Cherokees, who had about 50 villages over an area of 40,000 square miles in Tennessee, western North Carolina, northern Alabama, northern Georgia, and northwestern South Carolina. Their warriors, among the tallest and strongest of Indians, were estimated to number about 6,000 in 1735. Undoubtedly the Cherokees were the most influential tribe in South Carolina, if not in the Southeast. They were the last Indians to significantly resist white encroachment, fighting bloody wars from 1760 to 1761 and in 1776. Defeated in these conflicts, they were forced to give up all their South Carolina lands except a small strip along the state's northwestern mountain border, which they later surrendered.

A century and a half earlier, numerous tribes of Muskogean people lived south of the Santee. Most of these tribes were small and disappeared within a few years after the English settled at Charles Town in

1670. The most powerful of the Muskogeans were the Yemasees, near the Georgia and South Carolina coast. Influenced by the Spanish and the Creek Indians and feeling mistreated by the Carolina settlers, the Yemasees made a concerted effort from 1715 to 1718 to drive out the whites. This was the most serious Indian attack ever made on the province. After the war the Yemasee remnants fled to Florida.

Of the Souian Indians the Catawbas and the Cheraws were the most important tribes. They lived along the upper reaches of the Catawba and Pee Dee rivers, respectively. The Catawbas were said to have 1,500 warriors in 1700, but the number had dwindled to only 150 by 1787. The Catawbas were friendly to the Carolinians, except during the Yemasee War. By the time of the American Revolution the Cheraws appear to have been absorbed into the Catawbas. A few Catawba descendants live today on a small reservation in the southeast corner of York County.

Of the Yuchian stock the Westos were briefly of importance. They were fierce warriors living along the Savannah River, feared by other Indians and whites alike. In 1681 the white settlers, with some Indian allies, drove the warlike Westos from the province.

In general, the tribes in the lowcountry were numerous and small; in the backcountry, few and large. More than 40 tribes have been identified by whites as having lived in South Carolina.

One prominent authority on Indians commented that "war, pestilence, whiskey, and systematic slave hunts had nearly exterminated the aboriginal occupants of the Carolinas before anyone had thought them of sufficient importance to ask who they were, how they lived, what were their beliefs and opinions." As a consequence,

Seven "Chiefs of the Cherokee Indians" were taken from Carolina to England in 1730 by Sir Alexander Cuming, and were royally entertained there before signing "Articles of Friendship and Commerce." This contemporary print of the group is a copy of one in the British Museum. Courtesy, South Caroliniana Library

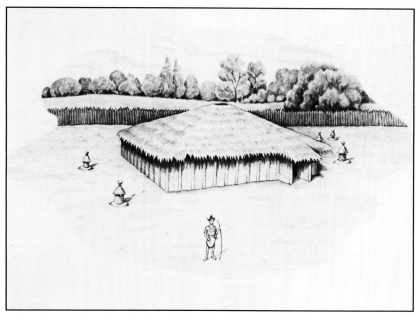

had a written language or metal implements prior to the coming of the whites. Their clothing usually consisted of skins, feathers, and leather moccasins.

Houses of the lowcountry tribes were generally round huts of cypress or cedar bark, often with tall palisades around each village. A large meeting house might be situated in the center of the village. The Cherokees, by contrast, constructed imposing buildings some 60 to 70 feet long and divided into compartments. Sometimes these buildings were two stories high. Construction materials consisted of sticks, posts, clay for plastering, and bark shingles for roofs, sewn together with wet rawhide. The Cherokees also had small conical-shaped winter houses covered with dirt. A large council house capable of accommodating several hundred persons was part of each village.

Evidence indicates that Carolina Indians enjoyed dancing, playing ball, and gambling. They believed in a variety of gods, or powers residing in animals or other objects. Their conception of the "Great Spirit" was apparently derived from contact with Christianity.

In daily routine Indian women usually performed the housework and tilled the fields, while the men bore the burden of the hunt and the defense of the tribe against enemy assault. However, Indian women often held high positions in the tribe. Indian government was essentially democratic; the chiefs acted as leaders rather than as dictators.

The Indians were charitable to their fellow tribe members; much of their livelihood was on a communal basis. They were likewise hospitable to strangers, including whites, until the latter began to exploit and abuse them. The whites' aggression led to a number of serious conflicts. Unfortunately for the Indians, the tribes were never united in their wars against the white Carolinians. In most conflicts the whites enjoyed some Indian allies.

The Indians frequently feuded with neighboring tribes for revenge or prestige or over trade with the whites. It was these wars, plus the whites' "firewater" and diseases, that decimated the tribes more than battles between the Indians and the whites.

Although relatively little is known about the Indians, their presence during the colonial era left a mark on white civilization, enduring far beyond that of occasional bloody warfare. South Carolinians relied heavily on Indians as guides, hunters, traders, and laborers. Indian crops and

Top: This Cherokee warrior is outfitted in a traditional costume. Drawing by Darby Erd. Courtesy, South Carolina Institute of Archeology and Anthropology

Above: This replica of an Indian temple was erected at Charles Town Landing. Drawing by Darby Erd. Courtesy, South Carolina Institute of Archeology and Anthropology

present-day knowledge of the early Indian civilization is not as complete as one might wish.

Although the Indian tribes in South Carolina came from at least five general stocks, they all shared traits in common. They lived in villages, hunted, practiced agriculture, and employed crude implements of stone, bone, shell, and clay. None

Theodore de Bry made this engraving of a Jacques Le Moyne de Morgues painting of Indians preparing a feast. Courtesy, Gibbes Art Gallery/Carolina Art Association

forest lore were invaluable to early white settlers, and many Indian words entered the English language.

De Ayllon's expedition to the Carolina coast in 1521, unfortunately for the Indians, stirred the Spaniard's interest in the region. He approached King Charles V for a charter to establish a colony there. In a grandiose undertaking, de Ayllon departed from Hispaniola in 1526 with about 500 settlers, including a few black slaves, plus many horses and a large store of provisions.

After a brief stay near the Cape Fear River, the colony moved southward to another location. Exactly where they established themselves is a matter of dispute. On the basis of Spanish records, historians usually locate the first European settlement in the general area of Winyah Bay and Georgetown, or some 25 miles south of that area.

Ill luck befell the settlement from the outset. Disease took a heavy toll, and de Ayllon himself died in October. The general misery which followed led to a mutiny against de Ayllon's successor; provisions became scarce, slaves attempted arson, and the winter of 1526-1527 was unusually severe. These difficulties induced the survivors, now reduced to about 150, to abandon the enterprise.

Hernando de Soto was apparently the next Spaniard to arrive in South Carolina. In search of gold, de Soto moved northward from Florida with a troop of soldiers

and reached the Savannah River a few miles below the fall line in April 1540. The Spaniards then marched as far east as the Wateree River. The Indians were hospitable and invited the white men to tarry; but de Soto, upon finding no gold, was soon on his way west. Another Spanish expedition, this one under Villafane, who bore the title of governor of Florida, briefly touched the Port Royal area in 1561 before sailing farther up the coast.

By this time the Spaniards seem to have lost interest in a settlement as far north as South Carolina. They were more interested in colonies elsewhere, some of which were proving to be lucrative. In the absence of a Spanish presence on the South Carolina coast, French Huguenots in 1562 attempted a settlement in the region. The Huguenots, who were Protestants, at that time were engaged in bloody civil strife with the Catholics, the dominant religious group in France, and in danger of complete subjugation. Huguenot leader Admiral de Coligny therefore organized an expedition under Jean Ribaut to settle a colony in Florida as a place of refuge for these persecuted Protestants. The French government approved the enterprise both as a potential solution to the Huguenot problem and as a move against Spain's New World empire.

The Spaniards meanwhile became alarmed, fearing for their small Florida colony at St. Augustine. They need not have been; Ribaut had only 150 men, and after

Hernando de Soto entered South Carolina in the spring of 1540 on an expedition in search of gold. Recent research indicates he may have traveled as far east as the Wateree River before turning west by way of the Blue Ridge Mountains. He died in 1541 shortly after reaching the Mississippi River. De Soto was probably the first white man to explore the interior of South Carolina. From Narratives of the Career of Hernando de Soto, *1866*

a brief stopover in northern Florida he sailed up the coast. The Frenchmen landed on what is now called Parris Island, built a crude stockade of logs and clay, called Charlesfort, and settled down to a life of idleness.

Meanwhile, Ribaut returned to France, promising to come back within six months with more supplies. The 30 soldiers who remained at Charlesfort took advantage of Indian hospitality to continue their leisurely ways. Instead of clearing land and planting crops, they depended on the Indians for food.

This strategy got the Frenchmen in trouble. Their storehouse burned at a time when their Indian friends were likewise short of food. Their autocratic and cruel leader, Captain Pierria, hanged one of their company for a petty crime and exiled another to a nearby island. Fearing for their own safety, the remaining soldiers mutinied, murdered Pierria, rescued their comrade, and deserted the colony in a leaky, makeshift vessel. The Indians, anxious to rid themselves of the parasitic visitors, willingly aided in the construction of the getaway ship.

A mid-ocean calm soon found the survivors without food. Their official chronicler leaves an account of how they resorted to cannibalism: "They agreed therefore that one should die to sustaine the others. Which thing was executed in the person of La Chere . . . whose flesh was divided equally among his fellows; a thing so pitiful to recite that my pen is loth to write it." The unlucky La Chere is the person who suggested they draw lots to see who would die. The survivors were later rescued and eventually reached France.

Not easily discouraged, Ribaut and Admiral de Coligny attempted another colony. This expedition included a much larger number of Frenchmen along with wives and children. They settled at Fort Caroline in northern Florida, an unfortunate location near the newly founded Spanish colony of St. Augustine. With a superior force the Spanish leader Pedro Menendez de Aviles, an ardent Catholic, wiped out the Huguenot colony, killing men, women, and children alike without mercy.

After eliminating the French at Fort Caroline, the Spaniards tried to maintain a presence on Parris Island for about 20 years. Due to Indian hostility their existence at that location was precarious. After Sir Francis Drake raided St. Augustine in 1586, the Spanish abandoned the Carolina coast completely. They did, however, maintain a few Catholic missions in Georgia for another century and, for four decades after the English settled Charles Town in 1670, they periodically threatened the new colony.

Above: Table Rock Mountain is one of the few South Carolina peaks that rise above 3,000 feet. The state's highest peak is Sassafras Mountain on the North Carolina border. It rises 3,554 feet above sea level Photo by Ted Ramsaur

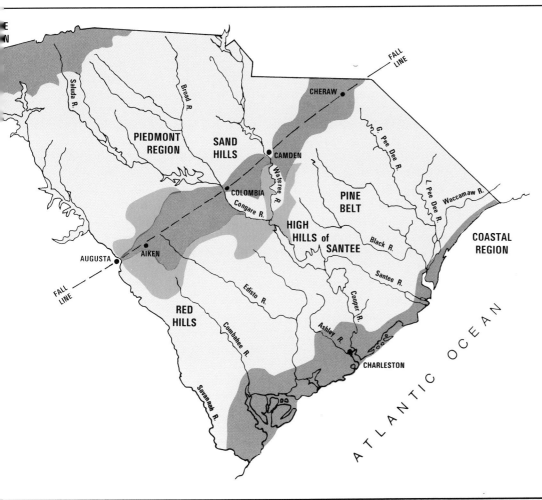

Left: The various geographic regions of South Carolina are shown in this map drawn by Jim Mehserle.

Chapter II

The Colonial Era: 1670-1763

For many years after the Spaniards left the Carolina coast, no other attempts were made to establish a colony in the region. In 1629 King Charles I of England granted a charter to Sir Robert Heath for a colony, but Heath made only a half-hearted effort to send over settlers. In 1663 King Charles II, recently restored to the throne, annulled Heath's charter and granted the same land to others. The significance of Heath's charter is the name he gave to the territory. He called it Carolana in honor of Charles I ("Carolus" in Latin).

In annulling Heath's charter, Charles II granted Carolina to eight well-known political leaders and businessmen who had aided in his restoration in 1660. The "Lords Proprietors," as the eight men were styled, were led at first by Sir John Colleton, a Barbadian planter. The other proprietors were Sir William Berkeley, Baron Anthony Ashley Cooper, Lord John Berkeley (Sir William's brother), Edward Hyde, William Craven, General George Monck, and Sir George Carteret. For these men Carolina was purely a business venture.

The 1663 charter was modeled on Heath's, and it granted the Lords Proprietors full rights over an area which included both North and South Carolina. Two separate colonies developed, and because of poor communications and the great distance between the two they established separate governments. The two settlements were soon referred to as North Carolina and South Carolina, and their development as distinct colonies was officially confirmed by the proprietors in 1712.

The charter contained the provision that the proprietors were to govern and legislate "with the advice, consent, and approbation of the freemen of the province." Nevertheless, with little active support from the proprietors, few settlers were attracted to the colony. A scattering of Virginians drifted down into the Albemarle region and a handful of New Englanders temporarily moved into the Cape Fear area. A few Barbadians, anxious to escape their overcrowded island, were also encouraged to try their luck on the Cape Fear River. After two years of hardship they gave up and returned to Barbados.

After several false starts and the death of Sir John Colleton, the proprietors were saved from utter failure by Baron Anthony Ashley Cooper. In 1669 he persuaded each proprietor to contribute 500 pounds sterling to start a Carolina settlement and give it initial financial support. With assurance of financial means, Baron Ashley Cooper laid plans for a colony. He received assistance from his philosopher and physician friend John Locke in drafting the Fundamental Constitutions of Carolina. This elaborate frame of government sought to establish a modified feudal land system and a "balance of government" between aristocracy and democracy. Although somewhat inappropriate for a frontier society, the search for "balance" had an influence lasting into the nineteenth century. The Fundamental Constitutions also contained several shrewd promotional devices to attract settlers, including cheap land and religious tolerance.

In August 1669, 3 ships and 92 passengers under the command of Captain Joseph West sailed for Barbados to pick up additional settlers and supplies. Only one of the three original vessels reached Carolina. The *Carolina*, accompanied by a small ship picked up en route, arrived at Port Royal in March 1670 for a brief stay. Fearful of the fierce Westo Indians and the Spaniards, the colonists decided to move farther north. In April they settled on the west bank of the Ashley River. There they

*Robert Johnson, son of Governor Na-
thaniel Johnson, served as the popular governor of the Charles Town
province under the proprietors,
1717-1719. His return in 1730 to
serve under the king is depicted
here. Courtesy, Bettman Archives*

This map of Charles Town was drawn by Edward Crisp in 1704. It represents the "Grand Model" designed by Ashley Cooper. He proposed a walled city with streets laid out in a perpendicular pattern. The streets in the old city today reflect the original plan. Photo by A. V. Huff, Jr.

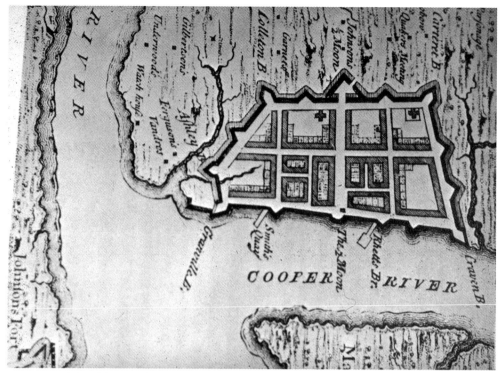

were soon joined by another of their fleet, the *Three Brothers*, that had been blown north to Virginia and overhauled by Spaniards off the Georgia coast.

Later that year only a formidable storm prevented a Spanish attack on the infant colony. The Spanish menace forced the settlers to live much like a besieged army garrison for the first few years.

The Charles Town settlement began with 148 people mainly of English background. They were a mixture of newcomers from England and colonists from Barbados. There were freemen and indentured servants, a few women and children, and at least three black slaves. The colony's chief attraction was land: 150 acres for each free adult male and lesser amounts for women and minors.

Once settled, the colonists began to clear small plots of land near the town and plant crops. The Barbadians soon learned that the Carolina climate was too cold in winter for their tropical crops. The newcomers were thus forced to shift their agricultural emphasis to crops for a temperate zone. This change notwithstanding, poor growing seasons in the early 1670s made it difficult for the Carolinians to produce sufficient food. Meanwhile, they embarked on other ventures: naval stores (tar and pitch produced from pine rosin), cattle raising, and most significantly, Indian trade.

The Carolinians secured alliances with nearby Indian tribes and even came to terms with the warlike Westos (whom they later crushed in 1681). Much of their early success in the Indian commerce was due to the guidance of Dr. Henry Woodward, an unusual adventurer who had lived with the Indians for several years just prior to the settlement at Charles Town.

By 1680 the colony had grown by about 1,000 people, with settlements beginning to spread along the Ashley and Cooper rivers. At that juncture colonial leaders decided to move Charles Town from the west bank of the Ashley to Oyster Point at the tip of the peninsula between the two rivers, the Ashley and the Cooper—a more promising port site. Present-day Charleston dates from that time.

The Carolina government was centralized under a governor, a council, and a popularly elected Commons House of Assembly. Nevertheless it was soon under the control of a group of Barbadians, eventually known as Goose Creek Men because of their settlements near Goose Creek, a tributary of the Cooper River. Strong Church of England followers, they opposed religious tolerance for dissenters. They opposed Baron Ashley Cooper's Fundamental Constitutions, traded with pirates, and sold probably more Indians into slavery than the settlers of any other English colony in North America.

In these matters the Goose Creek Men were frequently at odds with their overlords but managed to dominate the colony during most of the proprietary period. Whenever the proprietors tried to assert control over the Goose Creek faction, their efforts usually provoked political quarrels that hampered smooth running of the colony.

Middleburg Plantation was built circa 1697 near Huger, probably by Huguenot planter Benjamin Simons. It is the oldest building in South Carolina. Courtesy, Gibbes Art Gallery/Carolina Art Association

As a consequence, there were 22 governors in the 50 years of proprietary rule.

In the midst of nagging problems the energetic Lord Ashley Cooper was accused of treason and imprisoned by King Charles II. The disheartened proprietors, having spent £10,000 sterling in the first 10 years, almost let their enterprise fail before John Archdale and William Craven assumed leadership and persuaded the rest to continue their efforts.

The proprietors did enjoy a measure of success in acquiring new immigrants. King Louis XIV of France inadvertently aided them when he revoked the Edict of Nantes in 1685, withdrawing the royal guarantee of religious and civil liberty for Huguenots. Once again suffering cruel persecution, these French Protestants sought refuge in other lands. Some 500 came to South Carolina and took up land mainly between Charles Town and the Santee River.

At first the new settlers found frontier life extremely harsh. Judith Manigault left an account of the hardships of the voyage to South Carolina and the suffering on arrival. "I have been here for six months together without tasting bread," she wrote, "working the ground like a slave." Yet her son Gabriel became probably the richest merchant in the province before his death in 1781. Indeed, as a group, the Huguenots furnished a disproportionate share of South Carolina leadership.

English and Scottish settlers were also attracted by the liberal land policy, in one case with tragic results. A group of about 150 Scots, led by David Erskine (Lord Cardross), took up land near present-day Beaufort in 1683 and named their settlement Stuart Town. The Florida Spaniards, ever wary of Carolina encroachment, launched a surprise attack on Stuart Town three years later and, according to a witness, "having plundr'ed the houses, destroyed the [plantations], killed a great quantity of hoggs and cattle, they burnt the towne down to the ground and took away two men and a boy prisoner." The other settlers escaped by fleeing into the forest. The Spanish force next moved against Charles Town, but a storm drove off the invaders and saved the town from a serious attack.

The colony continued to attract settlers. To more closely supervise the colony, the proprietors organized three counties: Colleton (south of Charles Town), Berkeley (Charles Town and vicinity), and Craven (north of Charles Town), each with 10 representatives in the Commons House.

As a measure against the troublesome Goose Creek Men, the proprietors tried to build a loyal following among the dissenters, who were strongest in Colleton County, the main Indian frontier. Nonetheless the Goose Creekers retained control over the Commons House. During the "Glorious Revolution" in England in 1688 and the outbreak of war with France, they undermined the authority of Governor James Colleton, banned him from the colony, successfully supported rival claimant Seth Sothel, and further strengthened

St. James Goose Creek, built between 1708 and 1719, is the oldest church building in South Carolina. It is one of several Anglican churches or chapels built in the eighteenth-century South Carolina lowcountry. Several others have been preserved in original form. Courtesy, T. Benton Young

themselves by disenfranchising the Huguenots.

In 1692 the proprietors ousted the notorious Sothel (reputed to be a pirate trader), suspended the Fundamental Constitutions, and reorganized the legislature into two houses, the appointed Grand Council and the popularly elected Commons House of Assembly. For the remainder of the decade the colony continued to grow in relative harmony. During these years the proprietors made a concerted effort to placate the settlers, whose legislature they realized was gaining power at their expense.

Another noteworthy accomplishment in the 1690s was the codification of the colony's laws, which included comprehensive provisions for regulating slavery. These were thought essential because of the rapidly increasing number of slaves in the province. By 1708 blacks slightly outnumbered whites 4,100 to 4,080. Twenty years later blacks were in a two-to-one majority.

The growing slave population was due largely to importation of blacks to meet the needs of South Carolina's expanding economy. Highly significant in these early years, according to historian Clarence L. Ver Steeg, were naval stores, necessary for the British shipping industry. More than 52,000 barrels of tar and pitch were exported from 1718 to 1719 alone.

"Furthermore," contends Ver Steeg, "naval stores acted as a catalyst, which, in the second decade of the eighteenth century, brought prosperity to the white population of South Carolina and converted a fundamentally subsistence economy to one of boundless commercial growth." Thus it was the naval stores trade that initially led to a large influx of slave importation.

The colony's economy was also strengthened by the deerskin export trade, which nonetheless was erratic because of Indian wars. Skins shipped ranged from 121,000 in 1707 to only 4,000 in 1716. Colleton County was the center for a growing cattle industry until the Yemasee War; over 3,000 barrels of beef and pork were exported from June 1711 to June 1713. Rice, introduced about 1685 when a ship captain gave Dr. Henry Woodward a bagful of seed, was likewise becoming an important export item.

This growing prosperity at the beginning of the new century was counterpoint to trouble. The colony became deeply involved in England's war with Spain, known as the War of the Spanish Succession, and experienced internal political strife. During the war Governor James Moore led an unsuccessful expedition against St. Augustine. Somewhat later Moore, no longer governor, and other South Carolina adventurers led successful forays against Spanish and French Indian allies in Alabama and Mississippi. These victories extended English influence as far away as the Mississippi River. A French-Spanish naval expedition, with Indian support, attempted to retaliate against Charles Town in 1706 but was driven off by the local militia.

Meanwhile, quarrels arose between members of the Church of England and its Protestant dissenters. With the advent of Governor Nathaniel Johnson, a staunch Goose Creek Anglican himself, the Anglicans ousted dissenters from the Commons House and in 1706 established 10 parishes. The proprietors interceded the next year to restore the dissenters to their seats in Commons, but they failed to disestablish the Church itself. Nevertheless, the religious controversy soon began to wane.

The war with Spain called for a reexamination of the colony's Indian policy. The colonial House of Commons in 1707 passed a far-reaching Indian trade law that required the licensing of all traders, outlawed the sale of firearms to hostile tribes, and forbade the sale of friendly tribes into slavery. The leader against whites' abuses of Indians was Indian agent Thomas Nairne, a farsighted planter of the Port Royal region and a friend of the native Americans.

The new Indian trade law was unpopular with the Indian traders, and Governor Johnson, an ill-humored autocrat, refused to enforce it. He disliked Nairne, replaced him as Indian agent, and arrested him on charges of treason. (Nairne was later cleared.) Johnson's actions on this and other matters were so high-handed that the proprietors felt compelled to replace the stern old warhorse in 1709. Nevertheless, factional bickering continued. By this time the growing mercantile community was beginning to challenge the supremacy of the Goose Creek faction.

In 1712 Governor Charles Craven arrived in Charles Town, and during his tenure the colony was faced with the most serious Indian outbreak in its history. The Indian conflict began with an uprising of the Tuscaroras in under populated North Carolina in 1711. Upon frantic appeals from its hard-pressed neighbor, South Carolina sent two successive expeditions, and in time the Tuscaroras sued for peace. In South Carolina the main blow fell in April 1715 when the Yemasees rebelled against the injustices of white traders, who had cheated them, debauched them, forced them to work without pay, and sold their relatives into slavery. Many Indians concluded that their only recourse was to kill the traders who came out from Charles Town each spring.

Upon first hearing of threatened difficulties, Governor Craven sent a delegation under Thomas Nairne and Indian agent John Wright to Pocotaligo to negotiate with the Indians. The parley proceeded smoothly, and the whites retired for the evening with the belief that the Indians were ready for reconciliation. Before daybreak, however, the Yemasees burst in upon the sleeping whites, seized them, and tortured them to death. They then wiped out the white settlement at Pocotaligo; only 2 of 90 whites escaped. Nor did the Indians spare their longtime friend Thomas Nairne. They tormented him by thrusting burn-

Above: The irascible Sir Nathaniel Johnson was the governor of South Carolina between 1703 and 1709. He successfully defended the colony against a Spanish attack in 1706. At odds with the proprietors and the Commons over several issues, he retired in 1709 to his nearby plantation, named "Silk Hope" because of Johnson's experiments with silk culture. Courtesy, Gibbes Art Gallery/Carolina Art Association

Far left: The Powder Magazine, built in 1703, is Charleston's oldest preserved building. St. Philip's Episcopal Church, built in 1838, is in the background. Courtesy, National Archives

ing splinters into his flesh for two days before he finally died.

Yemasee bands then fanned out over the southern corner of the province, destroying plantations and killing all whites they could seize. Governor Craven had probably no more than 1,200 militiamen available for duty, and the Indians had several times as many warriors. The Yemasees had the support of several smaller tribes and the powerful Creeks, who in turn were pressuring the Cherokees to join them.

After the initial Indian onslaught Governor Craven's militia drove the Yemasees south across the Savannah. Meanwhile, Catawbas and other Indians to the north and west attacked from that direction. When the governor turned his attention to the new danger, the Yemasees recrossed the Savannah. Raids reached within 30 miles of Charles Town. Craven was forced to keep the militia on continuous service, arm some of the slaves, and appeal to other colonies for aid.

The Cherokees' refusal to join the Creeks saved the day for the whites. Impressed by a force of 300 Carolinians sent into their territory, the Cherokees decided instead to war against the Creeks. This relieved the pressure on the province and by the spring of 1716 the crisis had passed. Peace was not concluded with the Creeks until two years later, however, and small raids continued intermittently for several years.

The Yemasee War was the costliest Indian conflict in the history of the colony. The southern parishes were devastated, and about one-half of the cultivated land in the province was temporarily abandoned. Over 400 settlers had died and others had fled. The conflict had left the colony deeply in debt and, except for some sparse aid from Massachusetts and Virginia, South Carolina had borne the burden alone. The South Carolinians were particularly angry with the proprietors, who had furnished no assistance.

The Carolinians' Indian troubles were hardly settled before a wave of piracy beset the colony. An estimated 1,500 sea robbers began to operate along North Carolina's sparsely settled shore at the end of the War of the Spanish Succession. Among the pirates who preyed on Charles Town commerce was the notorious Edward Teach, better known as Blackbeard. He and other pirate captains seized ships and cargoes and ransomed passengers. Their nefarious activities became especially troublesome in the summer of 1718. In order to meet the challenge Governor Robert Johnson commissioned Colonel William Rhett as vice-admiral to deal with the marauders. The governor of Virginia also promised cooperation.

While the Virginians were running down Blackbeard, Colonel Rhett chanced upon gentleman pirate Stede Bonnet in the Cape Fear River and forced his surrender after a fierce encounter. After some delay Bonnet was finally hanged along with some 29 other buccaneers. Meanwhile, in November, Governor Johnson himself led a small fleet, disguised as merchant ships, against another pirate gang off the Charles Town bar. The pirates were taken by surprise; 19 of the survivors were hanged. These expeditions, along with British naval activity in the Caribbean, ended the pirate menace. Again, the proprietors had furnished no help.

For their part, the proprietors were about ready to surrender the Carolinas to the Crown. From the provincials' standpoint, the proprietors had neglected their duties, so that the Carolinians had been forced to shift for themselves. Military expeditions, Indian wars, and the campaign against the buccaneers had been extraordi-

narily expensive. Of necessity the colony had turned to paper money as early as 1702. Lacking sufficient revenues to retire the issues on schedule, the Carolinians saw their currency devalued to the point that the value of British sterling quadrupled by the end of 1717. This depreciation was unsettling to London merchants in particular. The proprietors came to loggerheads with the colonial assembly over currency and several other issues. They therefore ordered Governor Johnson to dissolve the assembly and call for new elections.

Johnson, son of the former governor Nathaniel Johnson, sympathized with the colonists and did his masters' bidding reluctantly. The new assembly, elected in November 1719, was clearly at odds with the proprietors. Complaints and grumblings throughout the port town indicated that a revolt was in the offing. It was eventually triggered by a false rumor that a Spanish fleet was about to attack Charles Town. Backed by swelling popular support, the assembly declared itself a convention and chose James Moore, Jr., to be provisional governor when the popular Johnson, ever loyal to the proprietors, refused to cooperate with the rebellion. They then asked the king to make South Carolina a royal colony.

Upon recommendation of the Board of Trade, King George I agreed to assume control of the colony. In 1729 he bought

Built in 1714, Mulberry Plantation in Berkeley County had its bastions defensively armed during the Yemasee War. Courtesy, Charles N. Bayless

The execution of "gentleman" pirate Stede Bonnet took place in Charles Town in November 1719. Bonnet was captured by William Rhett in a battle in the Cape Fear River and was sentenced to be hanged with members of his crew. After winning some sympathy in Charles Town, Bonnet escaped, but he was later recaptured and hanged. Courtesy, Special Collections, Clemson University Library

out the proprietors' interests in both North Carolina and South Carolina. The colonists obviously believed their interests would be served better under royal than proprietary rule.

South Carolina's first royal governor was Sir Francis Nicholson, an experienced colonial official who had served previously as governor of four other colonies. This capable and learned administrator exercised sound judgment in dealing with the South Carolinians. In view of the vexing prob-

lems he inherited, great skill was needed. There were problems involving land grants, taxes, regulation of Indian trade, frontier defense, British restriction of rice shipments to Europe, increasing currency inflation, and the disturbing growth of the slave population.

Governor Nicholson, with an appreciation for the colonists' viewpoints, adopted a conciliatory approach and in time won the Council's support for most of his policies. The governor faced an especially thorny problem in the currency issue. During Nicholson's administration South Carolina paper money dropped from four-to-one to seven-to-one compared with sterling. The governor's compromise currency bill failed to stem the bitterness that had arisen between creditors and debtors.

Colonial tensions were further heightened by an imperial act of 1724 that ended the bounty for all naval stores except that produced by the efficient Swedish method. Within two or three years the small landowners, engaged in gathering rosin and making tar and pitch, began to suffer financially. They therefore joined the rice planters in seeking more paper money. Nicholson's successor let the matter drift; the legislature became deadlocked and refused to act.

At this critical time Samuel Wragg, London agent for the Commons, and ex-Governor Robert Johnson cooperated to save South Carolina from anarchy.

Prompted by their urging, the British government agreed to appoint Johnson governor, resolve the currency dispute, restore the naval stores bounty, permit rice shipments directly to Spain and Portugal, and expand the Carolina settlements.

The remarkable Johnson had retained the good will of the colonists and upon his return in 1730 enjoyed a successful term of office. His political tact and evenhandedness produced political harmony; the change in British policy brought prosperity. Whereas currency had been the chief issue in the 1720s, land policy was the main cause of excitement in the 1730s. Nearly all land bordering tidewater streams was taken up during the latter decade, primarily by the wealthier classes. However, the poor had an opportunity to move farther inland to one of the new townships set up by Governor Johnson.

These townships were Johnson's best-remembered work. Prior to their establish-

Limerick at Cordesville on the Cooper River was built circa 1713 by Daniel Huger, son of Huguenot immigrants. The plantation produced naval stores and rice. This photograph was taken shortly before the house burned down in 1945. Courtesy, Library of Congress

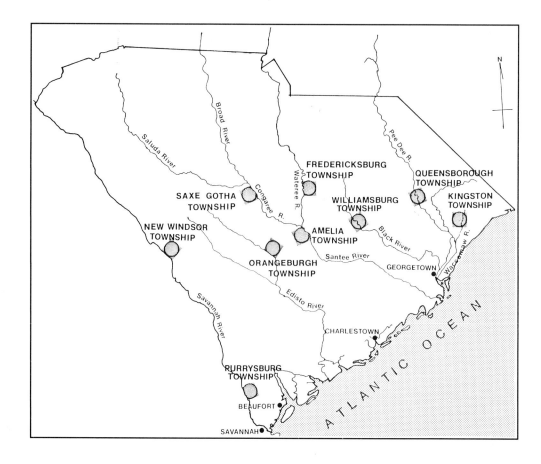

ment few settlements reached farther than 30 or 40 miles inland, except at Fort Moore near Augusta and Congaree Fort near Columbia. Johnson's plan called for nine townships in South Carolina and two in Georgia. Each township was to contain 20,000 acres and be situated on a river. Each settler was to be given transportation, land, tools, and provisions for a year. The governor's purpose was to encourage white immigration to offset the rising slave population and to promote defense against Indian attacks.

The most successful settlements were at Saxe Gotha (Lexington County), Amelia (Calhoun County), Orangeburgh—later spelled Orangeburg (Orangeburg County), Fredericksburg (Kershaw County), and Williamsburg (Williamsburg County). German-Swiss were the chief settlers at Saxe-Gotha, Amelia, and Orangeburgh. They spread their farms across the Saluda River into what is today called the Dutch Fork section. Irish settled at King's Tree in Williamsburg, and several nationalities made their way into Fredericksburg at Pine Tree Hill (Camden). Purrysburg, a Swiss-German colony and first to be settled, quickly withered and died because of its unhealthy location on the lower Savannah River. New Windsor, Queensborough, and Kingston similarly failed to flourish in the early years.

Wherever settlements were made, colonists were encouraged to move on to yet other lands throughout the pine belt. By 1750 settlers were beginning to look beyond the fall line for land.

These years of rapid expansion were not without strife. Even in peacetime French, Spanish, and British agents among the Indians conspired against rival colonists, each trying to subvert the others' Indian allies. The Spaniards in Florida at times also tried to encourage South Carolina slaves to rebel by offering freedom to runaways who might reach Spanish territory. This policy may have been partly responsible for a serious slave uprising in South Carolina in 1739.

On Sunday, September 9, a group of slaves began a rebellion on the Stono River within 20 miles of Charles Town. After murdering several whites and gathering recruits, the rebel gang grew in strength to about 100 blacks by late afternoon. While drinking, the slaves were caught off guard by a mounted contingent of planters. In the ensuing battle 14 slaves were killed or wounded. Several others were taken prisoner and shot. Many of the rebels who escaped became caught in an intensive manhunt which within two days killed about 20 and rounded up another 40, all of whom were shot, hanged, or gibbeted alive to die of exposure. A few days later the last large body of rebels was dispersed, thus breaking the backbone of the uprising. Outlying fugitives were still being brought in for execution the following spring, and one rebel leader remained at large for three years. About 20 whites were killed the first day of the insurrection. There is no reliable estimate of the total black casualties.

Although slaves in South Carolina were subject to restrictions and severe punishment for crime, the slave code was loosely enforced before the uprising. Slaves often congregated for recreation and came and went as they pleased. Some served in the militia until the end of the Yemasee War. South Carolina slaves also enjoyed a certain amount of autonomy, probably more than in any other English colony in North America.

After the Stono uprising South Carolina authorities drew up a new and stricter slave code, tried unsuccessfully to reduce slave importations while encouraging white immigration, and attempted to ameliorate the condition of slaves on plantations. The new slave code remained the basic law in South Carolina until 1865. But the fact of the black majority caused whites thereafter to live in fear for their safety.

Despite this fear, when James Glen arrived in Charles Town to assume the gov-

ernorship from 1743 to 1756, tranquility prevailed. South Carolina politics had undergone a transformation. The government was at last stable and largely under the control of the colonists themselves.

The chief executive was the governor, appointed by the British sovereign. He acted according to instructions from London. Since British policy was sometimes at odds with the wishes of the colonists, the governor often had to exercise great skill and tact to please both masters and "servants."

Assisting the governor in his administrative duties was a Grand Council of 12 men, also appointed by the Crown and serving on good behavior. In addition, the Council served as the upper house of the assembly and the highest court of appeals in the province. In order to secure a position on the Council, a man needed wealth and political influence in London. During the royal period the Council was dominated by six planter families—the Blakes, Bulls, Draytons, Fenwicks, Izards, and Middletons—and a few elite merchants.

By and large, the governors and the Council represented the interest of the British government, while the Commons House of Assembly voiced the feelings of the people of the colony. Any freeman could vote if he owned 50 acres of land or paid 20 shillings currency in taxes. Elec-

These unusually well-built slave houses were located at Nieuport Plantation, in Beaufort County. Most slave quarters were one-room buildings constructed of wood, sometimes with only dirt floors. Photograph by Carl Julien in Sea Islands to Sand Hills, *reproduced by permission of the University of South Carolina Press*

The birthplace of William Henry Drayton, Drayton Hall was built in 1738 and is a fine example of Palladian architecture. It is said that the building was spared Sherman's torch in 1865 because it was used as a hospital for blacks suffering from smallpox. Courtesy, South Carolina Department of Parks, Recreation, and Tourism

tions were held by secret ballot at parish churches over two-day periods. However, to be eligible to sit in Commons a man had to own 10 slaves or real estate worth £1,000. Consequently, as in the Council, interlocking families of wealthy planters and merchants ruled.

As already noted, when Governor Glen arrived in 1743, many of the colony's earlier problems had been largely settled and factionalism was on the wane. For the next 20 years the main issue seems to have been a struggle among the governor, Council, and Commons over prerogative and power. In these battles the Council and the governor both suffered from Commons' aggrandizement. No tax bill ever passed without Commons' consent, and Glen complained that the lower house had usurped "much of the executive part of the Government."

By mid-century South Carolina had developed a thriving and diversified economy. Rice had become the colony's chief export. Cattle ranching and hog production continued to be widespread and reasonably profitable, as were tobacco, hemp, and grain products.

Indian trade and naval stores, lucrative in earlier years, were on the decline. In place of naval stores many South Carolina farmers turned to indigo which, unlike rice, required no large amount of capital to produce. For its successful introduction as a market crop, South Carolina was indebted to Eliza Lucas, a talented young woman who successfully experimented with its growth on her father's plantation in the late 1740s. A British bounty for the blue dye made from the indigo plant was a further inducement to its production.

The 1750s and 1760s were a period of heady prosperity for South Carolinians. By 1770 an estimated 3,000 wagons carrying wheat, indigo, tobacco, and other products traveled the road to Charles Town annually. During these years colonial merchants began to replace English merchants as chief furnishers of long-term credit in the colony. The prosperity was also enhanced by low taxes, which Governor James Glen estimated in the 1740s to be no higher than 5 percent for any colonist.

Charles Town was indeed a wealthy place for the times. With some 10,000 inhabitants on the eve of the Revolution, the city was the largest in the Southern colonies. Its earliest buildings had been replaced because of the deterioration of these early wooden structures, plus destructive fires in 1698, 1700, and especially 1740. After the fire of 1740 the town was rebuilt along English Georgian architectural lines with Barbadian modifications.

Charles Town was cosmopolitan, tolerant, and central to colonial politics and society. A bright social season lit up the city during winter months, when outlying planters settled their families into townhouses. The whirl of activities included formal dinners, theatrical productions, dances, musical concerts, horse races, and other forms of recreation. The Dock Street Theatre originated in 1736, the Charles Town Library Society in 1748, the St. Cecilia (musical) Society in 1762, and the Charles Town Museum in 1773. The city had one or more weekly newspapers from 1732 on.

Yet the city's wealth and cosmopolitan atmosphere could not disguise its unhealthy location. Within a decade of settlement the town began to earn its reputation as a charnel house. Poor diet, dysentery, malaria, and occasional yellow fever epidemics took a heavy toll.

Away from Charles Town, life on the plantations was more leisurely. In their isolation planters were nearly always happy to welcome visitors. One foreigner visiting from 1733 to 1734 wrote: "The gentlemen in general, in this country, are exceedingly civil to strangers, so that a man . . . may go from one plantation to another, for a year or two, and keep his horse, and never cost him a farthing."

In religious matters South Carolinians generally exhibited indifference, which the Church of England apparently did little to correct. The Bishop of London sent out clergy from England but not in sufficient

Left: Rice fields are shown being prepared for planting in this black and white print of a watercolor painting. The artist is Alice Ravenel Huger Smith, a lowcountry resident well acquainted with the rice culture. Courtesy, Gibbes Art Gallery/ Carolina Art Association

Below: Bishop Roberts' Prospects for Charles Town, *engraved by W.H. Toms, was published in London on June 9, 1739. It is the earliest known drawing of the Charles Town waterfront. Most of the buildings in the picture were later burned, demolished and replaced by other structures, or destroyed by hurricanes. Courtesy, New York Public Library*

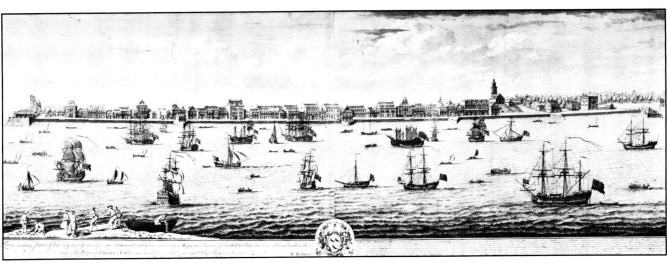

Gabriel Manigault (1704-1781) was the son of poor Huguenot immigrants. A prime example of social mobility in colonial South Carolina, he became one of the richest merchants in North America during his lifetime. For over two centuries his descendants have also perched on the top rungs of the social, cultural, and economic ladders in Charleston society. Courtesy, South Caroliniana Library

numbers to attend to the needs of rural parishioners. In Charles Town itself a visitor in 1773 noted that the Sunday service in St. Philip's lasted less than 18 minutes, during which time several members of the small congregation did not cease their casual conversation.

For those Charles Town residents who were church members, a majority do not appear to have been Anglicans. Besides the two Anglican churches, St. Philip's and St. Michael's, the city had six meeting houses of other denominations. Outside the city, the farther one traveled from the lowcountry, the weaker the support for the Church of England.

South Carolina society had a large number of slaves, working-class whites, and indigents, much of whose time was taken up with drudgery for their own maintenance or that of the well-to-do. These people enjoyed entertainment less frequently and on a modest scale. On the other hand, class lines in South Carolina were not rigid; economic prosperity enabled many persons to move into the upper-class gentry. Gabriel Manigault and Henry Laurens, two of the province's richest merchants, were prime examples of social mobility. The son of poor immigrant Huguenots, Manigault was worth, by 1988 standards, $2 million at the time of his death in 1781.

During James Glen's long rule as governor of South Carolina, from 1743 to 1756, he gave liberally of his own funds for public service, was constant in his duties, and

remained reasonably popular. Indian relations were his main concern. The frontier was never quiet for long, and King George's War (1744-1748) sharpened the English-Spanish-French contest for control of the Old Southwest territories.

In order to pacify the Indians, Governor Glen, accompanied by a force of 500 men, marched to the trading settlement of Ninety-Six in the summer of 1746 for a parley with the Cherokees, and later to Fort Moore for a similar meeting with the Creeks and Chickasaws. Except for some of the Tennessee tribes, the Cherokees, though disgruntled over the war's disruption of their English trade, remained peaceful.

Glen tried to strengthen English ties with the Lower Cherokees in South Carolina and Georgia by erecting Fort Prince George at the Indian town of Keowee, in present-day Oconee County. The governor completed the fortifications in December 1753, and a contingent of 17 soldiers moved in. The following year the French and Indian War erupted, and the governor sought funds to build a fort in Overhill

Cherokee territory in Tennessee. Before he could complete his mission, William Henry Lyttelton arrived to replace him as governor. The new executive was able to procure the necessary legislative support to build Fort Loudoun the following year.

The problems with the Cherokees were compounded by the advance of white settlers into Cherokee territory. As early as 1750 a few whites were drifting into the Piedmont and, with the coming of the French and Indian War, a flood of back-woodsmen began to flee southward from Pennsylvania and Virginia to escape the savage onslaught of Indians who supported the French.

Shortly, two attacks by settlers on Indian bands caused the Cherokees to take to the warpath. As Governor Lyttelton and the Council prepared for a general war, news arrived of the British capture of Quebec. The victory stirred a martial spirit among South Carolinians. More than 1,300 men volunteered to follow the governor into Indian territory. At the height of this agitation an Indian delegation arrived in

The original structure of Johns Island Presbyterian Church was built in 1719, and in 1823 it was lengthened by 20 feet. It is one of the oldest Presbyterian church buildings in America and the oldest non-Anglican church building in South Carolina. Photo by Carl Julien. Courtesy, South Caroliniana Library

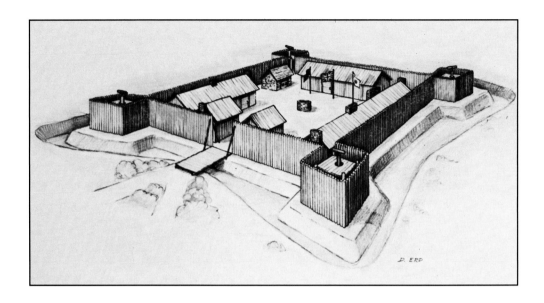

Charles Town seeking peace, they said, and munitions to protect themselves from their enemies.

After some parleys with the Indian peace delegation, Governor Lyttelton in November 1759 set out for Fort Prince George, meanwhile holding the Indian peace delegation hostage. Cold winter rains, measles, smallpox, and wholesale desertions destroyed his army. The governor decided it would be wise to confer rather than to fight. He reached an agreement which apparently did not satisfy the Cherokees, for in February 1760 they launched a major attack on the frontier and besieged Fort Prince George. Some 75 traders and settlers died in the initial onslaught. Among the victims were 23 settlers at Long Canes, including several members of the Calhoun family, caught fleeing in wagons toward Augusta.

In retaliation, whites at Fort Prince George murdered the 21 Indian hostages. Settlers at the Ninety-Six fort, having been forewarned, repulsed a Cherokee attack, whereupon one white jubilantly wrote the governor: "We now have the Pleasure Sir, to Fatten our dogs with their Carcasses and to Display their Scalps, neatly ornamented on top of our Bastions." The Cherokees were more successful elsewhere. They besieged and captured Fort Loudon, whose garrison they tortured and killed, sparing only Captain John Stuart's life upon the intercession of Little Carpenter, an Indian chief long friendly to the British.

The war was brought to a close in 1761 by two military invasions of Cherokee territory. The first suffered heavy losses, but the second exacted terrible damage among Cherokee crops and villages. Afterwards,

Little Carpenter and several other chiefs signed a peace treaty that surrendered additional land to the whites, retaining in South Carolina only what is today mostly Anderson, Pickens, Oconee, and Greenville counties.

The opening of new land to white settlement was one of the most significant results of the Cherokee War. Settlers poured into the region, and by the American Revolution whites in the Piedmont outnumbered those in the lowcountry. The newcomers, generally of Scotch-Irish ancestry, included small farmers, herdsmen, hunters, artisans, land speculators, and rogues.

The Piedmont settlers usually lived in crude one- or two-room cabins of rough-hewn logs chinked with mud. The foundations, if there were any, consisted of rocks. The chimneys were likewise of rocks chinked with clay wherever necessary. The newcomers dressed in homespun and leather, adorned their cabins with simple homemade furniture, and traveled mainly on foot. The itinerant Anglican clergyman Charles Woodmason noted: "Their Cabbins quite open and expos'd—Little or no Bedding, or anything to cover them—Not a drop of anything, save Cold Water to drink . . . The Indians are better Cloathed and Lodged." Later he added: "As for Tea and Coffee they know it not."

Here and there an occasional backcountry settler acquired considerable wealth in a short period of time. Moses Kirkland, for example, moved onto the lower Saluda River before 1752 and operated a gristmill, a sawmill, and a ferry. He amassed over 3,000 acres of land before the Revolution, including an indigo plantation in the

Ninety-Six District. A visitor in 1767 to Andrew Williamson's place on Hard Labor Creek (Edgefield District) reported it was "one of the finest plantations in South Carolina."

Most backcountry people were of Presbyterian, Baptist, or Lutheran stock, although few belonged to an organized congregation. Their church buildings were crude; their ministers, usually poorly educated, held services irregularly. Although frequently quarreling among themselves over religious matters, they reserved their greatest dislike for the Church of England, as the Reverend Charles Woodmason discovered while trying to minister to Anglican parishioners on the upper Wateree, Catawba, and Lynches rivers from 1767 to 1768.

In his journal Woodmason noted that his services were disrupted by rowdy Scot Presbyterian gangs. On one occasion they threatened his life, saying they wanted no "Black Gown Sons of Bitches" among them. The timely arrival of a group friendly to the Anglicans prevented a tragedy. Woodmason, not without prejudice, filled his journal with references to backcountry poverty, ignorance, and immorality. But shortly thereafter, he became the backwoodsmen's champion in their search for law and order and for a voice in the colonial government in Charles Town.

South Carolina had come a long way in the century since Charles Town's founding. Not only had the colony moved from proprietary to royal rule and, to a considerable extent, self rule. It had also developed a growing commercial economy built largely on slave labor; Charles Town was a thriving, cosmopolitan city; the Indians had been driven from all but the northwest corner of the province; and the backcountry was rapidly being populated.

Shown here is the William Nix house, on an old Cherokee path that passed through Nine Times Gap in Pickens County. Nix, an Indian trader, built the house circa 1780. Courtesy, Pickens County Museum

The Revolutionary Era: 1763-1789

British policy changes helped succor the revolutionary spirit in South Carolina as well as in other colonies. With the end of the French and Indian War in 1763 the British government tried to tighten colonial administration, enforce the Navigation Acts that restricted colonial commerce, and tax the colonies to help pay for administrative expenses that included keeping a standing army in America. Almost immediately American colonists, including South Carolinians, began to protest.

However, before the colony's relations with Great Britain reached the breaking point, a serious crisis arose in the backcountry. At the close of the Cherokee War of 1760-1761, backcountry South Carolina included the Piedmont, the sandhills, and much of the upper pine belt. With the conclusion of the war, settlers once more began pouring into the backcountry. The colonial government further encouraged their migration by setting up four new townships south and west of Ninety-Six in 1762.

It was a chaotic situation into which new backcountry settlers came. The Cherokee War had disrupted this frontier society. Some 1,500 persons had taken refuge in 30 backcountry forts during the winter of 1760 to 1761, and crowded living quarters, poor provisions, and a smallpox epidemic made life miserable inside these stockades.

To make matters worse, some of the post commanders robbed their charges of supplies sent by the government. Ruffians moved into the forts in some places, and the rangers when idle spent much time in debauchery. Many settlers complained that they sustained more damage from their protectors than from the enemy. While they endured the discomforts of the forts, often

their homes and farms were pillaged by outlaws. Stealing became a way of life in the backcountry.

After the Cherokee War the backcountry lawless element became even bolder in their crimes. They had connections in other colonies and among some of the frontier storekeepers. Owners of property found it necessary to cooperate lest their own stores and plantations be pillaged. The few officers of the law in the region were powerless to arrest the outlaws even if they dared.

Heinous crimes became so prevalent in the summers of 1767 and 1768 that backcountrymen organized a vigilante or "Regulator" movement to punish suspected perpetrators of evil-doing. In November 1767 about 4,000 backcountrymen sent an eloquent protest and petition, written by the Reverend Charles Woodmason, to the General Assembly to redress their grievances. This message, along with their vigilante activities, prompted Governor Charles G. Montagu and the Commons House into action. They sent two companies of rangers, with Regulator officers, into the backcountry to quell the disturbances.

The Regulator-ranger bands vigorously hunted down the rogues and by early spring of 1768 the worst of the criminal activities had stopped. Flushed with success, the Regulators sought to correct the moral conduct and indolent ways of the "lower people"—the dregs of frontier society. Soon the Regulators were guilty of severe floggings and general mistreatment of n'er-do-wells. These excesses led to a movement of Moderators in 1769, but some of the Moderators seemed intent only on revenge for having been "regulated" themselves. A

This painting of the Battle of Camden on August 16, 1780, depicts the death of Baron Johann de Kalb, a German officer enlisted in the patriot cause and commander of General Horatio Gates' Continental Line. Gates' army was destroyed by Lord Cornwallis. Courtesy, National Archives

serious clash between Regulators and Moderators was narrowly averted when both sides agreed to disperse and resort to legal means to settle their differences.

As the threat of violence subsided, backcountry people began to make progress in remedying another grievance: control of their own destinies. Although greatly underrepresented in Commons, the backcountrymen elected six members to that house in 1768, and the Circuit Court Act of 1769 promised an improved system of justice. The legislature provided for courthouses at Ninety-Six, Camden, Cheraw, and Orangeburg, with court to be held twice each year. Court would also be held twice yearly in coastal Beaufort and Georgetown and three times in Charles Town. After some delay the new court system went into operation in 1772.

As the backcountry's internal problems subsided, relations between the colony and Great Britain grew steadily worse. When Great Britain began to tighten colonial administration in 1763, one might not have expected South Carolina to raise serious objection, for the colony prospered within the empire. Although an annoyance, the new trade restrictions were not seriously damaging to South Carolina's economy, and the British bounty on indigo was actually quite beneficial. Nevertheless Charles Town was soon seething with discontent.

During the Cherokee War friction had arisen between British and colonial military leaders. One of these colonial leaders was Christopher Gadsden, whose polemical attacks on two British military leaders in the Cherokee War made him many enemies. A technical irregularity was discovered in Gadsden's election to the Commons House in 1762, and Governor Thomas Boone refused to administer the oath of office to Gadsden. Furthermore, Boone dissolved the Commons for declaring Gadsden elected. The newly elected house censured Boone and shortly thereafter refused to have further dealings with him. The quarrel continued until Boone, increasingly unpopular, gave up the struggle and sailed for England in 1764.

Having successfully challenged a royal governor, Commons leaders were not willing to back down when faced with a sterner test the following year. A major crisis arose between Britain and the colonies when Parliament proposed the Stamp Act, an attempt by London authorities to tax a wide variety of official and unofficial papers.

The Commons House directed its London agent to oppose the proposed tax or any other that Parliament might impose on the colony. Despite this and other colonial protests, Parliament went ahead and passed the Stamp Act, to become effective November 1, 1765.

For the moment Commons was content to send three delegates to a Stamp Act Congress in New York. Lieutenant Governor William Bull, serving in the interim between royal governors, was determined to enforce the act, and prominent Charles Town merchants advised compliance with the law until it could be repealed. But news of resistance in the North galvanized the Charles Town radicals into action.

On October 19 a mob of some 2,000 persons burned a stamp collector in effigy and buried a coffin labeled "American Liberty." Then, led by Gadsden and port city artisans, the crowd hunted for stamps in order to destroy them. Bull, anticipating their plans, had secretly placed the stamps in a fort. Frustrated in its efforts to locate the despised stamps, an unruly and half-drunken mob ransacked the homes of the stamp inspector and his tenant.

A few nights later the mob invaded the homes of Henry Laurens and Chief Justice Charles Shinner, a loyal officer of the Crown. By that time no one dared use the stamps, no matter what the law required. The port of Charles Town was soon in the midst of a crisis; business came to a standstill, ships in the harbor could not clear port, and some 1,400 idle and disgruntled sailors milled about the city. Under much public pressure, Lieutenant Governor Bull agreed to permit ships to depart without stamped papers. Fortunately for the colony, word soon arrived that Parliament had repealed the Stamp Act.

During the Stamp Act crisis, Christopher Gadsden rapidly rose to a position of leadership among those opposed to British policies. He served with John Rutledge and Thomas Lynch as a delegate to the Stamp Act Congress and skillfully harangued his artisan and mechanic friends to form the "Sons of Liberty," meanwhile winning the support of Charles Town printers.

Still in need of additional revenues, Parliament passed the Townshend measures in 1767, which taxed tea, lead, paint, and several other articles customarily imported by American colonists. Prompted by the Sons of Liberty and lowcountry planters, a general meeting in Charles Town agreed in July 1769 to embargo the importation of slaves and most British manufactured products. Although unpopular with most South Carolina merchants, the embargo was fairly effective; imports dropped about 50 percent. For his part the public-spirited Gadsden seemed quite willing to sacrifice his warehouse and wharfage business for the greater cause.

Lord North, the leading British minister, soon regarded the Townshend measures as an ineffective source of revenue and an impediment to commerce. At his request Parliament repealed the measures, all except the tax on tea. At the same time Parliament asserted its right to tax the American colonies by passing the Declaratory Act. In response to the repeal of the Townshend measures, South Carolinians in a general meeting on December 13, 1770, repealed the colony's embargo on all goods but tea.

Meanwhile, an ugly controversy erupted between the Commons House and the immature and unstable Governor Charles G. Montagu over the John Wilkes fund. Commons had voted £1,500 sterling to aid the demagogic Englishman Wilkes, imprisoned for sedition and now loudly defending the right of free speech. The British ministry was outraged that the South Carolina Commons had voted funds without approval of the governor and the Council. While the ministry was determined to make the Commons repudiate the gift, the house was equally stubborn in declining to do so. The feud between Montagu and the Commons continued over Wilkes and other matters until 1773 when the governor departed for England and soon resigned.

The issue over the tea tax came to a head in December 1773 with the arrival from England of several ships—one destined for Charles Town harbor—laden with tea. The British East India Company, in dire financial straits, was trying to sell its oversupply of tea in the colonies. Boston responded with its "tea party," and an angry Parliament decided to punish the colony of Massachusetts until it made restitution.

There was no tea party in South Carolina, although there was talk of staging one. Instead, leaders of a mass meeting secured promises from Charles Town merchants not to sell the tea. Afterwards customs officials quietly locked the tea in a public warehouse. It was later sold to help finance the Revolution.

British punitive measures against Massachusetts prompted a call for a colonial congress to meet in Philadelphia. Gadsden, the *Gazette*'s editor Peter Timothy, and other radicals managed to organize a general meeting in Charles Town on July 6, 1774, against the wishes of the Charles Town merchants. Attendants at the meeting named Henry Middleton, John and Edward Rutledge, Thomas Lynch, and Gadsden to attend the congress.

The First Continental Congress, after petitioning Britain to redress colonial grievances, agreed on a Continental Association to embargo imports from Britain, as well as exports except rice, unless grievances were redressed. The entire South Carolina delegation except Gadsden threatened to walk out unless both rice and indigo were exempted from the embargo. Gadsden, ever willing to make personal sacrifices to obtain united action, persuaded his colleagues to compromise; rice was exempted but indigo was not. Back in South Carolina a general meeting in January 1775 endorsed the embargo over merchants' protests. Indigo planters were compensated from rice sales.

The general meeting of January adopted the name Provincial Congress. Planters and artisans, realizing the need for strong backcountry support in the crisis, arranged for 46 backcountry delegates to be seated among the 184 members of Congress. A committee was set up to enforce the embargo and a "Secret Committee of Five," headed by William Henry Drayton, was quietly authorized to collect arms. Drayton's committee acted promptly. On the night of April 21 it raided military stores in Charles Town and made off with a quantity of arms.

The ambitious William Henry Drayton is a strange case. Once a great defender of prerogative, he became such an effective spokesman for the radicals that his kins-

William Henry Drayton (1742-1779) was a bold and energetic leader for independence. Drayton was elected chief justice of South Carolina in 1776 and elected to the Continental Congress in 1778. An early death cut short his promising political career. Courtesy, South Carolina Historical Society

*Born in Charles Town of Hugue-
not parents, Henry Laurens
(1724-1792) spent several years in
England, rose to prominence in
the colonial business world, and
held numerous colonial offices. Always public-spirited and conservative in outlook, Laurens was gradually won over to the rebel cause
and was elected president of the Continental Congress in 1777. Courtesy, South Caroliniana Library*

man, Lieutenant Gover-
nor Bull, felt it necessary
to dismiss him from the
Council a few weeks be-
fore the clash at Lexing-
ton. Why did Drayton
change? Perhaps he re-
sented the arrogance
and condescension of
"placemen," or office
holders from Britain.
Several South Carolina
revolutionary leaders
had returned from En-
glish schools with resentment at being treated as
inferior colonials; per-
haps Drayton harbored
such resentments as
well, though these did
not manifest themselves in his early career.

Others, such as Henry Laurens, had
more concrete grievances. Laurens' shipping business had suffered from what he
considered grossly unfair actions of imperial officials. In their opposition to British
policies Americans thus felt they were standing up for their principles—and their self-
interest.

The South Carolina Provincial Congress, with Henry Laurens as president,
met again on June 1, 1775, and immediately
acted with bold resolution. It issued money
and recruited soldiers; it organized an association pledged to sacrifice lives and for-
tunes "against every foe"; and it created a
"Council of Safety," again with Laurens as
president.

In mid-June a new royal governor,
Lord William Campbell, arrived in Charles
Town. Instead of being welcomed with
booming cannon and parading troops, as
was customary, Campbell was greeted with
restraint and quickly found he had little
support in the Commons. This was of little
importance, however, for the house ceased
to meet within a few weeks.

During this time partisan bands occasionally tarred and feathered a loyalist.
Laurens deplored mob violence but could
do nothing to stop it. Lord Campbell was
likewise helpless amid mounting mob activities. With rumors abroad that he intended
to arm Indians against the colonists, he
feared for his own safety and took refuge
on a British warship in mid-September.
Thereafter lowcountry loyalists generally
ceased any activity on behalf of the king.
A few who openly supported the Crown
were hastily punished by the revolutionar-

ies. Their property was seized and they
themselves banished or imprisoned.

In the backcountry the situation was
somewhat different. Among the Scotch-
Irish and Germans the Crown had many
loyal supporters. Since the Cherokee War
these settlers had developed grievances
against the coastal region, not all of which
had been satisfied by lowcountry concessions. Alarmed over backcountry discontent, the Council of Safety sent Drayton,
the Reverend William Tennent, and several other partisans to organize rebel militia, to win over neutrals, and to crush
loyalism above the fall line.

Drayton was the most audacious and
successful of these emissaries. From his
Ninety-Six headquarters he boldly sent out
parties to arrest loyalist leaders. He himself
without hesitation faced several hostile audiences and called up additional trust-
worthy militia from the Wateree region.
His troops, numbering about 1,000, soon
faced a similar number of loyalists under
Colonel Thomas Fletchall. Both sides were
reluctant to force a showdown, and at a parley Drayton induced the gullible Fletchall
to sign an agreement of neutrality. With
that, Fletchall disbanded his militia, gravely
weakening loyalism in the backcountry.

However, the Fletchall-Drayton truce
was shaky, and from November 19 to
November 22, blood was shed between
loyalists and rebels at Ninety-Six. The clash
resulted from loyalist Patrick Cunningham's seizure of a wagon train of powder
the Provincial Congress was sending to the
Cherokees. The Council of Safety immediately ordered Colonel Richard Richardson with about 2,500 patriot militiamen into
the Tory backcountry. Fletchall and other
loyalist militia leaders were rounded up
and imprisoned. Only one Tory band of
about 130 men fought back, and Richardson surprised and defeated them on the
Reedy River in Cherokee territory in late
December.

By now the rebels were referring to the
loyalists as Tories and to themselves as partisans, Whigs, or most often, patriots. The
rebels might not have succeeded if Fletchall had shown resolution, if Lord Campbell
had moved into the backcountry with
troops, and if British Indian agent John
Stuart had incited the Cherokees.

Shortly after Colonel Richardson's return from the backcountry, South Carolina's second Provincial Congress met on
February 1, 1776, and drew up a constitution for a government during "the present

This drawing shows Sergeant William Jasper rescuing the patriot flag that was shot down during the Battle of Fort Moultrie on June 28, 1776. Jasper, a color bearer, was killed in an unsuccessful American attack on Savannah on October 9, 1779. Courtesy, Harper's Monthly

dispute." It was completed and signed March 26, and Congress designated itself the first General Assembly under the new document. The chief executive, chosen by the General Assembly, was called president and given veto power. He was eligible for reelection. The backcountry, with about 60 percent of the white population, was apportioned about one-third of the seats in the General Assembly. John Rutledge was selected as president and William Henry Drayton as chief justice. Drayton's promising political career was cut short by his untimely death in 1779.

While the Provincial Congress was discussing the terms of the new constitution, word arrived that Parliament had declared the colonies to be in a state of rebellion; colonial ships and cargoes were now lawful plunder. Parliament's action dampened moderates' hopes for reconciliation between England and America.

Nevertheless, even at this late date there was little open talk of independence, and the spring was relatively quiet in South Carolina.

The calm was shattered in June by the appearance of a large English fleet off the Charles Town harbor. Under the command of Sir Henry Clinton and Sir Peter Parker, the fleet had stopped at the Cape Fear River to aid North Carolina Tories, only to learn that these loyal followers of the king had already been defeated and dispersed at Moore's Creek. The British commanders then turned their attention to South Carolina, where Lord Campbell had

long pleaded for a powerful force.

The British plan of attack was faulty. They landed troops off Long Island, not knowing that the inlet separating it from Sullivan's Island was too deep to wade. Rebel militia riflemen kept their boats at bay. With his fleet Clinton next attacked the unfinished fort on Sullivan's Island. The fort's spongy palmetto logs withstood British cannon fire surprisingly well, while the American gunners, commanded by Colonel William Moultrie, inflicted heavy casualties on the British. The rebels suffered about 40 casualties and the British over four times that number. After the costly engagement Clinton called off the campaign and ordered the badly mauled fleet back to New York. South Carolina came to be called the Palmetto State in memory of the palmetto logs that had protected the rebels on Sullivan's Island.

Meanwhile the war was being fought furiously in the North, and sentiment for independence was gaining strength in all 13 colonies. In June the Virginians introduced a resolution in Continental Congress calling for independence, and on July 4, 1776, that body proclaimed the Declaration of Independence.

In the early months of 1776, sentiment for independence had likewise gained support among a few South Carolina leaders. When the vote for independence was taken in Congress, the South Carolina delegation of Thomas Lynch, Jr., Thomas Heyward, Jr., Arthur Middleton, and Edward Rutledge, with varying degrees of re-

luctance, gave their assent. The Declaration of Independence signified that South Carolina's temporary constitution was now its legal government.

While these events were occurring in Philadelphia, the Cherokees attacked frontier settlements from Virginia to Georgia. The Indians paid dearly for this action. Some 6,000 militiamen from three states invaded their land and marched for several weeks, destroying villages and crops. The devastation was so complete that more Indians starved to death in mountain hideouts than died at the hands of whites. On May 20, 1777, at DeWitt's Corner the weary survivors surrendered all their remaining South Carolina lands except a small alpine strip in what are now Oconee and Pickens counties.

From 1776 through 1778 most of the military campaigns of the Revolution took place in the North, with inconclusive results. The British, having failed to crush the rebellion, by mid-1778 also faced a strong French adversary. They thus withdrew from Philadelphia and planned a major campaign in the South. In December a British army captured Savannah, and when a combined patriot and French force bungled efforts to recapture the town, the emboldened British turned their attention to Charles Town.

In the winter of 1779-1780, Sir Henry Clinton sailed south with 8,500 troops to invade Charles Town. He landed a large contingent on John's Island and moved over-

land to the west bank of the Ashley River. General Benjamin Lincoln had 6,000 continentals and militia to defend the city. However, it soon became apparent that Charles Town, situated on the lower end of a peninsula, was indefensible against attack by a superior enemy force. In view of his perilous situation General Lincoln considered evacuation, but Christopher Gadsden, General C.C. Pinckney, and other leading Charlestonians encouraged him to stay. While Lincoln hesitated, British troops under Colonel Banastre Tarleton and Major Patrick Ferguson cut off his last escape route north of the city. To save Charles Town from destruction by heavy bombardment from the British navy, the American general surrendered with 5,500 troops on May 12, 1780. British forces quickly overran the state and won many waverers to their side, including several erstwhile patriot leaders.

The rebel cause suffered further with General Horatio Gates' crushing defeat by Lord Charles Cornwallis at Camden in August. In his effort to rescue South Carolina from British domination, Gates, a hero at Saratoga, rushed his tired, ill-fed, and poorly prepared army into battle against veteran British troops. At the first enemy attack the raw American militia dropped their weapons and ran. Two days after the debacle at Camden, Tarleton surprised Thomas Sumter's force at Fishing Creek in Chester County and captured 310 men. Sumter's militiamen had stacked their arms

and were bathing in the creek when Tarleton struck. The American commander barely managed to escape.

Lord Cornwallis' overwhelming victory at Camden and Sumter's defeat at Fishing Creek left South Carolina almost free for British and Tory forces to operate at will within its borders. Considering South Carolina conquered, Lord Cornwallis, now the British Southern commander, decided next to crush rebellion in North Carolina. As his main army moved northward toward Charlotte, he left garrisons in Charles Town and other posts throughout the state.

The dispirited patriots in South Carolina might have remained passive but for serious blunders by the British. Less than a month after rebel militiamen taken prisoner at Charles Town were released on parole, Sir Henry Clinton proclaimed that parolees must sign up with His Majesty's forces or be treated as enemies. This ill-advised command caused many patriots to violate their paroles and rejoin rebel bands.

The first of the partisan leaders was Thomas Sumter, a veteran militiaman temporarily in retirement. He gathered a force of patriots and took up arms again when Colonel Tarleton burned his Stateburg residence. Sumter's bold, dashing exploits and guerrilla tactics soon earned him the title "The Gamecock." He operated mainly in central South Carolina and the lower

Piedmont. On July 12 Sumter's men wiped out a Tory band under Christian Huck. This victory was the signal for a new uprising. Even Sumter's subsequent defeat at Fishing Creek in August did not sideline him for long.

While Thomas Sumter operated in mid-Carolina, Francis Marion emerged as the chief partisan leader in the Pee Dee. In that

In this painting by William Ranney, Francis Marion crosses the Pee Dee. General Marion (1732-1795) was known as "The Swamp Fox." He was probably the most romanticized American leader in the Revolution because of his successful guerrilla warfare against the British. Marion often operated from a hidden base on Snow's Island in the Pee Dee swamp. Courtesy, South Caroliniana Library

area Tory plundering and burning under Major James Wemyes had created much bitterness among the residents, and Marion had little difficulty recruiting soldiers. He usually operated with a small band of cavalry from a hidden base on Snow's Island deep in the Pee Dee swamp.

It is amazing that Marion was as successful as he was. His biographer Hugh Rankin notes that his men came and went as they pleased, and that he "seldom had the same people under his command for as long as two weeks." As the civil government had practically ceased to operate after the fall of Charles Town, Marion had little authority over his men. Moreover, he had no steady source of military supplies. Nevertheless, during the summer of 1780 Marion's swift-striking exploits earned him the name "The Swamp Fox." In time he became probably the most romanticized rebel militia leader of the American Revolution.

The first significant patriot victory after Gates' defeat came on August 19, when some 200 North Carolina militiamen soundly trounced a much larger loyalist force at Musgrove's Mill on the Enoree River in present-day Spartanburg County. This stinging blow caused Cornwallis to send Major Patrick Ferguson from Ninety-Six to deal with the partisans. As Ferguson moved into the area with about 1,100 loyalists, he learned that a slightly larger force of mounted rebels was searching for him. He tried to beat a hasty retreat to Ninety-Six before the partisans could overtake him. En route he took refuge on a hilltop near King's Mountain and dispatched a mes-

senger to Cornwallis for aid. The patriots reached Ferguson's encampment before relief arrived.

On that day, October 7, these skilled frontier riflemen struck from three sides of the mountain, moved up slowly behind natural cover, and picked off Tories as they went. Although obviously in a hopeless position, Major Ferguson refused to surrender and fought unto death. Afterwards the surviving Tories surrendered. The partisans, incensed over previous Tory atrocities, summarily executed several prisoners and brutalized others on their long march to a North Carolina prison.

The Battle of King's Mountain was an important turning point in the American Revolution, and it had a shocking influence on the British leadership. Lord Cornwallis, alarmed and ill with fever, gave up his Charlotte post and retreated into South Carolina to await reinforcements.

On December 3 General Nathanael Greene replaced the discredited Gates as commander of the continental forces in the South. Greene dared not confront the strong enemy army under Cornwallis with his own poorly equipped force of 1,500 men.

Awaiting a buildup of his strength, Greene sent one-half of his army, under General Daniel Morgan, to operate in the western Piedmont, while he marched into the Pee Dee with the remaining half. In due course both detachments were strengthened when General "Light Horse" Harry Lee joined Greene and Colonel Andrew Pickens teamed up with Morgan.

Pickens, South Carolina's third great partisan leader, had been captured and paroled at Charles Town. He took up arms again, like Sumter, because of Tory humiliations: Tories had ransacked his plantation and insulted his family. Pickens, known as the Fighting Elder, joined the rebels at great risk, for he knew that if captured again he would be executed. Indeed, the British later executed Colonel Isaac Hayne for violating his parole.

Lord Cornwallis hoped to deal with Greene's army while it was divided. He or-

dered Colonel Tarleton to attack Morgan while he pursued Greene. Tarleton overtook Morgan at Cowpens as the latter was trying desperately to reunite his force with Greene's. With further retreat impossible the American commander halted and arranged a trap into which the careless Briton rushed.

Morgan stationed Pickens' militia in front of his continentals to receive Tarleton's first blow. The militia then retreated as planned through the continental line, which stood its ground against Tarleton's force. The militia re-formed in the rear to sweep alongside the enemy while Colonel William Washington's cavalry struck Tarleton's other flank. The British commander noticed the trap too late; only he and a handful of his men escaped.

The American victory at Cowpens on January 17, 1781, was another heavy loss for the British. Afterwards their scattered garrisons from Georgetown to Ninety-Six came under increasing patriot attacks. In the meantime Greene and Cornwallis marched and counter-marched in North Carolina and Virginia. The American commander, upon receiving reinforcements in Virginia, took the offensive and attacked Cornwallis at Guilford Courthouse. The British army, though claiming victory, was so weakened by the bloody encounter that Cornwallis could no longer effectively maintain the offensive. He thus retreated with his battered army to Wilmington and left Lord Rawdon in charge of British

forces in South Carolina. With an inferior force Rawdon boldly attacked Greene at Hobkirk's Hill near Camden. Again the British claimed victory, but again heavy losses forced a retreat.

With the main enemy forces licking their wounds on or near the coast, South Carolina patriot bands began to reduce British garrisons one by one. Only at Ninety-Six did they encounter prolonged resistance. General Greene, aided by Pickens and Lee, besieged the star fort the British had built. All efforts to take the bastion failed, however, and Greene was forced to lift the siege upon learning that Lord Rawdon was approaching with reinforcements. Upon arrival Rawdon quickly decided that the post was too difficult to hold. He thereupon burned the town and evacuated the defenders. His retreat left upcountry South Carolina firmly in the hands of the patriots.

On September 8, 1781, the last important engagement in South Carolina oc-

Above left: General Andrew Pickens (1739-1817) was one of South Carolina's great patriot leaders. He was captured by the British at Charles Town, paroled, and then took up arms again when Tories plundered his backcountry plantation. Courtesy, South Caroliniana Library

Above right: Mrs. Rebecca Brewton Motte presented a bow and arrows to General Marion and Colonel Henry Lee to shoot at her Mount Joseph Plantation home (Fort Motte) near the Congaree River in present-day Calhoun County. Her home had been invested and fortified by the British. After the Americans ignited the roof, the British surrendered. Mrs. Motte then entertained officers of both armies with a dinner. Courtesy, Harper's Monthly

curred. At Eutaw Springs General Greene's army fought a British force under Colonel Alexander Stewart. Thereafter the British did not venture far from their Charles Town base. With Lord Cornwallis' surrender at Yorktown on October 19 the major fighting ended. Minor clashes and skirmishes continued, however, until the Treaty of Paris was signed in 1783. All in all, South Carolina, with approximately 150 military engagements, was one of the most fought-over states in the American Revolution.

The fighting was almost over before the colonies had a national constitution. Congress had of course been obligated by the Declaration of Independence to devise a frame of government. Named the Articles of Confederation and approved by Congress on July 24, 1778, the new constitution essentially preserved state sovereignty. The South Carolina delegation assented, but it was not until 1781 that the last of the 13 states gave its approval.

In the interim the South Carolina General Assembly, in March 1778, had framed and approved a new state constitution to replace the temporary one drawn up in early 1776. Under the 1778 constitution the president (now governor) could no longer veto bills; the upper house (now Senate) became elective; and the suffrage requirements of 1721 remained essentially the same: white males, 21 and older, owning 50 acres, or paying about 65 cents in taxes. In the legislative apportionment the lowcountry was again favored at the expense of the backcountry, and only persons of substantial wealth were eligible for high office. The lowcountry gentry, in control of the government since early colonial days, had no intention of surrendering their power.

The legislature busied itself with the war until the British capture of Charles Town in May 1780 disrupted its sessions.

It did not meet again until January 1782, when it convened at the small town of Jacksonborough on the Edisto River.

At Jacksonborough the legislature faced many problems because no peace treaty had yet been signed and a sizable British force still occupied Charles Town. General Greene's continentals, encamped at the High Hills of Santee, were another cause for concern. These soldiers were ill-clad, poorly provisioned, and unpaid. Their pitiful condition was described by their commander: "Near one-half of our soldiers have not a shoe to their foot and not a blanket to 10 men through the line." South Carolina was faced with almost the sole support of Greene's army.

The legislature also had to deal with Tory bands still roaming the state. One Tory leader, William Cunningham (alias Bloody Bill), became so notorious that the legislature put a price on his capture, dead or alive. Throughout 1782 a number of senseless clashes occurred between patriots and Tories or British foraging parties in the surrounding areas of Charles Town.

After a preliminary peace treaty was signed, the British evacuated Charles Town on December 14, 1782. They departed with much booty, over 5,000 slaves, and about 4,000 loyalists. The latter gave up their homes and possessions rather than face the wrath of the victorious patriots.

For the Tories who remained, the question of their treatment proved to be a hot political issue. John Rutledge and many other leaders urged confiscation of their property, whereas Francis Marion, young Charles Pinckney, and Christopher Gadsden, who had suffered in a British prison, urged forgiveness. By and large, propertied people were inclined toward leniency; commoners were not. The radicals in what was now, after the war, called Charleston suspected that the wealthier Tories, if not proscribed, would side with the lowcountry gentry to stifle democracy.

As for legal action, the General Assembly severely punished Tories who had been most active in support of the king. With the passage of time the legislature became more merciful. Almost yearly it restored some confiscated estates and welcomed back a few of the lesser offenders. However, an estimated 5,500 Tories never returned to South Carolina.

Another major problem involved debts and paper money, both continental and state. Thousands of citizens were poverty-stricken because of wartime destruction

At the battle of Cowpens, on January 17, 1781, American Brigadier General Daniel Morgan decisively defeated a British force commanded by Lieutenant Colonel Banastre Tarleton. This painting by William Ranney shows American cavalryman Colonel William Washington in hand-to-hand combat with some of Tarleton's retreating dragoons. Courtesy, South Caroliniana Library

and high inflation, which had rendered paper money worthless. To aid the impoverished debtors, the legislature enacted stay laws to postpone forcible collection of debts until 1787, and it legalized payment in goods as well as coin.

The controversies over postwar problems gave birth to a radical party that was highly critical of the "nabobs," as they called the gentry. Led by Commodore Alexander Gillon and Isaac Peronneau, the radicals hoped to win control of the government by uniting backcountry farmers with Charleston working-class voters. For a time they created much excitement in the port city. However, they failed to rally enough support to prevent the return of well-to-do Tories or to capture control of the Charleston municipal government. In July 1784 the frustrated radicals took to the streets with demonstrations and mob violence. Colonel William Washington's militia quickly restored order, Peronneau was imprisoned, and the "nabobs" remained in control.

The appearance of similar problems and resultant radical groups in other states, especially in Massachusetts, led many Americans to search for ways to strengthen the national government. Delegates at a meeting in Annapolis, Maryland, issued a call for a constitutional convention to meet in Philadelphia in the spring of 1787. The South Carolina legislature supported the move and chose John Rutledge, Pierce Butler, General C.C. Pinckney, and Charles Pinckney to represent South Carolina. All four delegates were well-to-do property owners from the lowcountry.

The South Carolina delegation at Philadelphia rivaled those of Pennsylvania and Virginia in debate and in constructive work at the convention. Young Charles Pinckney brought the draft of a constitution that he had compiled on the basis of other state constitutions. Several of its provisions, as well as other contributions by Pinckney, were included in the final document. That document's drafting was overseen by the important Committee on Detail, chaired by John Rutledge. The South Carolinians successfully defended Southern interests with regard to slavery and the slave trade, but the Constitution as finally drafted was not as aristocratic as they would have preferred. Nonetheless they regarded it as an improvement over the Articles of Confederation and, despite differences among themselves, worked for its approval back in South Carolina.

A South Carolina convention met in Charleston in April 1788 to consider the work of the Philadelphia Convention. Probably a majority of South Carolina voters opposed the Constitution as giving too much power to the central government at the expense of the states. There was also fear of Northern domination of the new government. The small farmers in the upper pine belt and Piedmont were the chief opponents of the Constitution. However, these areas were underrepresented in the convention. Thus, after several days of debate, the Federalists, mostly Charlestonians and other lowcountrymen, won approval of the Constitution by a vote of 149 to 73.

Antifederalist Aedanus Burke credited the Federalist victory to the fact that all the leading men along the "rice coast," most of the Charleston merchants and professional men, and the former Tories favored the Constitution. In the city the leading supporters "kept open house" for convention delegates, gained the support of the printers, and brought pressure to bear on waverers. The Antifederalists, by contrast, were poorly organized and had failed to enlist any printer to ensure publication of their views.

South Carolina's approval of the Constitution led, Burke declared, to "disgust, sorrow, and vindictive reproaches" in the interior of the state. He believed the new government rested on a "sandy foundation." Despite such grave misgivings, the new constitution won nationwide approval, and the new government, under the presidency of George Washington, soon won the support of most Americans.

Fort Watson was a British post built on an Indian mound in present-day Clarendon County. American militia forced the fort to surrender on April 23, 1781, by constructing a tower and shooting down into the stockade. Such towers were called Maham towers, after Lieutenant Colonel Hezekiah Maham, who first devised one. Drawing by Darby Erd. Courtesy, South Carolina Institute of Archeology and Anthropology

Chapter IV

Cotton, Slavery, and Political Decline: 1789-1848

When Washington was inaugurated president, South Carolina's political leadership and economy made the state one of the most important in the American union. For some years thereafter it continued to play a highly visible and influential role.

The first census in 1790 reported 140,178 whites and 108,895 blacks for a total population of 249,073 in South Carolina. For the first time in over 80 years whites outnumbered blacks. However, by 1820 blacks were again in the majority and continued to be until the census of 1930.

In the early post-revolutionary years the state's economy underwent several changes. The Indian trade ceased, and Britain cut off American commerce to its West Indian islands. Independence also brought an end to the bounty on indigo, a severe blow to South Carolina growers. Rice continued to be the state's chief export crop. However, its position was soon challenged by cotton, first by the long-staple sea island variety and later by the short-staple inland type.

The major political issue in South Carolina was a continuation of backcountry-lowcountry rivalry over control of the government. In the 1790s the lowcountry was comprised of the rice-planting, coastal districts of Beaufort, Charleston, and Georgetown. Its economy was largely dependent on slave labor and foreign commerce. Its white inhabitants were mainly of English and Huguenot background; its outlook was international. The backcountry districts (or, "upper division") of Ninety-Six, Cheraw, Orangeburg, and Camden, covered the upper pine belt, sandhills, and Piedmont. The Scotch-Irish and Germans who dominated there owned few slaves, engaged in little foreign commerce, enjoyed a live-at-home economy, and were provincial in outlook.

Ever since the Regulator movement, the coastal gentry had grudgingly made concessions to the backcountry, but never enough to threaten lowcountry control of the government. In 1786 the General Assembly even agreed to move the state capital to Columbia in the center of the state, and shortly thereafter it yielded to pressure for a state convention to rewrite the Constitution of 1778.

The convention met in Columbia in 1790, and on a vote of 109 to 105 agreed to retain the capital in Columbia. On the question of legislative apportionment, the three "lower division" districts retained control of the House, 70 to 54, and the Senate, 20 to 17.

The lowcountry gentry would yield no further despite the fact that whites in the four "upper division" districts outnumbered "lower division" whites about four to one. The new document continued high property qualifications for membership in the General Assembly and payment of a modest tax for eligibility to vote. Generally, the provisions of the Constitution of 1778 were left unchanged.

In national affairs there were no regular political parties when Washington took office. Disagreement over foreign policy led to the development of the two-party system—initially Federalists and Republicans. From 1792 to 1815 Europe was almost continuously wracked by a war in which France and Great Britain were on opposite sides. Because the French had overthrown the monarchy and established a republic, that nation won much sympathy in America, especially among the small farmers and persons of liberal views. England had the support of the mercantile community and upper classes in general.

During his administration President Washington leaned heavily on the pro-

After a Day's "Picking" *is the title of this drawing by an unknown artist depicting life on a cotton plantation. Courtesy, South Carolina Historical Society*

English Federalist party for support. Within South Carolina the Pinckney brothers, Charles Cotesworth (C.C.) and Thomas, and the Rutledge brothers, John and Edward, became leading Federalists. These four men—lowcountry gentry and English-educated—held important judicial, diplomatic, and administrative posts in the federal government and were consulted on the federal patronage in South Carolina. They also held high position in the Federalist party.

The Pinckneys and Rutledges were closely connected through ties of friendship and marriage; they were known for their international outlook and moderately conservative views. Three of the four served as governor of South Carolina, and they were probably the most influential political clique the state has ever known.

In foreign affairs the Washington administration early faced the problem of dealing with France. The fledgling French republic, beset with numerous enemies, decided to send a new representative to America in 1793 to explain its position and seek whatever aid the United States government could render as a neutral. For this task they chose young Edmond Genet. Ordinarily South Carolina would not have been involved, but Genet, instead of going directly to Philadelphia to present his credentials,

landed at Charleston. He then proceeded to commission privateers to prey on British commerce and tried to organize an expedition against Spanish possessions to the south—all this in clear violation of American neutrality. Genet seems to have won support for his military schemes from certain Charlestonians who saw a chance for personal benefit. After having enjoyed a brief triumphal sojourn in the port city, the Frenchman set out for Philadelphia, where his continued indiscretions and defiance of Washington's proclamation of neutrality led to his recall.

As the European War continued, America—the chief neutral commerce carrier—found its ships, cargoes, and crews increasingly seized by the French and, even more so, by the British. British violations of American neutrality, coupled with unsettled disputes continued from the Revolution, generated war fever.

President Washington, in an effort to avoid war, replaced Thomas Pinckney, the American minister in London, with special emissary John Jay, who had instructions to negotiate all differences between the nations. Jay's Treaty (1794) won only minor concessions from the British, although the terms were the best Jay believed he could obtain. The treaty was a major factor in the rise of a new Republican party.

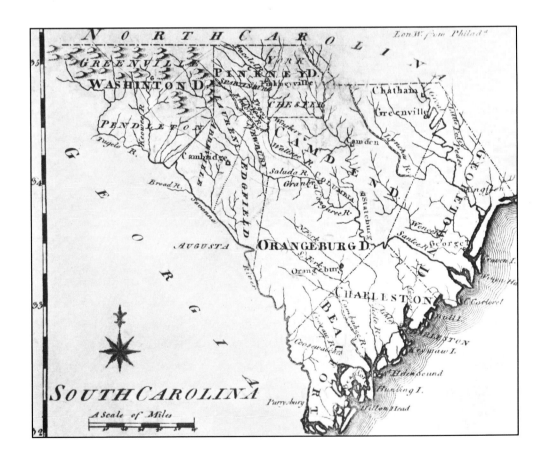

This map of South Carolina, circa 1790, is by an unknown cartographer. Several districts were later abolished or their boundaries were changed, and the northwestern boundary with North Carolina was not yet surveyed. The map mistakes the Broad River for the Wateree, and several names are misspelled. The settlements of Chatham and Greenville on the "Pedee" were early names for Cheraw and Long Bluff, respectively. Courtesy, Lewis Moorhead

In Charleston an angry mob burned the British flag in front of the British consulate. Leading supporters of the Washington administration were embarrassed and angry. John Rutledge was so incensed that he publicly denounced Jay's Treaty. His strong opposition caused the Federalist-controlled Senate to refuse confirmation of his appointment to the United States Supreme Court. Meanwhile, Thomas Pinckney's transfer from London to Madrid relieved him of a thorny problem. In Spain he gained new laurels by working out a treaty that led to the opening of the Mississippi River to American commerce, an object much desired by the South. In return, the Federalists, fearful of losing South Carolina in the 1796 election, placed Pinckney on their ticket as the vice-presidential nominee. However, he ran third in the contest, thus yielding the vice-presidency to Thomas Jefferson, a Republican.

The French government was offended by Jay's Treaty, in which it felt that the Americans had yielded too much on neutral rights to Great Britain. In order to appease the French, President Washington sent C.C. Pinckney to Paris as the new American minister. However, when the irate French government refused to receive Pinckney, John Adams, the new president, sent two additional diplomats to strengthen the minister's hand.

Further problems soon developed when it became clear that the three French emissaries who dealt with the Americans wanted a bribe before officially receiving them. Pinckney's indignant reply "no, no, not a sixpence" made him an immediate hero back in America. His fellow South Carolinian, Representative Robert Goodloe Harper, coined the phrase "millions for defense, but not one cent for tribute" that soon swept the nation. The incident became known as the "XYZ" affair because the American dispatches merely referred to the Frenchmen as Mr. X., Mr. Y, and Mr. Z. With jingoism running high in America, the United States and France tangled in a limited, undeclared naval war from 1798 to 1800.

It was during this naval war that the power of the South Carolina Federalists reached its zenith. In the election of 1798 they captured five of six congressional seats, and Edward Rutledge, their most capable politician, was elevated to the governor's office. The party faced a severe test two years later.

The presidential election of 1800 was

John Rutledge (1739-1800) was a Revolutionary leader, the president (governor) of South Carolina from 1776 to 1778, a member of the Philadelphia Convention in 1787, a U.S. Supreme Court justice, and a Federalist party leader. This portrait of Rutledge was painted by John Trumbull. Courtesy, Library of Congress

a rematch between President John Adams, a Federalist, and Vice President Thomas Jefferson, a Republican. C.C. Pinckney was Adams' running mate; Aaron Burr, Jefferson's. Alexander Hamilton, who heartily disliked Adams, tried to persuade several Southern electors to vote for Pinckney but not for Adams, with the hope that Pinckney would lead the ticket and become president. However, Pinckney refused to be a party to such a scheme.

Since presidential electors in South Carolina were chosen by the state legislature until 1860, the contests for legislative seats were hard fought. The Republicans' narrow victory in South Carolina in 1800 was due largely to Charles Pinckney's organizational work. Pinckney, a cousin of Thomas and Charles Cotesworth and known by his erstwhile upper class friends as "Blackguard Charley," was a former governor and current United States senator. The South Carolina vote was crucial for Republican victory in the presidential contest, but the party was embarrassed to find Burr and Jefferson tied in votes for the presidency. The tie had to be broken by the "lame duck" national House of Representatives, one vote per state. Many Federalist congressmen, including those from South Carolina, voted for Burr. Jefferson eventually prevailed, but the Federalists' efforts to make Burr president created further resentment against their party.

After the election of 1800 the Federalist party rapidly declined, except in New England. So weak did the party become that renowned Charles Cotesworth Pinckney,

Federalist candidate for president in 1804 and 1808, could not carry his own state.

The political revolution of 1800 reflected an economic revolution. Indigo growers, suffering from the loss of the British bounty, were searching for a new crop when Eli Whitney invented the cotton gin, patented in 1793. By 1800 cotton cultivation was sweeping the upper pine belt, and within another decade many backcountry farmers had become successful cotton planters.

The prime success story was that of Wade Hampton. A Virginian by birth, this skillful politician, soldier, and businessman acquired land in Richland District and began large-scale cotton production with slave labor. By 1811 he was able to purchase a sugar estate in Louisiana for $300,000. To a degree, Hampton's success was emulated by other cotton planters in middle and backcountry South Carolina, men who were mainly Jeffersonian Republicans. These men acquired slaves, and in some cases their sons cemented alliances with lowcountry gentry through marriage.

By the first decade of the nineteenth century the gentry of the "lower division" districts of Georgetown, Charleston, and Beaufort realized they could no longer hold back the political aspirations of the newly ascendant cotton barons in the more populous "upper division" districts. The influx of cotton and slaves into the "upper division" meanwhile changed attitudes of successful farmers. By 1808 black-belt planters in the "lower division" were ready to share their power. The "upper division" economic revolution cemented white support behind the institution of slavery. The legislature voted overwhelmingly to change representation.

The Compromise of 1808 provided one senator for each election district. House membership of 124 was to be apportioned evenly between white population and taxes paid. In the election of 1810 the "lower division" districts chose 22 senators (two from Charleston) and 54 representatives, while the "upper division" won 23 senators and 70 representatives. Since the census of 1810 revealed that much of central South Carolina, in the "upper division," was over 50 percent black in population, it was apparent that black-belt whites still controlled the General Assembly.

Meanwhile, in foreign affairs more than a decade of British depredations against American commerce and intrigues with Western Indians led to strained rela-

tions between Britain and America. South Carolinians were aroused primarily by British actions on the high seas. Rice and cotton planters and Charleston merchants all suffered from wartime disruptions of commerce. A new group of young leaders had come to the forefront, and when President James Madison asked Congress to declare war in June 1812, the South Carolinians unanimously joined other "war hawks" in granting his request.

While South Carolina played no direct role in the War of 1812, Governor Joseph Alston raised the 5,000 troops requested by the president and sent some to Northern battlefields, where most of the military action occurred. The state's chief concern was to defend its coast against minor enemy forays. Occasionally British raiders invaded inlets, looted plantations, captured ships off the South Carolina coast, and stirred up excitement in Charleston. The war ended in 1815 with South Carolina largely unaffected except for its commerce.

In fact, despite upheavals wrought by the Revolution, the cotton boom, and national political controversies, South Carolina had not changed in many important ways. According to Professor Kenneth Greenberg, probably in no other American state did eighteenth-century English political ideas remain so powerful so long into the nineteenth century as in South Carolina. The state's leadership, dominated by lowcountry gentry, staunchly believed in "virtual" representation in government rather than actual representation. There were no statewide elections for political office, not even for governor, as late as 1860, and there were restrictions on voting and office holding. Party politics, weaker in the South than in the North, was at its weakest in South Carolina. Palmetto leaders believed that party politics threatened white unity, so necessary in the face of the black majority.

These views survived even the transfer of leadership to new men, including David R. Williams, William Lowndes, Langdon Cheves, and John C. Calhoun. Williams and Lowndes were of the lowcountry gentry, while Cheves and Calhoun represented the backcountry.

These men were leaders under the "war hawks" against Great Britain, and during the war all four quickly gained important congressional committee chairmanships. Cheves succeeded Clay as Speaker of the House in 1814, the first South Carolinian ever to hold that prestigious post. With the close of the war the brilliant South Carolina quartet was supremely confident of their state's future. Williams was in the governor's chair; Cheves was soon to take over the Bank of the United States and guide it out of financial difficulties; Congressmen Calhoun and Lowndes were ably supporting President Madison's nationalistic program of internal improvement, the Bank of the United States, and a protective tariff.

A majority of the South Carolina leaders retained a broad view of the Constitution until the early 1820s. Meanwhile Calhoun removed himself from congressional debate in 1817 by accepting the position of secretary of war under President James Monroe, a post he held until 1825. Overall, a majority of South Carolinians seemed reasonably well satisfied with the national government: the state was prosperous, a Southern-dominated Republican party controlled Congress, and with one exception Southerners had served in the White House since the republic's inception in 1789.

However, in a brief period, two major forces changed South Carolina attitudes toward the national government. One was the Panic of 1819 and subsequent economic distress, and the other was slavery.

South Carolina's economy had undergone considerable change since the American Revolution. The Charleston merchants, riding high before 1775, suffered during the years 1808-1815 because of wartime restrictions and the permanent stoppage of the African slave trade.

With the relative decline of the Charleston merchants, agriculture emerged supreme. The years from 1816 to 1818 marked a brief golden period for the planters. Rice reached seven cents a pound, upland short-staple cotton peaked at 35 cents, and some of the finer grades of sea island long-staple cotton sold above one dollar. Then came the "bust"—the Panic of 1819—due largely to inflation, expansion of credit, and a land boom in the southwest. Bankruptcies were common and unemployment soared.

Prices in agricultural commodities in South Carolina dropped about one-half by 1822. Although the depression was over for most of the nation by that date, it lingered in South Carolina. Actually the state's planters were finding it difficult to compete with those exploiting the rich lands in Alabama, Mississippi, and elsewhere in the southwest opened up since the end of the War of 1812.

Wade Hampton I (1754-1835) was a Revolutionary War hero and a major general in the War of 1812. Hampton made a fortune growing cotton in the Richland District and producing sugar in Louisiana. His son, Wade Hampton II, held the family fortune together and was a strong behind-the-scenes political figure. Wade Hampton III, his grandson, was South Carolina's most illustrious Civil War general. Courtesy, South Carolina Historical Society

Moreover, credit was scarce; there was not a single bank above the fall line. Many South Carolina banks strictly limited their banknote circulation. Not surprisingly, many South Carolina farmers moved southwest with their families and possessions. The effect of the westward trek is shown in the census returns. Between 1820 and 1860 South Carolina suffered a net loss of 200,000 whites and 170,000 blacks through migration. In this climate the tariffs protecting Northern manufacturers were sharply resented by South Carolinians, who found themselves paying more for goods without any compensatory protection for their own products.

It was not that rice and long staple cotton planters suffered much decline in their standard of living in the 1820s. By improving the quality and quantity of their products, they had managed to hold their own, despite economic problems—long-term mortgages, debilitating malaria, and ineffective overseers. As planter and legislator Robert Barnwell Rhett explained: "The lands I own I have planted eleven years and have lost but one crop. Our tide swamp lands in the production of rice are the most certain in the world and the price of the commodity the least fluctuating."

The lowcountry planters were angry with the North, too, but as much on slavery's account as on economic grounds.

The census of 1820 revealed that blacks outnumbered whites in Charleston District three to one, in Colleton five to

one, in Beaufort six to one, and in Georgetown, the great rice-producing area, eight to one. As far inland as Sumter District blacks were in a two-to-one majority. The rapid growth of black population had been greatly accelerated by legislation, passed under pressure from cotton growers, reopening the African slave trade in 1804. From that date until the federal government stopped the traffic on January 1, 1808, about 40,000 blacks were brought into South Carolina. This racial imbalance made lowcountry whites uneasy about anything that might threaten their control of this vast slave population.

The same year of the census, a bitter debate over slavery in Missouri erupted in Congress. Although a compromise was worked out whereby Missouri entered the union as a slave state and Maine as a free state, thus preserving the balance in the Senate, South Carolinians were greatly alarmed over Northern opinions that, according to Governor John Geddes of Charleston, tended to reduce the value of slavery and "threaten our safety."

As an aftermath of the Missouri debates, the South Carolina General Assembly passed laws tightening whites' control over slaves and free blacks. Whites were particularly apprehensive of the latter as potential leaders of slave insurrection. Their fears were realized when in June 1822 a slave conspiracy was reported.

Charlestonians were horrified to hear that the blacks planned to seize the arsenals, murder all whites, and take over the city. Charleston was never the same again. Historian W.W. Freehling notes that in the nullification crisis "the man most responsible for bringing South Carolina to the boiling point was not a great planter-politician . . . but a lowly Charleston mulatto named Denmark Vesey." Vesey was a free black carpenter who had purchased his freedom with a lottery jackpot. It was in his shop that the plot was allegedly hatched.

How far the conspiracy went is unknown. Some of the suspects turned state's evidence and obviously lied in an effort to save their own lives. In any event, during the next two months 35 blacks were hanged (including Vesey and alleged chief henchman Gullah Jack) and 37 were banished from the state. How many innocent blacks were punished will never be known. The

Although this photo was taken in Georgetown circa 1900, the method of pounding rice shown was the same as that which was practiced in colonial days. After the grain had been threshed, it was polished by pounding, which removed the husk and bran. Unpolished rice was often eaten by slaves and poorer people. Courtesy, Morgan Collection, Georgetown County Library

accused leaders neither confessed nor revealed names.

The panic in the lowcountry set off by the alleged Vesey plot was heightened by several reports of slave arson in Charleston in the next few years, a reported slave conspiracy in Georgetown in 1826 (six blacks were executed), and the Nat Turner rebellion in Virginia in 1831. In the latter case the murder of some 60 whites sent a wave of fear throughout the South.

In South Carolina wild rumors were rampant; the slave patrol was strengthened and blacks were jailed on the slightest suspicion. Also suspect were Yankee peddlers, who were suspected of meeting slaves at night and selling them whiskey.

As the depression continued over the upland cotton belt and anxiety increased about slavery, South Carolina whites began to fear the growing power of the federal government. By the mid-1820s a majority of the state's voters had deserted a qualified nationalism in favor of states' rights. A further drop in short-staple cotton prices put South Carolina in a desperate mood by early 1827. It was on the tariff issue that upcountry and lowcountry planters closed ranks and sought ways to block what they considered unconstitutional federal encroachments on their rights.

President of South Carolina College Thomas Cooper, Charleston lawyer Robert J. Turnbull, Congressman George McDuffie, young legislator Robert Barnwell Rhett, and James Hamilton, Jr., led the vanguard of articulate proponents of state sovereignty. Cooper believed it was time for South Carolina "to calculate the value of the union." Having been unable to block

higher rates in the Tariff of 1824, South Carolinians were further frustrated by the Tariff of 1828, better known as the "Tariff of Abominations."

All the while, John C. Calhoun sat silently presiding over the United States Senate as vice president of the nation. After much study and thought Calhoun formulated a theory that he hoped would prevent more drastic measures, and he presented it to the General Assembly in the fall of 1828 under the title *South Carolina Exposition and Protest,* with the understanding that his name would not be made public—he still had presidential aspirations.

Calhoun's theory, based in part on the Virginia and Kentucky resolutions of 1798, was that sovereign states had joined a compact, the Constitution, through state conventions and that each state could be the judge of violations of that contact. He worked out an elaborate system for judging and remedying violations whereby states could preserve their sovereignty and minority rights. However, Calhoun did not envision states resorting to nullification of federal acts without considerable provocation. Nor did he concern himself much with other minorities, religious or racial.

The vice president's "nullification" theory quickly won great support in South Carolina, but Unionist leaders were able to forestall the Nullifiers' ambitions until 1832. Meanwhile, pressure from the Nullifiers "smoked out" the reticent Calhoun. In August 1831 the vice president published his "Fort Hill Letter" that committed him openly to the principle of nullification. He was thereafter marked as a sectionalist. His close admirer, Judge John McLean, sadly

CASH!

All persons that have SLAVES to dispose of, will do well by giving me a call, as I will give the

HIGHEST PRICE FOR

Men, Women, & CHILDREN.

Any person that wishes to sell, will call at Hill's tavern, or at Shannon Hill for me, and any information they want will be promptly attended to.

Thomas Griggs.

Charlestown, May 7, 1835.

PRINTED AT THE FREE PRESS OFFICE, CHARLESTOWN.

Advertisements for the sale of slaves were common in Southern newspapers. It is unlikely that anyone noticed the incongruity of such an ad being printed by the "Free Press Office, Charlestown." Courtesy, Black Charleston Exhibit, College of Charleston

Dr. Thomas Cooper (1759-1839) was a brilliant English-born scientist who served as president of South Carolina College from 1820 to 1834. His views on state sovereignty greatly influenced the generation of South Carolina leaders that came to power in the 1850s. However, his unorthodox religious views led to his removal from the presidency of the college. Courtesy, South Caroliniana Library

wrote: "Our friend Calhoun is gone, I fear, forever."

In 1832 Congress at last revised the tariff, but the new bill failed to give the relief South Carolinians sought. The Nullifiers girded for action and in a bitterly fought statewide election won two-thirds of the seats in the legislature against Unionist opponents.

Victorious at last, the Nullifiers called for a convention, which met in November and declared the tariff laws of 1828 and 1832 "null and void" within South Carolina, effective March 1, 1833. Robert Y. Hayne resigned from his Senate seat to become governor, and Calhoun relinquished the vice presidency to replace Hayne in the Senate. However, hoped-for support from other Southern states failed to materialize.

President Andrew Jackson moved cautiously but effectively. He kept in touch with South Carolina Unionist leaders and while he publicly voiced affection for his native state,

he warned of federal force. To avert a serious confrontation Congress passed a compromise tariff but at the same time enacted a force bill, which in effect endorsed the president's right to take military action to enforce federal laws in South Carolina. The Nullifiers, isolated from the rest of the South and facing opposition within their own state, seemed to welcome the compromise and the crisis passed.

But why did the Nullifiers seek to battle on the issue of tariff alone and not slavery? Governor James Hamilton, Jr., their organizer, explained: "However we might be united at home on slavery, we would have few confederates abroad—whereas on the subject of free trade and constitutional rights, we should have allies throughout the civilized world." No allies came forth.

After this brief flirtation with disaster, South Carolina remained on the defensive for the remainder of the antebellum period. At the outset of the nullification dispute Calhoun was overshadowed within his own state by other political leaders. But thereafter and until his death in 1850, Calhoun was South Carolina's (and the South's) foremost spokesman in defense of slavery and states' rights, making unceasing war on abolitionists, warning against their growing influence, and deploring the South's minority status. His opponents called him the Duke of Pendleton, and it was said that the whole state sneezed when

he took a pinch of snuff. Yet, he had no political machine; he lacked Jackson's charisma; and his hold on his state and most of the deep South, according to biographer Charles M. Wiltse, "was based on intellectual leadership."

Calhoun had greater ambitions—to become president of the United States—but he wanted the office to seek him. He briefly entered the presidential contest of 1824; however, upon seeing that other candidates had more support, he withdrew and ran for vice president instead. Successful then and again in 1828, he had high hopes of entering the White House following Jackson's presidency. Unfortunately for Calhoun, his break with Old Hickory over personal matters and his support of nullification doomed his chances for the Democratic party nomination in the 1830s.

In 1843, upon the urging of friends, Calhoun left the Senate to make one final effort for the presidency. Noting Calhoun's independence, Nullifier James H. Hammond commented: "It seems to me that Calhoun must be the man, unless he kicks over the pail of water, of which there is much danger." Calhoun's daughter, Anna Clemson, believed her father's chance was "at least a fair one." She noted that the entire Fort Hill household was excited over his prospects. No doubt, ambition and a sense of duty spurred Calhoun on, but later his brother-in-law, James Edward Calhoun, revealed that Calhoun had privately confessed that he was "too old to do justice to the office, and did not want it." Again, seeing his chances fade, he suddenly withdrew from the contest. However, even at this late date, Calhoun refused to publicly renounce his presidential ambitions.

The bitterness between Nullifiers and Unionists in South Carolina continued until the 1840 gubernatorial election, at which time Calhoun's forces supported Unionist John P. Richardson for the office. Above all Calhoun wanted political unity within the state on the issue of slavery. Palmetto politics had in the meantime become somewhat confusing. Most of the state's leaders were Democratic-Republicans, but because of their hatred of Jackson many, including Calhoun, left the party for a time. Many Unionists and a few Nullifiers joined the Whig party, organized in 1834, led in South Carolina by Senator William C. Preston and Congressman Waddy Thompson. This new party, however, was never strong enough to win control of the state. Calhoun himself made peace with the

James Henry Hammond (1807-1864) was an ardent Nullifier who served as a U.S. congressman from South Carolina in 1835 and 1836, state governor from 1842-1844, and U.S. senator from 1857-1860. A wealthy planter and slaveholder at Silver Bluff near Augusta, Georgia, Hammond became famous for his "Cotton is King" speech before the Senate in 1858. Photo by Mathew Brady. Courtesy, South Caroliniana Library

Democrats in 1837.

Of more significance than party alignments in the 1830s and 1840s was the pressure exerted by political cliques. The most prominent of these cliques was headed by secessionist Congressman Robert B. Rhett and lawyer-businessman Franklin H. Elmore. Their brothers, Albert and James Rhett and Benjamin T. Elmore, served in the legislature, and the Rhetts' brother-in-law, John A. Stuart, edited the influential Charleston Mercury. This clique usually supported Calhoun, who also had the support of his kinsmen Patrick Noble, Francis W. Pickens, and Armistead Burt, all prominent in politics. This was a formidable array of talent and almost impossible to beat so long as they cooperated.

There were as many issues to divide as well as unite these men. One of President Jackson's last acts before leaving the White House in March 1837 was to recognize the Republic of Texas. This act immediately led to difficulties between the United States and Mexican governments. For several years the United States government considered the annexation of Texas, much desired by Texans, but the slavery issue and obvious Mexican objections postponed a decision.

In early 1844, President John Tyler and Secretary of State Abel Upshur had cleared

John Caldwell Calhoun (1782-1850) was a South Carolina legislator, U.S. congressman, secretary of war, vice president, U.S. senator, secretary of state, and U.S. senator again, in that order. From the mid-1830s until his death, Calhoun was the South's foremost defender of states' rights and slavery. Photo of a miniature by Mueller at the Fort Hill mansion, Clemson University. Courtesy, Special Collections, Clemson University Library

icans obliged by attacking one of General Zachary Taylor's patrols in the disputed territory along the Rio Grande. Administration forces immediately introduced war resolutions in both houses of Congress.

In the Senate Calhoun and a few others pleaded for more time, for more discussion, and for a clearer picture of events on the Rio Grande. An administration steamroller crushed their amendments, and on the final vote of 40 to 2 Calhoun abstained. To his dying day he was convinced that the war was unnecessary and that the president had provoked it by ordering General Taylor into the disputed territory. He foresaw results that would weaken the South's defense of slavery. In spite of friends' advice, Calhoun broke with the Polk administration over the war. He opposed General Winfield Scott's march to Mexico City, and he proposed a defensive line along the Rio Grande to El Paso and then westward to the Pacific. As a result of his break with Polk, his longtime congressional colleague Dixon Lewis of Alabama remarked: "He reminds me of a great general, who wins great battles and then throws away his life in a street fracas."

In South Carolina the war was popular at its beginning, but after the first flush of victory subsided and Mexico stubbornly refused to come to terms, many South Carolinians began to have doubts about the wisdom of Polk's policy. When the secretary of war called the Palmetto Regiment to duty in November 1846, not a single company could be recruited in the backcountry districts of York, Spartanburg, Greenville, Pickens, Anderson, and Laurens. Nevertheless, the regiment raised its quota of 974 men mainly from the central districts of the state. It was an ill-fated regiment. Disease and privation took their toll before the men had a chance for glory at Churubusco and Mexico City. The regimental commander, Colonel Pierce M. Butler, was killed in action, and the second in command, Lieutenant Colonel John P. Dickinson, later died from his injuries in battle. In fact, almost half the regiment succumbed in Mexico in what was probably the highest casualty rate of any United States regiment in the war.

The change in attitude in South Carolina could be seen when the legislature in December 1846 unanimously reelected Calhoun to the United States Senate. By that time, Calhoun was supported by Governor David Johnson and two South Carolinians who had at various times served as the U.S.

the way for a treaty of annexation when the secretary was killed in a gun explosion aboard a warship. Calhoun succeeded Upshur in the State Department but was so blatant in his defense of slavery that he turned Whig senators against the treaty. Annexation was thus delayed until March 1845, at which time Texas was taken into the American union by a joint resolution of Congress just before Tyler and Calhoun left office. This act worsened relations between Mexico and the United States.

The new president, James K. Polk, had been elected on an expansionist platform that included annexation of Texas all the way to the Rio Grande, a disputed boundary. Polk also wanted California and New Mexico. After Polk was unable to get Mexican authorities even to discuss the issues, he decided on war. In April 1846 the Mex-

minister to Mexico, Joel R. Poinsett and Waddy Thompson. In addition, South Carolinians were worried about the Wilmot Proviso, first introduced into Congress in August 1846. The proviso called for the abolition of slavery in all territory that the United States might wrest from Mexico. During 1847 nearly every courthouse town in the state held an anti-Wilmot Proviso rally. At some places there was a hint of secession.

Yet even without the hated proviso, Calhoun and others believed that slavery would never flourish beyond the Rio Grande. A few South Carolina leaders, but not Calhoun, went so far as to call for no territorial annexation beyond the Rio Grande. As the war dragged on into early 1848 and anarchy seemed to threaten Mexico, nearly every newspaper in South Carolina voiced opposition to the president's war policy. The state's political leaders who supported Polk kept their silence. However, during the winter Mexican leaders, tired of the fruitless

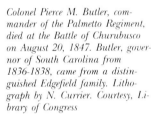

conflict, agreed to peace largely on Polk's terms. The large southwestern territory they surrendered was soon to cause a great conflict in America over slavery.

William Campbell Preston (1794-1860) was a Nullifier who later became South Carolina's foremost Whig party leader. As a U.S. senator from 1833 until his resignation in 1842, he broke with John C. Calhoun. Preston, a classical scholar and brilliant orator, served as president of South Carolina College from 1845-1850. Courtesy, South Caroliniana Library

Colonel Pierce M. Butler, commander of the Palmetto Regiment, died at the Battle of Churubusco on August 20, 1847. Butler, governor of South Carolina from 1836-1838, came from a distinguished Edgefield family. Lithograph by N. Currier. Courtesy, Library of Congress

Chapter V

The Mid-Nineteenth Century

However important, national affairs only occupied a small portion of the time, energy, and thought of nineteenth-century South Carolinians. Living in a rural, agricultural state, South Carolinians had to be as concerned about the weather, world market conditions, and farm management. For example, South Carolina had more large slaveowners than any other state, 484 of whom owned 100 slaves or more in 1850—the majority of these slaveholders being rice planters.

Like their long-staple cotton growing cousins, the rice planters were generally prosperous during the antebellum years. On the other hand, upland short-staple cotton growers fared poorly in the 1820s and again in the 1840s, when cotton prices dipped below five cents per pound. Buffering them was the fact that most also tried to produce sufficient foodstuffs for their own needs. John C. Calhoun, for example, with 1,100 acres on his Fort Hill estate and 50 to 75 slaves, planted about 75 acres of cotton as a cash crop, which he sent by flatboat to Augusta. He would be known today as a progressive farmer, for he put much more acreage in corn, wheat, rye, potatoes, and vegetables. He had success with two acres of rice on Seneca River bottomland. His pasture was filled with hogs and cattle, his barnyard had various kinds of fowl, and his orchard contained several varieties of fruit. To further promote self-sufficiency Calhoun had slaves trained in carpentry and mechanics. His example was emulated by large planters statewide.

Large planters employed overseers on their estates with varying degrees of success. James H. Hammond, a successful planter near Augusta, declared that the "present race of overseers are the greatest curse under which our Agriculture labours." His criticism was too harsh; overseers were isolated, poorly paid ($200 to $500 a year), and on duty around the clock.

With the severe agricultural depression in the 1840s, South Carolina farm leaders began to make serious efforts to improve agriculture. Local agricultural societies sprang up, several farm journals were published, and the State Agricultural Society took on new life. Although there was some improvement, there was no great wave of reform. Fortunately for the cotton growers, short-staple cotton prices rose above 10 cents a pound in the 1850s, thus bringing a reasonable measure of prosperity during that decade.

As for transportation, most commerce in colonial days had moved by water. Although there was wagon trade between Charleston and the backcountry, river crossings, lowcountry swamps, and poor roads made it difficult to move commerce by land. Where there were roads, they were maintained by local road commissions, and narrow-wheeled wagons quickly rutted them in bad weather to the point of impassability. In the 1820s a few plank toll roads were built, some with state aid, but expensive upkeep rendered them unprofitable. Also in the 1820s the state built a toll road from Charleston to Columbia and later extended it to North Carolina via present-day Greer. The roundtrip toll for a four-horse wagon from Charleston to Columbia was nine dollars.

In the meantime, Charlestonians, in an effort to tap interior trade, promoted the Santee Canal to connect the Santee and Cooper rivers. The canal was 22 miles long—the longest in the United States—when completed in 1800. Unfortunately the route was poorly chosen and construction costs soared to over $650,000, making the investment financially unsound. Begin-

The locomotive called the "Best Friend of Charleston" was manufactured in New York and made its first run in 1830 on the South Carolina Railroad. The line between Charleston and Hamburg was completed in 1833. This is a replica of the original locomotive. Courtesy, Pendleton District Historical and Recreational Commission

Adele Petigru Allston (1810-1896) was the sister of Unionist lawyer James L. Petigru and the wife of Robert F.W. Allston. Allston was the governor of South Carolina from 1856 to 1858 and the owner of seven rice plantations and hundreds of slaves in the Georgetown District. Mrs. Allston, a cultured lady and the mother of 10 children, epitomized the ideal of antebellum South Carolina womanhood. The war left her husband dead and his estate virtually bankrupt. With difficulty she managed to hold on to her Chicora Wood home and a few acres of adjoining land, on which she continued to plant rice until her death. Courtesy, South Caroliniana Library

During the 1850s the trackage was increased to 988 miles, split between 11 railroad companies. Charleston at this time was well served with lines to Wilmington, Augusta, Savannah, and Columbia, and as far inland as Walhalla, Greenville, Spartanburg, and Yorkville. The port city's foreign commerce increased from $13.3 million in 1850 to $22.8 million in 1860. The total cost of South Carolina railroads by 1860 was over $22 million. Of this amount the legislature had invested $2.6 million and endorsed $4.7 million of bonds; the Charleston city government had invested almost $3 million.

Public and private investors were not always as solicitous of agriculture. Banks were slow to be established in South Carolina, except in Charleston. Not until the 1830s did the legislature charter a bank outside the port city. By 1860, of the 18 banks in the state only two were above the fall line, one each at Winnsboro and Chester. The richest bank in the state was the Bank of Charleston, with $3 million in capital. It paid handsome dividends and was the only antebellum bank to survive to the present, the parent of the statewide South Carolina National chain. Next in importance was the Bank of the State of South Carolina, known as the State Bank, chartered in 1812 and financed and controlled by the state government.

All South Carolina banks printed and circulated their own currency, but they operated more for the benefit of Charleston businessmen than for the state as a whole. They failed to furnish sufficient credit for a growing economy, especially for agriculture. Charleston businessmen, fearing inflation, opposed chartering additional banks. Also, because the State Bank's profits were used to pay off the state's debt, the legislature was reluctant to charter new institutions that might cut into the State Bank's profits.

Besides agriculture, transportation, and banking, there was interest in industry. In this sector, too, Charleston took the lead. True, before 1815 almost all manufacturing in South Carolina was of the domestic type, dependent for power on human hands, animals, or water. Outside Charleston a mere handful of sizable plants existed in the state. Among these were William Hill's iron works in York District and Adam Carruth's gun factory below Greenville. Each employed 50 or more workers. There were many small sawmills, gristmills, tanyards, and distilleries scattered over the

ning in 1817 the state government embarked on an ambitious program of improving the state's main riverways. It soon became apparent, however, that it was too expensive to maintain sluices and canals in good condition on the swift-moving streams above the fall line. The coming of the railroads led to the abandonment of most such projects. Below the fall line necessary work was minimal, and by mid-century steamboats plied major rivers, such as the Pee Dee and the Savannah.

The railroad era began in 1827 when the legislature chartered the South Carolina Canal and Railroad Company. It was promoted largely by Charleston capitalists in an effort to lure backcountry Georgia and South Carolina trade away from Augusta and Savannah. When the line was completed to Hamburg, opposite Augusta, in 1833, its 136 miles made it the longest railroad in the world. It remained cheaper, however, to ship by water to Savannah than by rail to Charleston.

The depression of the 1840s slowed railroad construction in South Carolina, and there were only 289 miles of track in 1850.

state, and much spinning and weaving was carried on at home.

In the lowcountry several attempts were made to establish small cotton mills. None survived the War of 1812. It remained for several New England migrants to Spartanburg and Greenville districts to start textile manufacturing on a permanent basis after the war. The backcountry example was followed by entrepreneurs (mainly planters) elsewhere in the state in the 1820s and early 1830s because of the low price of cotton. By 1838 there were 16 small mills scattered throughout South Carolina. All operated with water power.

In iron production the backcountry industry reached its peak in 1838, with three companies—capitalized at a total of about $500,000—controlling the best ore and timber lands in Spartanburg and York districts. The South Carolina ironmakers, relying on charcoal and low-grade ore, could not compete with the iron industry of Virginia and Pennsylvania. Nor did they ever recover fully from the depression that began in 1839. Industry stagnated during the depression that lasted until 1844 over much of the nation and longer in the cotton belt.

Then, from 1845 to 1850, South Carolina enjoyed a flurry of industrial activity, chiefly in sawmilling, rice milling, carriage manufacturing, paper manufacturing, textiles, iron foundries, and two new industries: railway cars and turpentine distilling. The small boom in construction was accom-

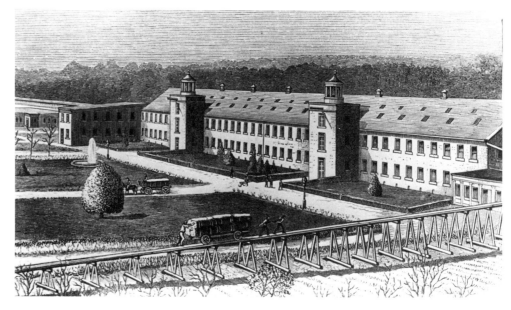

panied by a great deal of publicity. William Gregg, successful jeweler and businessman, was the chief contributer to the "Industrial Gospel" through numerous articles and speeches. He was convinced that poor whites could become useful factory workers, and he led the way in the establishment of the Graniteville Manufacturing Company, chartered in 1845. Charlestonians furnished most of the capital for Graniteville, the most successful cotton mill in the antebellum South.

Bankers, merchants, and planters joined the crusade and talked about the union of agriculture and industry, but the movement lost its momentum in the 1850s with the return of prosperity in the agricultural sector. By 1860 the total investment in South Carolina industry was only $7 million, which compared poorly with $27 million in Virginia, the South's leader, and $190 million in Pennsylvania, the national leader. South Carolina industry employed about 7,000 workers, of whom a considerable number were women, children, and slaves.

Charleston was the chief industrial center in South Carolina. Its plants, aided by the introduction of steam power, produced railway cars, machinery, foundry products, carriages and wagons, sawed lumber, distilled turpentine, flour, milled rice, and a

few ships, to name the most important. Apart from Charleston, railroads led to the development of industry in other places. Thus Columbia and Horse Creek Valley, across the river from Augusta, became small manufacturing centers. In 1860 Horse Creek Valley boasted not only the South's largest cotton mill but also its largest paper mill and largest porcelain ware factory.

South Carolina might have developed further in industry, but it was too difficult to compete successfully with well-established industry in the North. As early as 1830 former governor David R. Williams, a textile manufacturer, voiced the opinion that South Carolinians could preach "till the cows come home," but if they could not undersell the Yankees, they would not get the business. South Carolina entrepreneurs were also discouraged by a lack of experienced managers, skilled labor, and technical know-how.

In order to educate children of the poor and those of modest means, the legislature in 1811 enacted a law to establish 124 free schools, one for each member of the House of Representatives. However, an inadequate appropriation of $300 for each school assured only limited success. Moreover, many parents considered it a stigma to send their children to schools that gave first preference in enrollment to orphans and paupers.

Thus the free schools endured for years with poor attendance and poor instruction. James H. Hammond said that his neighbors at Silver Bluff were among "the most ignorant, vulgar, and narrow-minded set of people in the world." In the 1840s a traveler in the backcountry wrote: "I never met in my whole life so many white persons who could neither read nor write, who had never taken a newspaper, who had never travelled fifty miles from home,

or who had never been to the house of God." About one-half of Gregg's Graniteville factory workers could not even sign their own names. The general public was obviously not interested in paying taxes for a better system of public education.

Better schools were often operated by private philanthropy or by private school masters who charged tuition. By 1830 every district in the state had one or more private academies. A notable academy was the Reverend Moses Waddel's at Willington, opened in 1804. Although Waddel's students lived in crude log huts, enjoyed little recreation, and were rigorously disciplined, they studied hard and were usually well prepared for college. At the same time a number of well-to-do parents still employed tutors for their children, especially daughters they did not wish to send to boarding schools.

Whether in free schools or private academies, instructors were often poorly prepared. Promising young men found other professions and vocations more rewarding than teaching school. In the entire state, only Charleston had a school system nearly adequate to the needs of its children, and this through a tax-supported system begun in 1856. There was no public education for slaves or free blacks.

In higher education the South Carolina legislature chartered six colleges prior to 1802, but only the College of Charleston and South Carolina College survived. The College of Charleston did not really achieve collegiate status until the mid-1820s. It was later aided by municipal support and private philanthropy.

Much better known was South Carolina College. From 1821 to 1834 its president was Dr. Thomas Cooper, one of the ablest minds in America. He was eventually forced out because of his then unorthodox religious views; he regarded Old Testament stories as largely myths. The college later regained prestige under presidents William C. Preston, a cosmopolitan planter-lawyer-politician, and James H. Thornwell, a noted theologian, and a renowned staff. To provide formal military training for the state's youths the legislature in the early 1840s established The Arsenal, a military academy in Columbia, and The Citadel, a military college in Charleston.

Except for Erskine, founded in 1839 by the Associate Reformed Presbyterians, religious denominations did not open colleges until the 1850s. Then followed Furman, Wofford, and several more. Their teaching staffs usually consisted of only three or four professors, headed by a clergyman. The facilities were poor and student bodies small. Females were schooled separately from males, usually in private academies. Limestone College dates from an academy founded in 1845. Columbia Female College and Greenville Female College also had their origins in academies opened in the 1850s. Barhamville, a prestigious school near Columbia, educated female students from many parts of the United States. However, in antebellum days daughters even of well-to-do families were not expected to go to college.

Before 1860 The Citadel was located on Marion Square in Charleston. The college was later moved to a new site on the Ashley River, and the original building now houses offices of the Charleston County School District. Courtesy, South Caroliniana Library

The main building at Wofford College, a Methodist institution, was constructed in 1853 and 1854. The building is still in use, with a renovated interior. This daguerrotype, made shortly after the building's construction, is believed to be the oldest extant photograph of a building in Spartanburg County. Courtesy, Special Collections Division, University of Georgia Libraries

In male institutions discipline was often a serious problem. At South Carolina College students insulted professors, mistreated servants, dueled and fought each other, and even attacked the police. Privately, Dr. Cooper complained: "Every student in College holds himself bound to conceal any offense against the Laws of the Land as well as the Laws of the College; the robbing of henroosts, the nightly prowling about to steal Turkies . . . are constant practices, among a set of young men who would never forgive you, if you doubted their honor."

In 1823 the Medical Society in Charleston established the Medical College of South Carolina and elected six professors. Both city and state offered financial support. However, the science of medicine was still in the "dark ages," and hospitals were hardly more than pest houses.

In 1835 Dr. Cooper was advising his friend James H. Hammond about the use of bleeding and purgatives, the apparatus for which he always kept handy. On one occasion, after bleeding and purging, he said he still felt dizzy, hence "I applied 4 cupping glasses to the nape of the neck and took away 3 oz of blood. While this was going on I took an oz of Epsom salts." With all that, he recovered.

As one reads of deaths from cholera epidemics, yellow fever, malaria, dysentery,

typhoid, diphtheria, measles, whooping cough, scarlet fever, pneumonia, cancer, dropsy, childbirth, tuberculosis, and alcoholism, it seems a wonder that anyone survived. When the Palmetto Regiment went to Mexico in 1847, almost half of the soldiers died of various fevers and complications of wounds, because physicians had little knowledge of causes of infection. As one writer later claimed, "It was the golden age of germs, epidemics, and intemperence."

Besides formal education in the classics and the field of medicine, many well-to-do South Carolinians showed considerable interest in science, particularly natural science. On a Southern tour, English geologist Sir Charles Lyell was astonished at meeting so many South Carolina planters who were well acquainted with the flora, fauna, and geology of their surroundings.

As might be expected, Charleston was the center of scientific education, study, and discussion. There was also a small coterie of scientists in Columbia centered around South Carolina College. The Charleston Library Society and the Charleston Museum predate the Revolution. In 1813 Charleston scientists, under the leadership of Stephen Elliott, organized the Literary and Philosophical Society of South Carolina, which flourished until Elliott's

The Williamsburg County Court-house was one of many buildings designed by Robert Mills (1781-1855), South Carolina's most famous architect. Courtesy, National Archives

death in 1830. A score or more South Carolina scientists gained national reputations for their publications in botany, geology, and other natural sciences.

South Carolina also had its share of prominent artists. In colonial days there were Henrietta Johnston, the earliest American woman pastelist, and German-born Jeremiah Theus, a noted portrait artist. As the colony gained in wealth, many portrait artists found patronage among the well-to-do. Washington Allston of Brookgreen Plantation was regarded by some as the greatest American artist of his day. He also inspired South Carolina's great miniaturist Charles Fraser.

Charleston boasted many notable architects, as surviving structures attest. Early in the nineteenth century South Carolinians adopted Greek classicism, with its tall columns, for their homes and public buildings. Robert Mills, an outstanding South Carolina architect, was in fact one of America's greatest. He designed the Washington Monument and other public buildings in the national capital and many public buildings in South Carolina, including jails, courthouses, and the Fireproof Building in Charleston.

South Carolina's best-known antebellum literary figure was William Gilmore Simms. His *Southern Quarterly Review* was

second only to Edgar Allen Poe's *Southern Literary Messenger* as the best literary journal in the South. Simms' novels about the American Revolution are judged by some critics to equal James Fenimore Cooper's *Leatherstocking Tales.* However, Simms wasted much of his literary talent defending slavery. He was leader of a Charleston group of writers that included Henry Timrod, the poet laureate of the Confederacy, and Paul Hamilton Hayne. Timrod's poem "Carolina," written during the Civil War, was later set to music as the state song.

Unfortunately for Simms and his coterie, South Carolina showed little appreciation for native authors. On the eve of the Civil War it appears that Palmetto hotheaded secessionists still preferred the *New York Herald* and *Harper's Magazine* to South Carolina publications. At that time Simms, who was poor and discouraged, pathetically wrote a friend: "I have been unsuccessful all my life; my books fail to pay me . . . I am resigned to obscurity, and can struggle no more, except to pay off creditors and feed and clothe my poor children." Hayne echoed Simms's views. He edited a journal for two years without pay and sold less than 200 copies of a small book of verse, published largely at his own expense. The war added to these woes, leaving all three—Simms, Timrod, and Hayne—dispirited and virtually penniless.

Charleston has been called the graveyard of literary journals. Newspapers, however, generally fared better. With a population of 42,985 in 1850, the city supported four daily newspapers, the most important being the fire-eating *Mercury* founded in 1822, and the conservative *Courier,* founded in 1803. In the 1850s Columbia, with a population of 6,060, had three daily and two weekly newspapers, but Columbia publishers still suffered financially.

Elsewhere in the state nearly every town of importance published a weekly paper. Most newspapers, weekly and daily, consisted of four pages, filled with advertisements and stale news, and their content reflected the opinions of their editors. When the telegraph arrived in the late 1840s, the influence of newspapers increased significantly.

As South Carolina's largest city, Charleston received much attention from both visitors and native Carolinians, many of whom left accounts of the city: its bright winter social season for the upper classes, its fine mansions, its literary and scientific interests, its commerce and industry, its educational institutions, its streets bordered with Pride of India trees, its gardens, and its political influence. However, not all of the impressions were flattering. The gentlest breeze would raise clouds of dust from its sandy streets; its brackish drinking water was barely potable; its deadly summer fevers frightened many away; and its slave market and slave prison, with its hated treadmill, upset visitors. Frances Hall, visiting in 1818, called the city "a noble monument of what human avarice can effect."

Farther north on the coast, Georgetown, while boasting two handsome churches and several attractive residences, was observed to have a "miserable collection of decayed wooden domiciles and filthy beer shops." A traveler to Beaufort in 1859 found no improvement over the past 20 years—same old sandy streets, hardly any sidewalks, no place of entertainment, no public accommodation for travelers, and no newspaper. He did note, however, several elegant private homes, two churches, a town hall, a jail, and a public library.

Inland, Columbia's broad and well-planned streets, its public buildings and college campus favorably impressed visitors. The Congaree Hotel on Main Street, with 114 rooms, a large dining room, and gas lighting, was the most elegant of the capital city's seven hotels in 1859.

A visitor to the Piedmont called Anderson "one of the prettiest little towns I ever saw." The courthouse stood at its center, surrounded with shade trees. The outer edge of the square was paved with brick. Nearby Greenville was reported in 1843 to have three churches, two academies, and a doz-

en stores. A few years later its coach and wagon factory employed 60 or 70 workers as the largest business of its type in the South. However appealing and prosperous, these towns were unsanitary; livestock roamed at large and fires were a constant hazard because most buildings were constructed of wood. Early in the century only Charleston and Columbia owned fire engines, operated by volunteer companies; Greenville bought its first in 1842.

Although not understanding the reasons, lowcountry residents learned early to minimize their chances of exposure to malaria and other vector-borne fevers by escaping in the summer to the seacoast, the pinelands, the High Hills of Santee, or towns and watering places in the upcountry. Many prominent Charlestonians acquired modest homes on Sullivan's Island at the town of Moultrieville, said to have 200 houses and several "hotels" by 1826. In 1850 the elaborate Moultrie House opened, offering good food, whiskies and wine, billiards, dances, music, and accommodations for 200 guests.

Legareville was the summer resort for John's Island planters. Edisto planters flocked to Edingsville, famous for its dueling grounds, two churches, an academy, the Atlantic Hotel, and about 60 houses

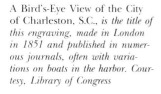

A Bird's-Eye View of the City of Charleston, S.C., is the title of this engraving, made in London in 1851 and published in numerous journals, often with variations on boats in the harbor. Courtesy, Library of Congress

with gardens and slave quarters. Other summer resorts were established up and down the coast.

Some resorts were modest; others were quite impressive, such as North Inlet, near Georgetown, with about 100 houses and a church. Planters would usually arrive at island resorts with their families in May and remain until October. The long summer days would be spent in swimming, sailing, dancing, giving parties, and entertaining visitors. Every piazza was the scene of much hospitality. Over time, several of these resorts were destroyed or damaged by hurricanes, never to be rebuilt.

Planters who did not live close to the seacoast often sought summer refuge in pineland villages such as Summerville, Gillisonville, Grahamville, Walterboro, McPhersonville, and Pineville. The residents spent much of their leisure as did their counterparts on the seacoast. The men enjoyed hunting and fishing and entertaining visitors. When ex-President Martin Van Buren visited Joel R. Poinsett at his plantation on Black River in 1842, the Planters Club of the Pee Dee extended him an honorary membership.

In the middle of the state were located a number of mineral springs and watering places: Bradford Springs (High Hills of Santee), Spring Hill (Marlboro), Cool Spring (Kershaw), and Diamond Hill Spring (Abbeville), to name a few. The best-known upcountry watering places were Glenn Springs and Limestone Springs, both in Spartanburg District. Besides these springs, such upcountry towns as Pendleton, Greenville, and Spartanburg became havens in the summer for lowcountry families, and resort hotels were built at Table Rock and Caesar's Head. Of course,

some of the rich spent summers at spas in Virginia mountains or in Northern states.

Politics, money, and leisure did not consume nineteenth-century Carolinians. Religion played a much larger role than in colonial times. The most numerous sect was the Methodist, followed by the Baptist. Both denominations were in evidence throughout the state but were strongest in the upcountry. The Presbyterians, less numerous, were widely scattered; the Episcopalians were concentrated in the lowcountry; the Lutherans in Charleston, Walhalla, and the Dutch Fork section; the Associate Reformed Presbyterians in Abbeville, York, and Chester districts; and a few Catholics and Jews in the cities and commercial towns, especially Charleston.

Episcopal services were usually sedate and attended with much ceremony, whereas Baptist and Methodist country ("cracker") congregations were completely informal in their services; while a poorly educated clergyman delivered an emotional sermon on the terrors of hell, people came and went, babies cried or crawled around on the floor, and much conversation went on outside the building.

Women constituted a majority of the membership of most congregations but, as

The Glenn Springs Hotel in Spartanburg District is pictured in this photograph taken about 1890. The hotel, built in 1838, was the most fashionable and successful spa in upcountry South Carolina before the Civil War. Courtesy, South Caroliniana Library

a rule, remained silent. Membership in most churches also included slaves, who were relegated to special sections, usually galleries. By mid-century a number of denominations had become active in the temperance movement, foreign missions, and higher education.

The great enlistment grounds were the annual revivals and camp meetings. These grew out of the "Great Revival" that swept the South from 1802 to 1805. In some places the church people established regular camp meeting grounds with outdoor tabernacles and cabins. Families would come prepared to stay for several days, complete with bedding, food, cooking equipment, and black servants, who also attended the religious services.

Antebellum Southern society has been said to have rested on the tripod of plantation, slavery, and romanticism (or chivalry); certainly the South Carolina gentry did. Men prided themselves on manliness, honor, and the ability to shoot and ride. In the lowcountry, tournaments came to be held with all the fanfare of medieval jousts.

The Waverly novels of Sir Walter Scott made vivid the ideals the South Carolina gentry tried to emulate. These folk gave romantic names to their plantations, boats, and servants. They were lavish in their hospitality and ever quick to defend their honor, especially when their word was questioned. The *code duello* prevailed although it was not universally supported. The South Carolina antidueling law of 1812 was largely ignored. Skill in killing or injuring an opponent was in fact secondary to proving one's ability to behave as a gentleman and making one's opponent take the same risk.

Nevertheless, a duel was a traumatic experience. Forty years after a duel in which he killed fellow editor Turner Bynum, Benjamin F. Perry called the incident "the most painful event of my life." But he said he could not have avoided it "without sacrificing character and usefulness in life." He blamed public opinion.

The gentry were not only planters, politicians, and duelists. They also engaged in law and medicine and served as the social, religious, and military leaders of their communities. Opposed to equal rights for women, as was most of the western world in the nineteenth century, South Carolina romantics placed their ladies on a pedestal. Journalist Wilbur J. Cash concluded: "At the last, I verily believe, the ranks of the Confederacy went rolling into battle in the misty conviction that it was wholly for her that they fought." This romantic vision conflicted with reality, however, for the "lily-pure maid," whether wife of a yeoman or a planter, had many demanding duties to perform and often died early from childbearing.

Immediately below the gentry in the social hierarchy were the yeomen, the great mass of South Carolina whites. They were most numerous in the Piedmont, the upper pine belt, and the towns. For their livelihood they were mainly artisans, shopkeepers, and above all, small farmers. Most had a rudimentary education and some owned a few slaves.

At the bottom of the whites' social ladder were the poor whites, often called "crackers," "sandhillers," or "po' buckras." Frequently ignorant squatters, they suffered from hookworm, pellagra, malaria, and malnutrition. They made up possibly 10 percent of South Carolina's white population. Slave owners looked askance at the poor whites, for they suspected them of engaging in illegal trafficking with slaves in return for pilfered produce from the plantations.

As a group, the blacks (57 percent of the state's population in 1860) existed in a society apart from whites. Therein, slaves were socially inferior to the state's 9,000 free blacks. Among the slaves, household servants, slave drivers, and craftsmen ranked above field hands, at least in the eyes of free society. One of the most important personages on the plantation was the black woman who cared for the master's children.

Among Charleston's 3,000 free blacks, a small class stood above the artisans and unskilled laborers. For instance, the Brown Fellowship Society, organized in 1790, admitted only well-to-do free mulattoes. Some prominent free blacks in Charleston were Jehu Jones, proprietor of a fashionable hotel that served a white clientele; Richmond Kinlock, millwright and landowner; and Daniel Payne, whose private school drew mainly white children. Elsewhere there was William Ellison, a prominent Sumter District planter and cotton gin man-

ufacturer who was probably the wealthiest free black in the state. In 1860 Ellison himself owned 63 slaves.

Free blacks were greatly restricted by law, more so after the Vesey plot. Although taxed, they could not vote or testify in court against whites, and there were no public schools for their children. They were prohibited from smoking or carrying a cane in public, and if they left the state they could not return. They were also required to have a white guardian to vouch for their conduct. Even so, they were in danger of being illegally arrested and beaten by the slave patrol. That they fared as well as they did was due largely to informal support from Charleston's upper classes.

This support began to evaporate in the 1850s when the aristocrats' political control of the city started slipping. There were several bills introduced in the legislature to expel free blacks from the state. So precarious had their position become on the eve of the Civil War that a handful requested the legislature to return them to slavery, while others departed for the North or Canada. However, with the coming of the war their desperate situation was soon alleviated by the Confederacy's need for their services.

Ashtabula, near Pendleton, was built circa 1825 by Lewis Ladson Gibbes, a descendant of Dr. Henry Woodward and father of Charleston scientist Lewis Reeve Gibbes. Ashtabula was one of many Pendleton homes built by Charlestonians in antebellum years. Courtesy, Library of Congress

In this drawing of Greenville in 1825 by Joshua Tucker, the courthouse is to the right of center and the Mansion House is to the left of center. The Mansion House operated for almost a century, much of the time as a resort hotel. Courtesy, Abby Aldrich Rockefeller Folk Art Center, Williamsburg, Virginia

Chapter VI

Civil War and Reconstruction: 1848-1877

After the Mexican War the South became increasingly defensive over the issue of slavery. The same year the United States acquired the Mexican cession, gold was discovered in California; before the end of 1849 that territory was requesting statehood as a free state. Within Congress a long debate erupted over slavery in California and the rest of the Mexican cession. Southerners foresaw their region, already a minority in the national House of Representatives, becoming outvoted in the Senate as well.

During the debate over the admission of California and the organization of the other newly acquired territory, many moderates urged compromise, but extreme views and dire warnings issued from both sides. Senator John C. Calhoun presented the extreme proslavery view. South Carolina was unified in defense of this peculiar institution, and men like the influential Dr. Thomas Cooper had effectively schooled a younger generation of South Carolinians in extremism.

Calhoun and others decided the time had come for the South to insist on equality within the Union, and he arranged for a Southern convention to meet in Nashville in June 1850 for the purpose of seeking unity on the issue. Meanwhile, the elderly senator from South Carolina was dying of consumption and could hardly participate in the congressional debates. Shivering though wrapped in flannels, he listened to another senator read his lengthy farewell speech on March 4.

Calhoun emphasized that the South could no longer protect itself against a Northern majority, but the Union could be saved, he wrote, if the North would concede equal rights to the South in the new territory, faithfully enforce the fugitive slave law, and cease its agitation of the slavery question. If the North were unwilling to grant this demand, he suggested peaceful dissolution of the Union. He was not sanguine; to one friend he predicted the breakup of the Union within the next 12 years. He died on March 31.

It was often asked why Calhoun remained in politics when his health was failing and he longed to be at home with his family. He answered the question himself some years earlier when he consoled his brother-in-law James Edward Calhoun upon the loss of the latter's wife. He wrote: "Your affliction has been great, but . . . while health and strength remain we have duties to perform, and we ought not to permit greif (sic) caused by incidents and afflictions that life is subject to, to prevent us from performing them."

Calhoun had not been able to achieve Southern unity. Too many Southern leaders had become suspicious of South Carolina's radicalism. South Carolina's political influence, so powerful a half-century earlier, was now on the wane.

The Nashville Convention met June 3, with only South Carolina sending a full delegation. After sharp debate the convention decided to adjourn and await congressional action. In the meantime Congress worked out a compromise. Although the only significant concession to the South was a stricter fugitive slave law, the South Carolina extremists' hopes were doomed. In other Southern states moderate views prevailed, and the Nashville Convention, upon reassembling, did nothing.

For the moment secession faded into the background, but the slavery issue, so prominent for 30 years, was still very much alive. The South as it stood recognized itself as a dwindling minority in an expanding Union. Hugh Swinton Legaré, a Charleston diplomat and literary figure, foresaw

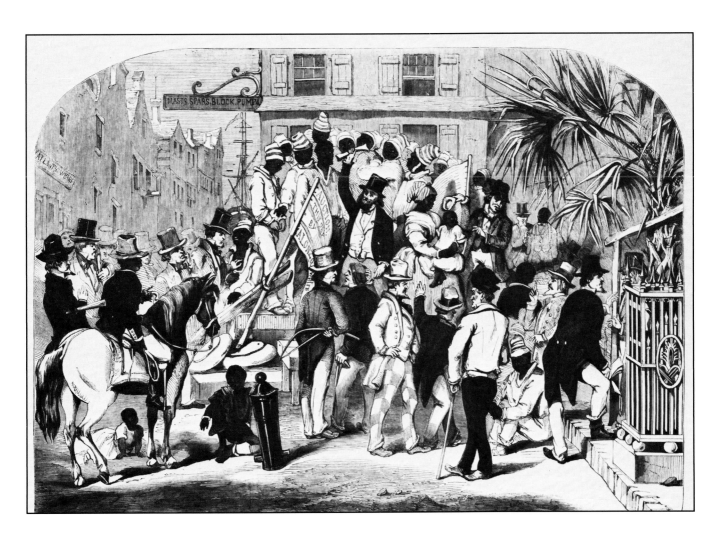

This Charleston slave sale was drawn by Eyre Crowe, secretary to William M. Thackeray during his 1856 American trip, for the Illustrated London News. *Probably no other aspect of slavery caused as much Northern and foreign criticism as the public auctioning of blacks. Courtesy, Library of Congress*

This satirical drawing depicts a raid on the Charleston post office in which abolitionist materials were destroyed. The $20,000 reward posted was for Arthur Tappan, a wealthy and outspoken New York abolitionist. Courtesy, Black Charleston Exhibit, College of Charleston

Robert Barnwell Rhett (1800-1876) is sometimes called the "Father of Secession." For almost 30 years he advocated disunion, and he was disappointed when the Confederate Convention in Montgomery failed to elect him president. Courtesy, Library of Congress

nothing ahead but "decay and downfall." James H. Hammond expected a new assault "upon our purses and liberty" within a few years, and Robert Barnwell Rhett, having no confidence in the national government, never ceased to preach secession.

For years, Northern and foreign visitors to the South had painted dismal pictures of the institution of slavery, giving accounts of cruel treatment of blacks. A Swedish visitor in Beaufort in 1832 wrote of seeing a young slave woman sold away from her husband. She bade "a tender farewell to her fellow slaves," he said, "and when at length she embraced her husband for the last time, she lost all power, and fell senseless in the arms of her unfeeling mas-

ter." The traveler noted that as the boat pulled away from the dock, the heartbroken woman waved her handkerchief for "as long as she could see her unhappy husband and a group of friends whom she left behind."

Reports such as these aided the abolitionist movement in the North, and in the 1830s abolitionists began to flood Congress with antislavery petitions and the South with antislavery propaganda. In South Carolina defenders of slavery raided post offices and destroyed abolitionist mail, while in Congress Henry Laurens Pinckney introduced a "gag resolution" to prevent discussion of abolitionist petitions.

With Senator Calhoun and Governor George McDuffie leading the way, South Carolinians began to rationalize slavery as a positive good for both races. Even in the slaves' subordinate position, Benjamin F. Perry told a Pickens audience, "the negro is not only a happier and better man than he is in Africa, but his condition *as a Slave* in the Southern States, is a great deal preferable to his situation in the North *as a freeman!*"

Within South Carolina there was one unusual family of antislavery advocates: the sons and daughters of Judge John F. Grimké. Whereas the two sons kept their antislavery opinions largely to themselves, the daughters Sarah and Angelina were outspoken advocates of women's rights and abolition. Well acquainted with the evils of slavery, they exiled themselves from their native state, and Angelina married Theo-

dore Dwight Weld, one of America's foremost abolitionist leaders.

After Calhoun's death, Robert Barnwell Rhett moved to the forefront as leader of the "fire-eaters" (secessionists). He was closely supported by Maxcy Gregg and Lawrence M. Keitt, two young hotspurs who had grown up indoctrinated with talk of secession. Moderates generally agreed with Charleston merchant Henry W. Conner that Rhett was "a rash and ultra man in his politics, frequently bent upon extreme and desperate courses, very excitable and unstable and intollerant and contemptuous of all about him."

The leader of the moderates was James L. Orr, an unlikely candidate for political success in South Carolina. He was a backcountry merchant's son and educated at the University of Virginia. He was neither orator, writer, nor constitutional theorist. He championed no cause, but he was a competent lawyer and a practical politician who believed in working within the national Democratic party. He built up a good political organization in South Carolina and persuaded his fellow Democrats to send a moderate delegation to the national convention in 1856. Because of his conciliatory attitude in Congress he was chosen

Speaker of the House in 1857, a position
no South Carolinian has held since.

A third political group in South Carolina was the Unionists, led by Greenville editor Benjamin F. Perry, lawyer James L.
Petigru, and Judge John Belton O'Neall.
The Unionists went back to the days of nullification and drew their chief support from
Charleston businessmen and small
farmers in northwestern South Carolina.

From 1851 to 1854 there had been a lull
nationwide in the slavery controversy, but
the Kansas-Nebraska Act, which repealed
the Missouri Compromise and opened territory north of the Missouri border to slavery, released a storm of criticism in the
North. Both Northerners and Southerners
sought by various means, both foul and
fair, to mold the territorial government in
Kansas to suit their purposes.

Meanwhile, in Congress acrimonious
debate turned to violence in May 1856 after
Senator Charles Sumner of Massachusetts
severely criticized and ridiculed Senator
A.P. Butler of South Carolina. Butler was
absent at the time, but later his kinsman,
Congressman Preston Brooks, a hothead
who had once been expelled from South
Carolina College for fighting, approached
Sumner's Senate desk, addressed a few remarks, and then beat the senator into insen-
sibility with a heavy cane. Although a hero
in South Carolina, the impetuous congressman was soon known as "Bully Brooks" in
the North, and his attack generated more
support for the abolitionist cause.

The presidential election of 1856,
which sent Democrat James Buchanan to
the White House, was a victory for moderation. Yet soon thereafter the Supreme
Court handed down the Dred Scott decision that legalized slavery in all federal territories, a victory for militant Southerners.
By that time some South Carolina leaders,
including Governor James H. Adams,
began to agitate for a reopening of the
African slave trade. Moderates were appalled and Orr used his influence in Congress to head off the move. Nevertheless,
by 1858 illegal slave traders found Charleston a safe haven for their nefarious commerce.

The influence of the moderates was further shaken by John Brown's raid on Harper's Ferry in October 1859. Although unsuccessful in stirring up a slave revolt, Brown received such widespread sympathy in the North that many Southerners were convinced that abolitionists would use any means to gain their ends. Brown's raid greatly strengthened the fire-eaters in South Carolina. Even Unionist Perry felt constrained to denounce Northern sympathy for Brown. Meanwhile, tension in Washington had reached such a height that Congress could scarcely conduct business. In early 1860 Senator Hammond said that he believed "every man in both Houses is armed with a revolver—some with two—and a bowie knife." It was in this volatile atmosphere that the 1860 presidential election took place.

By the time the party conventions met, the movement for Southern nationalism, with South Carolina in the forefront, had gained great momentum. In South Carolina there was a general feeling that only unprincipled men could be elected in the North and that antislavery politicians were the most corrupt of all. There was also fear that the corruption would seep into the South. In Charleston the Reverend William O. Prentiss exclaimed, "We cannot coalesce with men whose society will eventually corrupt our own and bring down upon us the awful doom that awaits them."

The first convention, the Democratic, met in Charleston on April 22, 1860. The city was a poor choice, for the weather was already hot, hotel facilities were inadequate, and the hostile atmosphere was not conducive to harmony between Northern and Southern delegates.

In Charleston William Lowndes Yancey and the Alabama delegation assumed leadership of the Southern extremists. Determined to have a platform plank that called for protection of slavery in the territories, Yancey and the Alabamians walked out of the convention when it adopted, by a close vote, the Northern plank of popular sovereignty. The Alabamians were followed by delegates from seven other Southern states, including 13 of 16 South Carolinians. The three South Carolinians who remained were Perry and two other longtime Unionists. Perry properly noted that his colleagues had not come to Charleston with any idea of walking out but had been swept into folly by a storm of emotion. However, neither Perry nor other conciliators

could undo the damage; the convention disbanded. In the end, in separate conventions, Southern Democrats nominated John C. Breckinridge for president, and Northern Democrats chose Stephen A. Douglas. Republicans picked Abraham Lincoln as their standard bearer, while a newly formed Constitutional Union party nominated John Bell.

As the summer wore on, the chief issue in South Carolina was whether to secede alone. Nearly every newspaper in the state agreed that Lincoln's election would be the signal for secession, and most felt that he would be victorious over the divided Democrats.

Governor William H. Gist, a secessionist, arranged for the legislature—meeting to choose presidential electors—to remain in session until the results were announced. The legislature thereupon called for the election of a state convention, to meet on December 17. Throughout the fall, excitement ran high in South Carolina with parades, military reviews, meetings of vigilante committees, and even sermons defending the state's position.

At some rallies, as in Abbeville on November 22, there was overwhelming support for immediate secession. There was a general feeling that South Carolina could leave the Union with little risk of war. Floride Calhoun, John's widow, expressed it well after attending a secession rally in Pendleton. She expected no war, she wrote daughter Anna, because "the South has always been dreaded by the North, when she is in earnest, which they now see she is." On the other hand, if war should come and secession be crushed, General James Jones, one of the ultras, predicted: "If we fail, we have saved our honour *and lost nothing.*"

By election time on December 6, moderates were fast yielding to the fire-eaters. When the convention met later that month in Columbia, the secessionists were confident of general support. Meeting in the First Baptist Church, the convention resolved that "South Carolina should forthwith secede from the Federal Union." It appointed a committee to draft an ordinance of secession and adjourned to Charleston to avoid, so it was said, an outbreak of smallpox.

In Charleston the convention reconvened in the South Carolina Institute Hall and for two days appointed committees, listened to impassioned speeches, and resolved to send commissioners to other

The Secession Convention met at the First Baptist Church in Columbia before moving to Charleston. During the Columbia session James L. Petigru, a strong Unionist, referred to the church as a lunatic asylum. Courtesy, South Caroliniana Library

Southern states. On Thursday, December 20, the convention voted 160 to 0 to adopt the Ordinance of Secession, drawn up by a seven-member committee. Within minutes the *Mercury* had a news extra on the streets.

Even Unionists like Benjamin F. Perry and industrialist William Gregg succumbed to the excitement. Perry explained: "They are now all going to the devil, and I will go with them." Not so for James L. Petigru. He viewed the scene with grim foreboding. "We shall have no more peace forever," he said.

With secession there was jubilation throughout South Carolina. Young James Gregg, manager of his father's Vaucluse cotton mill, wrote in January: "Georgia will go out of the Union this week, then our provisional Congress will meet and form a Southern Confederacy, not one state of us ever to join a New England State." They were now prepared for a Yankee invasion, he said, and would welcome them "with bloody hands to a hospitable grave."

Upon leaving the Union, many South Carolinians felt that statesmen rather than low politicians would control their new government. James H. Thornwell said of the

secession convention: "There were men in that convention utterly incapable of low and selfish schemes." South Carolina's new governor Francis W. Pickens wrote: "We must start *our Government* free from the vulgar influences that debauched and demoralized the Government at Washington."

With high hopes South Carolina and six other Southern states in February 1861 sent delegates to Montgomery, Alabama, to draw up a constitution and establish the Confederate States of America. They chose Jefferson Davis of Mississippi as president and Alexander Stephens of Georgia as vice president. Davis chose one South Carolinian to serve in his cabinet: Christopher G. Memminger, as secretary of the treasury.

In the meantime, a crisis was shaping up in the Charleston harbor. Major Robert Anderson, with a small, poorly supplied Union garrison at indefensible Fort Moultrie, secretly moved to Fort Sumter in the harbor, where he felt he could hold out until given relief. President Buchanan sent *The Star of the West* to reprovision Anderson, but Citadel cadets fired on the vessel and turned it back.

After some delay and unofficial promises to Confederates by Union leaders to

THE SECEDING SOUTH CAROLINA DELEGATION.—[PHOTOGRAPHED BY BRADY.]

"The Seceding South Carolina Delegation (Photographed by Brady)" was the caption accompanying this picture on the front page of Harper's Weekly on December 22, 1860. Pictured from left to right, top row, are Lawrence M. Keitt, John McQueen, and Milledge Bonham; second row, senators James Chesnut and James H. Hammond; and bottom row, Congressmen W.W. Boyce, John D. Ashmore, and William P. Miles.

withdraw Major Anderson's force, the new president, Abraham Lincoln, decided to hold Fort Sumter. Having been led to believe that the Union forces would evacuate Fort Sumter, Confederate officials in Montgomery regarded Lincoln's decision as an example of Yankee trickery. As a consequence, Davis and his cabinet decided to take Fort Sumter before a Union relief expedition arrived. When faced with a Confederate ultimatum, Major Anderson

stalled for time as long as he could. Ultimately, he was given one hour to surrender, a demand which he refused.

At 4:30 A.M., April 12, 1861, Confederate batteries began to shell Fort Sumter. Charlestonians and visitors climbed on top of their houses to watch the cannon flash in the darkness.

Following a 33-hour bombardment, Major Anderson, his ammunition exhausted, surrendered. After the battle Pres-

On January 9, 1861, a South Carolina battery fired on and turned back this Union supply ship, Star of the West, *which carried provisions for the Fort Sumter garrison. War might have followed the incident, but President Buchanan, soon to leave office, chose not to make an issue of it. Courtesy, Library of Congress*

ident Lincoln called for 75,000 volunteers to suppress the rebellion. The president's act forced other slave states to make a fateful decision. Virginia, North Carolina, Tennessee, and Arkansas joined the Confederacy, which now moved its capital to Richmond. Professor Bertram Wyatt-Brown has written: "Liberty, equality, and honor all had different connotations in the North and the South. For that reason, the nation went to war."

Meanwhile, thousands of South Carolina whites were volunteering their services for the Confederate army. South Carolina was more unified in its support of the rebel cause than any other Southern state. As a matter of fact, the South Carolina convention had been the only state convention to vote unanimously to secede. Palmetto soldiers participated in every important battle of the war. Several South Carolina officers rose to the rank of general, the best-known being Wade Hampton, III, who became General Lee's chief cavalry officer after the death of General "Jeb" Stuart in 1864. A plentiful number of South Carolina volunteers made it unnecessary for the state to

introduce conscription until well into the war. The state's desertion rate was less than one-half that of the Confederacy as a whole. During the last year of the war the South Carolina and Virginia troops bore the brunt of battle.

In the early part of the war the only important military action in South Carolina occurred in November 1861 when a Union naval flotilla invaded Port Royal sound and seized lightly defended Beaufort and the sea island in that area. From that time until the end of the war, much of Beaufort District remained under Federal control. Several thousand slaves joined the Union army, while others took over plantations their masters had deserted.

Colonel Thomas Wentworth Higginson, a Harvard graduate, abolitionist, and commander of a troop of ex-slaves, witnessed a memorable scene at a sea island ceremony on January 1, 1863, the day that Lincoln's Emancipation Proclamation went into effect. Spontaneously several blacks began to sing "My Country 'Tis of Thee." "I never saw anything so electric," Higginson wrote. "Tears were everywhere

Above: The Confederate bombard-
ment of Fort Sumter took place on
April 12, 1861. Harper's Weekly
published this drawing of the at-
tack as a two-page spread, which ex-
plains the dark line running
down the middle.

Left: Major Robert Anderson and
his Union troops stealthily entered
Fort Sumter on Christmas night in
1860, leaving Fort Moultrie,
which Anderson believed was indefen-
sible. Courtesy, Harper's Monthly

. . . Just think of it!—the first day they ever had a country, the first flag they had ever seen which promised anything to their people."

After the Federal capture of Beaufort in late 1861, there was only limited fighting in the state until General W.T. Sherman's invasion in 1865. Union troops from Beaufort made occasional forays against Confed-erate defenses on James Island and the Charleston to Savannah railroad. All were beaten back.

The chief military action in South Carolina before 1865 was the Union siege of Charleston. The Confederates had labored hard to strengthen the defenses of the city with shore batteries on Morris and Sullivan's islands and minefields and iron-

clads in the harbor. It was natural for Union forces to besiege Charleston, for after their capture of New Orleans early in 1862, Charleston and Wilmington became the chief ports of supply for the Confederacy. Fast blockade runners would sneak in and out under the cover of darkness en route to or from Nassau and West Indian ports.

In April 1863 a large Union fleet appeared off Charleston and began major operations to capture the port. Yankee troops landed on Folly Island and began an assault against rebel positions on Morris Island from which they drove the rebels and intensified the shelling of Fort Sumter.

In all, Fort Sumter suffered three major and eight minor attacks over a five-month period. The fort was almost battered to pieces, but its defenders dug in, repaired damages, and managed to hold on until Charleston fell to Union troops in February 1865. Union ships engaged in the bom-

bardment suffered heavy losses; they never ventured past Confederate batteries on Sullivan's Island.

During the war the state government underwent several changes. The people were shocked at the loss of the Beaufort District sea islands. The secession convention reassembled in the crisis and created an executive council with broad powers, composed of Governor Francis W. Pickens and four others. Thereafter the regular state government took a back seat. However, the council's high-handed, although effective, manner raised much protest, and when the convention was dissolved in December 1862, the legislature reasserted its authority and abolished the autocratic council.

Despite loyalty to the cause, many South Carolinians in time became dissatisfied with the lack of progress toward Southern independence. Their expected quick victory proved elusive. As the war dragged on and disappointment mounted, most people focused their blame on Davis. In South Carolina his chief critic was bitter Robert Barnwell Rhett. Even as early as 1861 Rhett's *Mercury* castigated the president for his "silly policy" of defensive war, poor management, and general ineptitude, from the loss of the sea islands to the commissary's poor rations. In 1861 most South Carolinians disagreed with the *Mercury's* scathing editorials. This attitude changed, however, as battlefield reverses became more common, and after Gettysburg in July 1863, nearly every newspaper in the state began to criticize the Confederate president. Only the Charleston *Courier* seemed to have a good word for Davis. In Congress, with the exception of Senator Robert W. Barnwell, the South Carolina delegation had turned against Davis.

On the home front murmurs arose that it was a "rich man's war but a poor man's fight." This complaint seemed valid, for a planter with 20 or more slaves was exempt from military conscription. Often his overseer was also exempt. It was the women whose plight was most difficult, however, especially rural, non-slaveholding women. Confederate army pay of only $11 per month for privates forced yeomen wives with small children to seek other means of support—from relatives, friends, or charity.

This Mathew Brady photograph depicts the ruins of Charleston in 1865, after fire and federal bombardment ravaged the city. The camera faced east, showing the damaged Circular Church (with scaffolding) and St. Philip's steeple to the rear. Courtesy, National Archives

As the war wore on, many of these female-led families received insufficient government aid or charity to make ends meet. As it was, many farm women plowed fields, chopped wood, tended livestock, and ran their households without adult male help. They also had to find substitutes for numerous staples that had become increasingly scarce.

Women who had the time aided the war effort insofar as they could. They sewed and sent clothing to the war front, worked in factories, managed plantations, and set up hospitals that aided thousands of Confederate soldiers.

The hardships of war markedly widened the gap between the rich and the poor, and before the conflict ended, the facade of social unity among whites had shattered. As for the slaves, it was only when Federal troops were near that they made a break for freedom because runaways, if caught, were likely to be executed.

The prospect of defeat hastened some of the older generation to early graves;

James H. Hammond, not yet 60, told his son that death would be a relief because he wished to escape the ordeal of defeat. He did escape. Duncan C. Heyward, in an account of his grandfather, a rice planter who took refuge on the Wateree, wrote: "All they [former slaves] said was that they were going home, and would look for him soon. He never returned to Combahee and did not see them again. Broken in health and staggered by his losses, Charles Heyward could not recover under the final blow of defeat." Actually, Heyward had little to go back to. The Yankees had burned his plantation, his livestock was gone, and his rice fields had flooded because of broken dikes.

At Chicora Wood in Georgetown District, former governor and ardent secessionist Robert F.W. Allston succumbed before the end of the war, as did his Unionist brother-in-law James L. Petigru. Petigru's niece said her uncle died "heartbroken, they said, at the suffering and distress for his own people that he saw ahead."

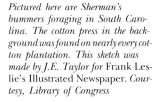

Pictured here are Sherman's bummers foraging in South Carolina. The cotton press in the background was found on nearly every cotton plantation. This sketch was made by J.E. Taylor for Frank Leslie's Illustrated Newspaper. *Courtesy, Library of Congress*

In January 1865 General William Tecumseh Sherman's army crossed the lower Savannah River, and soon many South Carolinians' worst fears were realized. As Sherman drove across the state, the demoralized Confederates, unable to determine on which Union columns to concentrate, failed to use their 33,000 available troops effectively against his advance. Only rain, mud, and poor roads slowed Union troop movements, and by February 16 Sherman's army was encamped on the west bank of the Congaree River, opposite Columbia. The proud capital, with its railroads and wartime industry, was a prime target for Sherman. Inside the city panic reigned as officials, Confederate soldiers, and private citizens scrambled to flee. The following day Federalist troops entered the city unopposed.

Sherman met and reassured Mayor Thomas J. Goodwyn of the city's safety, except for a few military installations. The Union commander visited prewar friends and in the late afternoon lay down for a nap. Just after dark several fires broke out simultaneously in the heart of the city, and because of a high wind were soon completely out of control.

For political reasons Sherman later blamed departing Confederates who had fired some cotton bales, but evidence indicates that the fires were started by drunken Union soldiers, escaped prisoners, and released convicts. Columbia's warehouses bulged with vast quantities of liquor that Confederate authorities had failed to destroy before evacuating. The tired and warweary Yankee soldiers simply helped themselves.

This Wilbur G. Kurtz painting portrays Jefferson Davis' last "cabinet" meeting in the residence of Armistead Burt (now the Burt-Stark house) in Abbeville. This took place in May 1865, as the Confederate president fled south from Richmond; he was later captured deep in Georgia. In the painting Davis is standing beside the picture of John C. Calhoun. Courtesy, Atlanta Historical Society

Once the fires got out of hand some 2,000 Union soldiers—even Sherman himself—worked hard to check the flames, but only a shift in the wind about 3 A.M. saved the city from greater destruction. Eventually General Sherman brought in a brigade of sober and disciplined soldiers to round up the disorderly men. Some 370 were arrested and 2 shot for resisting arrest.

Two days later Sherman's army resumed its march toward Winnsboro and North Carolina, leaving an embittered populace behind. While Sherman's main force moved on Columbia, one of his detachments captured Charleston; soon other Union troops moved over the state, often accompanied by pillage, destruction, and violence.

Upon hearing of General Lee's surrender at Appomattox on April 9, young Floride Clemson in Pendleton confided to her diary: "It is dreadful . . . I pray God may have mercy on us, for they have none . . . God only knows how we are to bear it, for the country is starving now." Her last faint hopes died with General Joseph Johnston's surrender to General Sherman on April 26.

The war left South Carolina in a wretched condition. Even where homes were not burned, Yankee foraging parties were often merciless. Lowcountry planter H.W. Ravenel recorded: "They used very threatening language with oaths & curses. They then proceeded to the stable & took my pair & Rene's horse . . . They then emptied the smoke house, store room & meat house, giving to the negroes what they did not want." He was lucky, for his plantation buildings were spared.

At Chicora Wood the Allstons sank their wine casks in the mill pond, but Yankee foragers found them out, broke the dam, drained the pond, and made off with them. The captain in charge delighted in threatening the frightened women: "We'll starve you out, not in one place that we have visited have we left *three meals*!"

Some destruction was also due to the foraging of retreating Confederates. One lowcountry woman remarked that General Joe Wheeler's cavalry had caused more damage than the Yankees. In early May, H.W. Ravenel noted that 300 discharged and penniless Confederate troops looted several stores in Augusta. Of course, much wartime destruction was due to simple neglect: fences, terraces, and dikes in disrepair, fields overgrown and livestock untended. The state's transportation system had almost completely broken down. Confederate bonds and currency were worthless, and Union officials seized thousands of bales of cotton, claiming it had belonged to the rebel government. It has been estimated that three-fourths of the state's wealth, not counting slaves, had disappeared in the war. Worst of all was the state's loss in manpower: 13,000 dead of 71,000 who participated in the service. Many others were broken in health and spirit.

The next years would scarcely be easier, thanks in part to the death of Abraham Lincoln from an assassin's bullet on April 15, 1865. Lincoln's successor, Andrew Johnson, no more desired vindictive reconstruction of his native region than had Lincoln; rather he wished to readmit the Southern states into the Union as quickly and as painlessly as possible. Johnson was also generous in pardoning ex-Confederates, but his actions were soon challenged.

On June 30 the new president appointed Benjamin F. Perry as South Carolina's provisional governor, and both agreed to the need for a state constitutional convention to abolish slavery, nullify the Ordinance of Secession, and provide for popular election of the governor and presidential electors. When the South Carolina convention met, it followed the lines laid down by Johnson and Perry. In the fall South Carolina voters elected a new legislature and chose James L. Orr governor.

In the meantime, South Carolina was in the throes of great social upheaval because of the emancipation of its 400,000 slaves. Members of both races were stunned by the dramatic suddenness of the event. There was some celebrating by the freed slaves, some wandering, stealing, following Union armies, or traipsing off to towns. But most blacks received news of their liberation quietly. Whatever course they followed, life was hard immediately after the war. Disease and hunger were a common lot, as many persons of both races were on the verge of starvation. Even genteel society was very poor.

Elizabeth Allston, staying in Charleston with her aunt, the widow of James L. Petigru, found life and entertainment very spartan. At private parties she noted that refreshments usually consisted of rolls "in dishes of exquisite china and water in very dainty glasses." At one or two homes, she said, they had "the rare treat of coffee, but that did not often happen."

Serving to look after the welfare of the freed slaves were federal army units and of-

ficials of the newly created Freedmen's Bureau. Both Bureau and army officials tried to alleviate suffering and endeavored to establish new workable relationships between ex-slaves and their former masters, to persuade the blacks to remain on the plantations and work the crops.

Whereas the freed slaves' chief goal was land, no federal agency had authority to confiscate ex-Confederates' property. As a matter of fact, several thousand sea island blacks who had acquired land temporarily through an order of General Sherman were in time forced to surrender their land. The ex-slaves' hopes for land died hard and sometimes violently. The federal government did hardly anything to supply these folk with means for obtaining land; "40 acres and a mule" was only a cruel rumor. In the end, most black field hands remained on plantations as sharecroppers. They could have hardly done otherwise.

Understandably, it was difficult for planters and their former slaves to adjust to the new situation. Distrust and misunderstanding arose frequently on both sides, and occasional violence flared. Many whites resented the Freedmen's Bureau's efforts on behalf of the blacks. They accused Bureau officials of corruption, partiality to ex-slaves, and politicking on

behalf of the Republican party. Recent historians have found that these accusations were much exaggerated. Moreover, in the general lawlessness prevailing at the close of the war, blacks needed protection, for they were sometimes victims of white atrocities. Bureau officials reported a number of wanton murders. In January 1867, for example, General J.C. Robinson reported that the Kingstree jail had been burned "and 22 colored prisoners smothered or burned to death, while the only white prisoner was permitted to escape."

When the new legislature met in the fall of 1865, its most notable work was the so-called Black Code, an elaborate set of laws to govern the conduct of the former slaves. While extending numerous rights to blacks, the Black Code greatly restricted them in various ways. Special courts were set up for blacks, who could be punished for a greater variety of offenses and with greater severity than whites. Furthermore, blacks could not testify in court except in cases involving blacks.

Other provisions of the Code forbade blacks to make or sell liquor or, excepting farmers, to own firearms. A special license was required of all blacks engaged in work other than farm labor or domestic service. There were also elaborate restrictions on

The hanging of a former slave for theft took place in the summer of 1865. The woman had belonged to Major A.C. Spain of Darlington. Until well into the twentieth century blacks were punished more severely than whites for crimes they committed. This sketch appeared in Harper's Weekly. *Courtesy, Darlington County Historical Commission*

Robert Smalls (1839-1915) was an outstanding black leader. After escaping with his family and several friends in the Confederate boat Planter, *Smalls joined the U.S. Navy. During Reconstruction he was elected to Congress three times and from 1897 to 1913 he served as collector of customs at Beaufort. Courtesy, South Caroliniana Library*

the nineteenth century, segregation in many areas became customary during Reconstruction. Many blacks resisted enforced segregation in public places and on common carriers, but in practice blacks tended to withdraw from confrontations with whites. They developed their own society and their own churches.

Besides the Black Code, the legislature passed an important "stay law" to rescue debtors from bankruptcy and loss of property. On this matter General Sickles was sympathetic and cooperated with South Carolina officials. In addition, he banned imprisonment for debt. With President Johnson's announcement, April 2, 1866, officially ending the rebellion, Union troop strength in South Carolina was reduced to about 3,000 personnel by November. Gradually Sickles relinquished more and more of his duties to the South Carolina government.

President Johnson's policies early came under attack from congressmen who became known as Radical Republicans. They resented Johnson's failure to consult them, and they objected to his leniency toward former rebels. They were determined not to permit the Democrats, with their errant Southern members, to regain control in Washington. Thus, when Congress met in December 1865, the Radicals managed to block the seating of members from ex-Confederate states and, throughout the winter and spring, to win several converts to their cause. They then completely broke with the president, and pushed the Fourteenth Amendment through Congress.

The amendment's first section, granting citizenship to blacks and guaranteeing civil liberties to all citizens, appalled ex-Confederates, even moderates such as Governor James L. Orr. The legislature almost unanimously agreed with the governor. Tennessee was the only ex-Confederate state to approve the amendment. Nevertheless, a sufficient number of Northern and Western states approved the amendment for it to be ratified.

When the congressional elections of 1866 assured the Radical Republicans of a continued two-thirds control of both houses of Congress, they moved forward with their program to reorganize state governments in the South. This included declaring the present state governments illegal, reimposing military rule, enfranchising black males over 21, disenfranchising whites who had voluntarily aided the

black servants contracted to white masters. Finally, interracial marriage was forbidden.

The Black Code clearly was intended to ensure white supremacy. Although blacks were now free, whites generally regarded them as inferior, indolent, and as having been better workers as slaves. A few legislators spoke for fairer treatment of blacks, but the sharpest critics were whites who thought the Code was too lenient. In view of its harsh provisions, on January 1, 1866, General Daniel Sickles, Union commander in South Carolina, declared the Code illegal. Within the next year the legislature, under pressure, made changes to assure blacks practically the same judicial rights as whites. However, the right to vote was still withheld.

Although strict segregation ("Jim Crow") laws were not enacted until late in

Robert B. Elliott (1842-1884) was a Massachusetts lawyer who came to South Carolina. One of the ablest black leaders in the state during Reconstruction, Elliott served in the U.S. House of Representatives from 1871 until his resignation in 1874. Courtesy, South Caroliniana Library

Confederacy, and requiring new state constitutions.

The South Carolina Constitutional Convention of 1868 was composed of 124 delegates, of whom at least 74 were black. While some of the blacks were illiterate former slaves, most black leaders came either from the free black community in South Carolina or other states. A number were outstanding in ability. For example, Francis L. Cardozo from Charleston had graduated with honors from the University of Glasgow, had studied theology, and had become an accountant.

The whites in the convention were mainly scalawags (Southerners who cooperated with Yankees) or carpetbaggers (Northerners who moved south in the war's wake). Among the scalawags were Columbia merchant Thomas J. Robertson and Dr. Albert G. Mackey. The latter was in no small way responsible for much of the constructive work of the convention. Among the carpetbaggers were Daniel H. Chamberlain and Justus K. Jillson. These two served ably as governor and as superintendent of

education, respectively.

The Constitution of 1868 was more democratic than any previous South Carolina constitution. In addition to instituting universal manhood suffrage, it outlawed dueling and imprisonment for debt, legalized divorce, and granted women greater equality before the law. Nevertheless, on race relations it did little to promote intermingling of the races. Most blacks were in fact more concerned with economic and educational opportunities than with racial integration. According to some critics, the convention's only serious error was its failure to place proper safeguards on the state's finances.

The new state legislature, meeting first in July 1868, was controlled by a combination of scalawags, carpetbaggers, and blacks. The latter were in a majority in the Lower house and remained so for six years. Jonathan J. Wright served on the South Carolina Supreme Court, and several blacks were also elected to Congress.

The Radical Republican legislature was not noted for distinguished service. It

This Thomas Nast cartoon was accompanied by the caption, "The Commandments in South Carolina." The black convict, just pardoned by Governor Franklin Moses, says, "We've pretty well smashed that; but I suppose Massa Moses, you can get another one." Courtesy, Harper's Weekly

never furnished sufficient funds to run the public schools properly and did little to secure land for the ex-slaves. It was extravagant with its limited resources in refurbishing the statehouse, adding extraneous employees to the state's payroll, and spending exorbitant amounts for printing. Its greatest expense came from endorsing millions of dollars worth of railroad bonds.

The Radical Republicans were also tainted with charges of corruption. For example, in 1872 John J. Patterson, scandalously known as "Honest John," reputedly paid out $40,000 to legislators to ensure his election to the United States Senate. Large business firms on occasion paid handsome sums to secure favorable laws, and there was corruption in the sale of state bonds. Without excusing Radical malfeasance, it should be noted that most South Carolina newspapers were edited by Democrats who despised Republican rule especially because of the blacks, and thus were determined to discredit the Radical regime in any way possible.

This was the only period in South Carolina history when blacks participated so broadly in the state government. Their presence in the legislature excited the curiosity of Northern newspapermen. After all,

South Carolina was the only Southern state where blacks were in a majority in either house of the legislature.

One of the best-known Northern journalists was James S. Pike, whose widely read book The Prostrate State gave an unflattering picture of garishly clad black legislators in unruly and irreverent action. Pike's report was accepted with little question for many years.

In recent times historian Joel Williamson and others have presented an alternate picture of the black political leaders. Williamson discovered that the average black legislator had little money, lived in an inexpensive Columbia boardinghouse, and daily followed a drab, dull routine. A few profited handsomely, but most of those who sought graft found the wages of sin pitifully small. Whites kept the choicest plums for themselves.

On the other hand, competent and honest blacks like Martin Delany and the Reverend R.H. Cain joined with some of their white colleagues in trying to stamp out corruption. By 1872 some Republicans felt the need for reform so strongly that the party split into two factions.

Republican governors during Reconstruction included Robert K. Scott, a carpetbagger from Ohio who lacked strength of character and common sense. He served two terms, from 1868 through 1872, and was succeeded by Franklin J. Moses, a corrupt and extravagant scalawag from Sumter. The third Republican governor was Daniel H. Chamberlain, a carpetbagger from Massachusetts. Although previously accused of corruption, Chamberlain, elected in 1874, made a conscientious effort to rid his party of wrongdoing.

Shortly after Chamberlain's election the moribund Democratic party was rejuvenated. For several years it had practically abjured politics, allowing the Republicans a free reign, contested only by extralegal groups such as the Ku Klux Klan. The latter was primarily interested in keeping blacks "in their place." By 1871 this loose-knit organization of night riders had become so notorious that President Grant declared martial law in nine upstate counties. This broke up the organization.

With Democratic party reorganization the Republicans in 1876 faced a serious challenge. At first the Democrats were divided between "fusionists" and "straight-outs." The former believed that Chamberlain had been a reasonably honest and effective governor and that there was little likelihood that he could be defeated for re-election. They were willing to cooperate with reform Republicans. By contrast, the straightouts wished to challenge the Republicans directly.

The differences remained unresolved until a riot broke out in the river town of Hamburg between black militiamen and a band of whites, angry because the blacks had obstructed passage of two white men down Hamburg's main street. In the shooting that occurred several days after the incident, one white and seven blacks were killed. When it appeared, correctly or not, that Governor Chamberlain sympathized with the militiamen, the straightouts quickly won control of the Democratic party. Under the leadership of generals Matthew C. Butler and Martin W. Gary the Democrats nominated General Wade Hampton for governor.

Hampton, far ahead of his day in his approach to race relations, appealed to both races for support, promising to hold "the scales of justice with a firm and impartial hand." His formula for victory was based on a plan used successfully in Mississippi the previous year, that is, "force without violence."

As the campaign got under way, large groups of well-armed Democrats dressed in red shirts roamed the countryside, appeared at Republican rallies, and demanded equal speaking time. The "Red Shirts" did not always adhere to nonviolence, and their Republican opponents sometimes replied in kind, especially in areas where blacks outnumbered whites. Citizens like Gary had no intention of following Hampton's policy of equal treatment for both races. Strangely, election day went by rather peacefully, though not without dishonesty at the polls.

After the ballots were counted both parties claimed victory in the governor's race. At the same time as the gubernatorial election there was a presidential contest between Republican nominee Rutherford B. Hayes and Democratic candidate Samuel J. Tilden. The results of the presidential election were also contested in South Carolina, as well as in several other states.

The situation became even more confused in South Carolina because both parties claimed they had won a majority of the seats in the legislature; hence, two legislatures emerged in Columbia, the Democrats meeting separately from the Republicans, who were in the statehouse. Before a legal decision was reached on the disputed state

election, five Republican lower house members deserted to the Democrats, giving the latter a legislative majority by any count. Surly crowds roamed outside the capitol, threatening a riot, but the Republicans refused to yield the statehouse in spite of a state supreme court decision on December 6 against them. With the support of federal troops, they inaugurated Chamberlain governor.

While this political controversy was boiling in Columbia, the Hayes-Tilden disputed election was finally settled in Washington. In the compromise national leaders worked out, Hayes was inaugurated March 4, 1877, after giving certain promises to the South, one of which was to remove federal troops from the three states remaining under Republican rule. On April 10 Hayes ordered Union troops out of Columbia, whereupon Governor Chamberlain and the Republicans yielded the statehouse to the Democrats. Finally, conservative Democrats, with Hampton as governor, were once more in political control of South Carolina.

General Wade Hampton III (1818-1902), a Richland County planter and Confederate hero, served his state as governor and U.S. senator. He led the Democratic party forces that overthrew Radical Reconstruction. Courtesy, South Caroliniana Library

The Political Scene: 1877-1917

The Radical Republican regime left a more democratic government for Governor Wade Hampton and the faction known as Conservative Democrats, or simply Conservatives. The Republicans laid the foundation for free public education for all children, rebuilt most of the state's railroads and added new lines, organized local government on a basis that largely permitted self-rule, and extended civil liberties and suffrage to black citizens. At the same time they dealt leniently with former rebels—none was brought to trial and little property was confiscated.

On the other hand, the Radicals deserve demerits for corruption, extravagance, and waste in handling public funds. They left a large debt unpaid and much wartime destruction unrepaired. The state was still largely poverty-stricken in 1877.

Radical policies embittered many South Carolina whites against their former slaves, even though the freed slaves received limited economic benefits under Radical rule and many were reduced to farm tenancy. Furthermore, educational opportunities fell far short of the blacks' needs, leaving blacks' high hopes largely unfulfilled. After 1877 the federal government made only token efforts to guarantee civil liberties and did almost nothing to help alleviate miserable economic conditions.

For South Carolina whites, the word *Republican* was anathema well into the twentieth century. White Republicans were often socially ostracized from well-to-do society.

Hampton and the Conservative leaders were primarily elderly Civil War veterans who wished to re-create the world as they had known it. They held their positions largely due to public respect for their services to the Confederacy. Although primarily agrarians, they welcomed railroads and manufacturing and offered low taxes and *laissez faire* policies in order to encourage both. Generally they envisioned no conflict between agriculture and industry. They promised efficient, low-cost government, and they were determined to undermine the Republican party and maintain white supremacy through Democratic party solidarity. Yet they disagreed among themselves how best to deal with the blacks.

During the early years of Conservative control there was no real class struggle in the state. On the other hand, there was friction in the Conservative ranks caused by General Martin W. Gary and a small coterie of his Edgefield County supporters. Primarily because of Gary's extreme racism and unwillingness to deal leniently with the Republicans, Hampton distrusted him and blocked his ambitions for high office. The frustrated Gary posed as the "poor man's friend" and lashed back at Hampton with a personal attack on his integrity. But Gary had neither program nor class appeal; he died a bitter and unreconstructed rebel in 1881.

There was also the appearance of an upcountry-lowcountry feud over scaling down the state's debt, because many of the bondholders were Charleston residents. The debt had soared above $25 million by 1873, and the Radical Republicans had begun to reduce it before losing control of the legislature. After Hampton's inauguration in 1877 the Conservatives vigorously debated the issue. For his part, the governor urged moderation. He and his Conservative allies were able to block extreme attempts at canceling. They compromised on some bond issues, and by the time refunding was complete in 1882, the debt had been lowered to about $6.5 million.

After his inauguration in 1877,

Woodrow Wilson, governor of New Jersey, was at the home of August Kohn of Columbia on June 2, 1911. He visited the city for two days as guest of the South Carolina Press Association. Mayor W.H. Gibbes is seated to Wilson's left. While in Columbia Wilson laid the cornerstone of the YMCA on Sumter Street and called on Mrs. James Woodrow, widow of his uncle. Wilson spent part of his boyhood in Columbia, and the house in which he lived has been preserved. Courtesy, Darlington County Historical Commission

Brigadier General Martin W. Gary (1831-1881) of Edgefield was known as the "Bald Eagle." A political opponent of Wade Hampton, Gary espoused racist views that were eventually adopted by many South Carolina white voters years after his death. Courtesy, South Caroliniana Library

Governor Wade Hampton sought black and Republican party support by following a moderate policy and invited blacks to join the Democratic party. He also agreed with Washington authorities mutually to drop state prosecution of South Carolina Republicans accused of corruption and federal prosecution of South Carolina Democrats involved in a bloody race riot at Ellenton in 1876, in which one or two whites and probably 40 to 50 blacks were slain.

In 1878 Hampton was reelected without opposition. Two days later he was gravely injured in a hunting accident when the mule he was riding crushed his leg against a tree, necessitating amputation a few days later. Then while the governor lay dangerously ill, the legislature elected him to fill the Senate seat of "Honest John" Patterson.

Senator Hampton, with enormous personal prestige, remained a strong leader of the Conservatives until about 1882. By then there was little likelihood of Republican resurgence. Thereafter Hampton's role in politics became less active, and his influence in South Carolina began to wane while he busied himself with affairs in Washington. Unfortunately for the Conservatives, they lacked a forceful leader to replace him.

Hampton's declining political influence could be seen in the state's racial policy. At first he apparently had the support of most upper-class, lowcountry Democratic leaders, but General Gary and others disagreed, for they wished to drive blacks out of politics altogether. Beginning in

1878 in Gary's home county of Edgefield, blacks were gradually excluded from most Democratic county clubs, conventions, and primaries. After Gary's death in 1881, his extreme racial views gathered further support.

In 1882 the legislature enacted an "eight-box" election law which, in effect, served as a literacy test for voters. It required that candidates for different offices be listed on separate ballots and that each ballot be dropped in the appropriate box in order to be legal. Election officials were required to instruct voters upon request as to the proper boxes, but they could easily misinform illiterates whenever they wished. The "eight-box" law was designed to eliminate large numbers of blacks, which it did. Nonetheless, some 15,000 to 20,000 blacks continued to vote and a few continued to hold office, including legislators mainly from Beaufort, Georgetown, and Berkeley counties.

The legislature enacted another measure in 1882 to reduce black political influence. The federal census of 1880 had granted South Carolina two additional congressional seats, bringing the total to seven. In redrawing congressional district boundaries, the General Assembly gerrymandered a group of black counties into one district, the "Black Seventh." Here, black voters outnumbered whites about four to one and controlled the district; whites controlled the other six.

The Conservative Democrats' policy of *laissez faire*, inexpensive government, and tax breaks for new factories encouraged a budding "cotton mill crusade" to pick up increased momentum. In 1900 there were 115 textile mills scattered over the state, nearly all in the upper Piedmont and along the fall line, where water power was most readily available.

The coming of industry was also helped by the postwar growth of Anderson, Greenville, Spartanburg, Rock Hill, and several lesser Piedmont towns. Both the towns and their industries were aided by the building of railroads, particularly the Atlanta and Charlotte Airline Railroad, and the increased raw cotton production in Piedmont counties. The state as a whole increased raw cotton production 45 percent between 1860 and 1880, but the five counties of Oconee, Pickens, Anderson, Greenville, and Spartanburg quintupled their production during the same period. The Piedmont merchants who marketed the expanded cotton crop found the business to be quite profitable, and a number turned to textiles to invest their newly increased wealth.

For many South Carolina farmers, the expansion of cotton cultivation involved a significant shift from a diversified live- at-home economy to one specializing heavily in production of a crop for international market. For a brief time high cotton prices encouraged this change, but after the Panic of 1873 cotton prices remained relatively low until the end of the century. The low price caused much dissatisfaction among the growers, many of whom (both whites and blacks) were soon reduced to farm tenancy. It was largely from poor and dissatisfied white farmers that the new textile magnates drew their labor supply.

Among the landowners were many who stubbornly clung to the soil. They looked forward to better times, and through various organizations they hoped to find means of improving their lot. One such farmer was Benjamin Ryan Tillman, an Edgefield cotton grower in economic dis-tress primarily for having borrowed to expand his operations. He burst upon the scene in 1885 with a sensational speech at Bennettsville before a statewide meeting of farmers and mechanics. On that occasion Tillman strongly condemned the state legislature for its failure to aid suffering agrarians. He proposed a number of measures to aid farmers and for the next three years agitated to push farmers into political action against what he called the "polluted atmosphere" of the statehouse and "lawyers in the pay of finance." His barbs extended to aristocrats in general and Charlestonians in particular.

Ben Tillman and his newly organized Farmers' Association generated much interest and support from the agrarians, but they were frustrated by state Democratic party leaders who refused to endorse their program. Discouraged, Tillman was about to give up politics when Thomas G. Clemson's death on April 6, 1888, offered new hope. Clemson's will left the state a fund of $80,000 and John C. Calhoun's former

Benjamin Ryan Tillman (1847-1918) was a governor of South Carolina and a U.S. senator from 1890-1918. Known as "Pitchfork Ben," Tillman dominated South Carolina politics for three decades. He is shown here as governor working at his desk. Courtesy, Special Collections, Clemson University Library

The burning of Tillman Hall at Clemson College occurred on May 22, 1894. The building was restored according to the same architectural plan. The administration building at Winthrop College was of similar design. Courtesy, Special Collections, Clemson University Library

estate of 814 acres for the establishment of a separate agricultural college, a project dear to Tillman. The founding of Clemson College the following year, after a difficult legislative battle, was a signal victory for the farmers.

In January 1890 Tillman, with encouragement from farm leaders, announced his intention to run for governor on the Democratic party ticket. At a well-attended farmers' convention in March, Tillman spoke on behalf of his candidacy.

The campaign that followed quickly degenerated into bitter diatribes, slanderous remarks, near-violence, and howling mob action. Joseph H. Earle, the Conservatives' choice for governor, was a poor match for Tillman's vitriolic onslaught. Tillman's Reformers, as they were known, dominated the state Democratic convention and nominated their candidate. Some Conservatives, unwilling to accept convention results, bolted and nominated Alexander C. Haskell to face Tillman in November. The Haskellites, called Straightout Democrats, made a poor showing; Tillman won the election by a four-to-one majority. Most blacks remained aloof from what appeared to be a no-win situation.

The undoing of the Conservatives was due to poor leadership, their reverence for the past, and the generation gap. Their leaders apparently did not comprehend the seriousness of the agricultural depression and, to their political peril, denied its existence.

Benjamin R. Tillman was inaugurated governor on December 4, 1890, before a large audience of enthusiastic supporters. He called his election a victory for democracy "unparalleled in its magnitude and importance." He reassured his listeners of continued white control of the state government "at any and all hazards." He immediately used his influence to unseat Senator Wade Hampton with henchman J.L.M. Irby and then turned his attention to a number of legislative proposals.

The new governor's accomplishments were modest: establishment of Winthrop College for women, reorganization of the University of South Carolina, tax reform in favor of small landowners, increased funds for state institutions, and reorganization of the state asylum. In a legislative reapportionment the more populous upstate counties benefited, primarily at Charleston County's expense.

To secure these results Tillman at times dealt harshly with recalcitrant legislators. His arbitrary tactics caused resentment among some of his supporters and eventually led to defeat of part of his program. In 1892 Tillman, dissatisfied with partial success, appealed to voters to give him a new legislature in place of the "driftwood" lawmakers they had elected in 1890, and he himself stood for reelection against John C. Sheppard, the Conservatives' choice.

The campaign was reminiscent of that of 1890, with near riots at several speaking engagements. In the end the Tillmanites swept once more into the statehouse. Subsequently, as Tillman sought to round out a modest program of reform, he became more tyrannical than during his first term.

These militiamen, pictured in front of the Darlington courthouse in April 1894, were sent by Governor Tillman to enforce the Dispensary Act. A bloody riot had taken place and a mob had driven state constables from the town. However, the governor prevailed. Courtesy, Darlington County Historical Commission

One especially controversial measure was the Dispensary Act of 1893. For several years South Carolinians had debated various methods of controlling the manufacture and sale of alcohol. Many favored outright prohibition. The controversy was raging when Tillman took office. After studying the issue he decided on state control through strictly regulated dispensaries.

The Dispensary Act was never popular with either prohibitionists or Conservatives, but to the governor enforcement of the law became an obsession. It led to bloodshed in Darlington the following year when a state constable killed a local citizen during a heated quarrel. In the riot that followed, several people were either killed or wounded, and an angry mob of Darlingtonians destroyed the local dispensary and drove the state policemen from the town.

When news of the "Darlington War" reached Columbia, mob action in ugly defiance of authority threatened the capital city. Governor Tillman was embarrassed because several militia companies refused orders to go to Darlington. Undaunted, the governor declared Florence and Darlington counties to be in a state of insurrection. Meanwhile, several rural militia companies from Edgefield came to the governor's rescue. No further violence occurred, for before the loyal troops reached Darlington, emotion had subsided and the mob had dispersed. So intense was the hatred of the dispensary system that several of the leading Conservatives' newspaper editors

sided with the mob, for which Tillman summarily castigated them.

In the 1894 elections South Carolina voters sent Ben Tillman to the United States Senate with the nickname "Pitchfork Ben." This sobriquet resulted from a Tillman statement calling President Grover Cleveland "an old bag of beef" and promising to go to Washington and prod him in "his old fat ribs" with a pitchfork. In the same elections the state's voters also approved the calling of a constitutional convention, supported by Tillman for the primary purpose of eliminating black suffrage and thereby destroying what he called an "unholy alliance" between blacks and dissident Conservatives.

When the Constitutional Convention of 1895 assembled on September 10, Senator Tillman and the Reformers were in control. Tillman's new voting requirements received little opposition except from six black delegates to the convention. The most important provision of the new voting regulations was the literacy test. Upon registering, prospective voters were required to read to the satisfaction of their registration boards any section of the state constitution. However, until January 1, 1898, voters merely had to "understand and explain" any section when read to them—a neat escape favored by registration boards for illiterates. After the new constitution went into effect, Republican votes in the state gradually dropped to less than 5,000, and no blacks were elected to the General Assembly between 1900 and 1970.

Aside from discriminatory suffrage provisions, the constitution legalized customary Jim Crow practices and separate, but not necessarily equal, educational systems and prohibited interracial marriage. The convention adjourned on December 4 and decreed the constitution would go into effect January 1, 1896, without a popular referendum.

In the Senate "Pitchfork Ben" spoke often, loud, and long. He became notorious for his demagogic speeches against blacks. He declared that blacks were biologically inferior to whites, deserved to be lynched for rape, and had been demoralized by Reconstruction. He opposed education for blacks, favored the repeal of the Fourteenth and Fifteenth amendments, and urged the arming of Southern whites. He could foresee no end of racial troubles, and he accused Yankees of hypocrisy about race. But on this and other matters his influence was minimal, for the Republicans controlled the Senate until 1913. By then Tillman's health was broken, and he was therefore unable to play a strong role in the Democratic administration of Woodrow Wilson. At times Tillman's popularity within his state wavered, though it never fell so low as to prevent his reelection, and he died in Washington, D.C., in 1918.

An especially unpleasant episode in his senatorial career was his feud with his colleague John L. McLaurin. The latter cooperated with President William McKinley's economic policies and in return was consulted about federal patronage in South Carolina. This infuriated Tillman. He turned against his fellow senator, denounced him with abusive language, and later, on February 22, 1902, came to blows with him on the Senate floor. For this fistfight the Senate formally censured Tillman, and the White House withdrew an invitation for Tillman to attend a state dinner honoring Prince Henry of Prussia.

In 1903 Ben Tillman became involved in another ugly affair, the defense of his nephew James H. Tillman, on trial for the sensational murder of editor N.G. Gonzales of *The State* newspaper. Jim Tillman, elected lieutenant governor in 1900, had his eye on the governorship. At this juncture Gonzales, in repeated editorials, sought to expose the younger Tillman as a "proven liar, defaulter, gambler, and drunkard." The editor achieved his purpose, whereupon the embittered Tillman openly shot him down in cold blood on a Columbia street on January 15, 1903. The

senator felt constrained to defend his nephew, and his influence was probably not inconsequential in bringing about acquittal by a Lexington County jury.

It was events, however, not Tillman's Senate notoriety, which were changing South Carolina. In 1895 long-standing Cuban discontent against Spanish rule broke into open revolt. Because of increasing American sympathy for the rebels, in April 1898 President McKinley and Congress yielded to the public demand for intervention. Governor William H. Ellerbe quickly organized two regiments of volunteers in South Carolina, but the war was of such short duration that neither regiment saw action. On the other hand, several South Carolinians served with distinction in other units.

In the 1902 state elections, the Conservatives once more won control of the legislature and the governorship. For the latter position Duncan Clinch Heyward defeated W. Jasper Talbert, a Tillmanite. Heyward's victory came as a surprise, for the charismatic and aristocratic rice planter was an amateur in politics and little known outside Colleton County. Once in office, the new governor supported a moderately progressive policy that included improvements in the state's education system, elimination of child labor in factories, and the removal of certain county financial offices from politics. Above all, he advocated strict law enforcement.

Governor Heyward's greatest difficulty lay in the enforcement of the Dispensary Act. The growing opposition to "Ben Tillman's Baby" made this task almost impossible. Corruption arose in liquor contracts; there were violations of dispensary regulations; illegal saloons abounded in some towns and cities—with Charleston apparently the worst offender. State constables encountered judges and juries who sympathized with offenders, and, of course, there were the prohibitionists who wanted no legal sales at all.

With the move for statewide prohibition gaining headway, Senator Tillman, growing more cautious, submitted to the dispensary system's inevitable extinction. The election of 1906 settled the issue. Though Tillman was elected to a third term in the Senate, Martin F. Ansel of Greenville, a prohibitionist, became the new governor. The following year the legislature began to dismantle the dispensary system, and in 1915 the "drys" won a statewide referendum ending all legal sales of alcohol within the state.

Except for the dispensary issue, South Carolina was relatively quiet from 1903 to 1910. With blacks almost totally excluded from politics, there was little agitation. During that time the old Tillman forces split up and there emerged a "new Tillman." He was Coleman Livingston Blease—"Coley" —an ambitious, sociable lawyer from Newberry. He had first served in the House of Representatives in the 1890s as a Tillman supporter. From there he rose to the state senate and twice ran unsuccessfully for governor.

In 1910, on Blease's third try for the governorship, he was elected. His opponents underestimated his voter appeal, and their sometimes wild, unsubstantiated statements about his character backfired to his advantage. But more than that, Blease capitalized on labor unrest among the new "cracker proletariat" or "lintheads" in the mill villages. As historian David Carlton recently noted, the town bourgeoisie became alarmed at the "lawlessness" of the mill operatives and sought to uplift them by educating their children.

In the ensuing debate over compulsory education and restricted child labor in factories, the workers had little voice. They regarded the middle-class program for social control as an attack on their independence. Their major avenue of resistance was through the ballot, and their champion

was "Coley" Blease. But Blease could not have won the election with only mill workers' votes. Luckily for him, many poor farmers also supported him.

"Coley" developed no specific program for the welfare of mill workers and tenant farmers. He was a flamboyant demagogue of the Tillman style. He understood his constituency well, used their language, and made these relatively inarticulate people feel important in the election process. He never hesitated to play on racial, religious, or class prejudice to obtain votes, and his outlandish speeches entertained his audiences.

As the state's chief executive, Blease frequently defended lynching, opposed education for blacks at white taxpayers' expense, and on one occasion condemned a political opponent for acting as a trustee of a school for blacks. He was often at odds with the newspapers and praised Jim Tillman for shooting Gonzales. Blease's legislative program called for more aid to education and improved health services, but he was strictly *laissez faire* about labor legislation. He frequently squabbled with the General Assembly, with whom his influence fluctuated, and he sometimes defied the courts. Above all, he wielded his pardoning power. "I want to give the poor devils a chance," he said, and he set free some 1,500 to 1,700 prisoners. It was rumored

In 1898 volunteers for the Spanish-American War marched on Main Street in Columbia. An electric streetcar system had already been installed in the city. Courtesy, Security Federal Savings, Columbia

that any friend of "Coley" was safe from punishment.

In 1912, when Governor Blease ran for reelection, Senator Tillman, though in wretched health, decided to run for another term. By this time Tillman was convinced that Blease was morally unworthy of the governor's office and had injured the good name of the state, although he was reluctant to express that view publicly. However, at the last minute he endorsed Blease's opponent, Judge Ira B. Jones. Blease was greatly angered by Tillman's "eleventh-hour stab" and suggested that the senator's mind was diseased. Nevertheless, both Blease and Tillman won their respective offices. Ironically, Senator Tillman was now appealing to the very voters who had opposed him in 1890.

In 1914 Blease tried to unseat United States Senator Ellison D. Smith, who was running for a second term. The enfeebled Tillman dealt Blease another "eleventh-hour stab." This time Tillman's efforts were successful. Not only did Blease fail, but so did his candidate for governor. For the next 10 years "Coley" was out of office, but not out of politics.

The winner of the 1914 gubernatorial contest was reform-minded Richard I. Manning, prominent Sumter County planter, banker, and legislator. Viewed in broader terms, Manning's victory marked South Carolina's efforts to catch up with progressive currents sweeping the nation, and he appeared to be the first South Carolina governor to recognize the seriousness of the new social and economic problems created by the industrial era. Like many progressives of his time, Manning believed the government should attempt to ensure the economic welfare of all its people and should undertake those functions neither individual citizens nor smaller governmental units could effectively perform.

Governor Manning first directed the attention of the General Assembly to the pathetic condition of the state hospital, where

Far right: Governor and Mrs. Coleman L. Blease are pictured on a campaign tour, circa 1912. Blease served two controversial terms as governor, from 1911-1915. Courtesy, Anderson Independent

Below: President William H. Taft visited Charleston on April 5, 1909, and journeyed by rail to Columbia the next day. In the capital city he addressed several thousand people at the state fairgrounds and was honored with a parade and a luncheon before departing for Augusta. This picture shows the president seated with, left to right, Columbia Mayor W.S. Reamer and Governor Martin Ansel. Standing beside the automobile is Captain Archibald Butt, the president's military aide. Dr. E.M. Whaley is the driver. Courtesy, Security Federal Savings, Columbia

some 1,700 mental patients were crowded into dilapidated and unsanitary firetraps and fed a poor diet. The hospital had only two full-time and two part-time doctors to treat this horde of inmates, a number of whom suffered from tuberculosis or other diseases. The legislature agreed to a complete reorganization.

Manning's progressive forces next were able to secure legislative approval of a three-man tax commission authorized to equalize tax assessments throughout the state. That measure drew fire from some of the business community, as did a local option law for compulsory school attendance and laws to protect employees from fraud. In 1916 Manning secured a worker's compensation act and a law raising the minimum age for factory workers from 12 to 14. In keeping with this progressive trend, the legislature took a step in introducing the secret ballot for the Democratic primary, at least in Richland and Charleston counties.

Manning's sincere efforts to improve the welfare of workers, including their right to organize, and his attempt to me-

diate several labor disputes were resented by factory owners. But his conservative background, honesty, and impartial enforcement of the law held their support in his fight for reelection in 1916 against veteran "Coley" Blease. The latter predictably had the support of mill workers. Although Blease led on the first primary ballot, Manning won the runoff—by a narrow margin. At the same time, certain Bleaseite candidates for the legislature were victorious, and in 1917 the General Assembly scuttled the governor's proposals for further progressive measures.

Overall, political changes in South Carolina were modest during the 1877-1917 years, even under the governorships of Ben Tillman, "Coley" Blease, and Richard Manning.

At no time did the legislature render significant help to tenant farmers. Moreover, it took away many rights that blacks had enjoyed in 1877, and Manning's progressive forces did nothing to restore those rights. In effect, Conservative views retained a strong hold on the South Carolina electorate during most of the period.

This rare frontal photograph of the aging Senator B.R. Tillman was taken in June 1915, in the Panama Canal Zone. Tillman is pictured with his wife and daughter Sallie May; the man in the white suit is Brigadier General Clarence R. Edwards, commander of U.S. forces in the Canal Zone. Because Tillman lost an eye as a youth he usually objected to frontal photos. Courtesy, Special Collections, Clemson University Library

Economy and Culture: 1865-1917

When James H. Hammond informed the United States Senate in 1858 that "cotton is king," he could hardly have envisioned the dominance of the crop in the post-Civil War years. In South Carolina, cotton production rose from 224,000 bales in 1870 to 837,000 bales in 1900. Thereafter, until World War II, annual output occasionally topped the million-bale mark. Its value was greater than that of all other South Carolina agricultural products combined. Nearly all South Carolina cotton was the short-staple variety. The long-staple cotton was grown in a limited area on sea islands.

By contrast, rice production never regained its antebellum status after the Civil War destruction of rice fields and dikes and the freeing of the slaves. In the 1880s the South Carolina growers, dependent on intensive hand labor, began to face serious competition from new producers in the southwest who made extensive use of machinery. Two devastating autumnal storms in 1910 and 1911 administered the *coup de grace* to the few remaining rice growers along the Edisto and Combahee rivers and in Georgetown County.

Meanwhile, bright leaf tobacco was making its way in the Pee Dee region as a new commercial crop. Before 1890, F.M. Rogers introduced the crop into South Carolina, and within 10 years its annual production was valued at $1 million. The expansion of the bright leaf tobacco belt was due to the increased consumption of machine-made cigarettes.

Because of postwar hardships during Reconstruction and low cotton prices after the Panic of 1873, some South Carolina farmers tried to organize to improve their lot. During the early Reconstruction years they joined the Patrons of Husbandry (the Grange), a national organization strong in the Midwest. But the Grange never gained much support in South Carolina, probably because of political turmoil, and all but disappeared before the end of Reconstruction.

In 1885 Ben Tillman took the lead in establishing the Farmers' Association, an organization primarily interested in political action. Two years later the Farmers' Alliance entered South Carolina. The Alliance, a national organization, supported a broad economic program that included the establishment of farm cooperatives for buying and selling. A number of county exchanges were set up and experienced limited success. Then, following the Panic of 1893, several exchanges failed, and the Alliance declined rapidly thereafter.

With the rise of cotton prices at the end of the century, South Carolina farmers began to enjoy somewhat renewed prosperity and to lose interest in further organizations. Moreover, it was difficult for landlords and tenants, whites and blacks, to cooperate for their common good. Farm life was hard, featuring as it did rural isolation, an inadequate diet, no electricity, and hardly any labor-saving machinery. John Andrew Rice remembered the ordeal of picking cotton as a 14-year-old boy on his grandmother's farm in Colleton County in 1900. September, he wrote, was the worst time of the year:

Food began to run low; pork by now was rancid, cabbage was burned by the heat of the sun and collards had not yet felt the sweetening touch of frost, turnips were tasteless and beans rattled in the pod. Moreover, this was the time of dysentery; heat-weary bodies became so ill that they could barely drag themselves out of bed to do the necessary tasks for keeping alive, and still work had to be done. There was little fruit on the neglected trees and we had no milk, for the cows had long ago gone dry, and butter was distant memory.

This sketch by H.A. Ogden in Frank Leslie's Illustrated News-paper *in 1878 shows cotton being shipped from North Commercial Wharf in Charleston to foreign and domestic ports. Courtesy, Library of Congress*

This cotton market was located on the square in Anderson in the 1890s. The courthouse is to the left. This setting was typical of cotton markets in South Carolina courthouse towns prior to World War I. Courtesy, South Carolina State Museu

These cotton pickers in Lexington in the 1930s used a back-breaking method that did not change from earliest times until after World War II. Courtesy, South Carolina State Museum

Between the Civil War and World War I, farmers' lives were also affected by the expansion of South Carolina's railroad system. By the time of World War I, nearly every town in the state was reached by rail. A great deal of railroad consolidation took place in the late nineteenth century, and by the time of World War I three major systems operated in South Carolina: Southern Railway, Seaboard Air Line, and Atlantic Coast Line. All operated fast-moving passenger trains as well as "locals" that stopped at every hamlet. In addition to the three major systems, there were about two dozen smaller lines.

Interest in improving South Carolina roads began in 1895 when the state govern-ment permitted counties to use convict labor. Three years later a Good Roads Association was organized, but progress was slow because counties annually spent less than a million dollars on roads. By 1917 the number of registered vehicles in the state surpassed 40,000, but to handle this increased traffic there was hardly a paved road outside city limits. At that time the General Assembly established the State Highway Commission and began a more serious effort to improve the state's road system.

In manufacturing, textiles were relatively unimportant during Reconstruction years. At that time sawmilling, turpentine distilling, and phosphate mining, all heavily dependent on black labor, were important to the state's economy.

South Carolina's rich forests encouraged sawmills to locate along the coast prior to the Civil War, and during the 1850s turpentine distillers began to drift down from North Carolina, where pine forests were becoming depleted. The distillers found a livelihood in South Carolina well into the twentieth century.

But phosphate mining was of shorter duration. It began shortly after the Civil War when beds of rich phosphate rock were discovered in the Charleston vicinity. A number of firms quickly sprang up to mine the rock and process it for agricultural use. The peak of operations was reached in 1885, at which time 673,000 tons of rock were mined, valued at over $4 million. About five years later richer deposits were discovered in Florida, Tennessee, and elsewhere, thus hastening the decline of South Carolina mining operations.

Beginning as Reconstruction ended, textile manufacturing underwent several years of phenomenal growth, and by 1900 it had dwarfed all other industries in South Carolina. There were now in the state 115 cotton mills, with over $39 million in capital investment, 30,201 workers, and an annual production valued at almost $30 million. With rare exception all cotton mills were dependent on water power to propel their machinery. However, a hydroelectric power project at Portman Shoals on the Seneca River in 1897 began successful transmission of power over several miles. Similar

projects were tried successfully elsewhere. With this new source of power, cotton mills could be located most anywhere. By 1920, capital investment had increased to $140.3 million in 184 mills with 54,629 workers, and annual production was valued at $286 million. The textile expansion was also aided by further railroad development, improvement in communications via the telephone, and the continued plentiful supply of cheap white labor. State law did not permit blacks to work alongside whites in cotton mills.

In an effort to attract workers, most textile companies practiced a system of paternalism. Pelzer Manufacturing Company, founded in 1881, was a leader in paternalistic practices. In 1906 veteran newsman August Kohn reported that the company had contributed $9,500 to build local churches; also, it supplied parsonages and contrib-

Above: In this circa 1913 photo, two men near St. Matthews promoted the "Good Roads" movement. At that time South Carolina had no hard-surfaced roads and few roads covered with topsoil outside its cities. Courtesy, National Archives

Below left: Workers in phosphate diggings near Charleston are shown, circa 1880. This industry, begun during the Reconstruction, died before World War I. Courtesy, South Caroliniana Library

uted to their upkeep. The company had spent $12,000 for school buildings and paid the salaries of the teachers. It supported a night school, a kindergarten, and a library, and it paid the wages of YWCA workers. The company built a large social hall, a roller skating rink, and was in the process of building a park pavilion and a swimming pool. All facilities were free for Pelzer workers and their families.

The same year, a flyer, distributed by the Pacolet Manufacturing Company in Spartanburg County to draw workers, stated in part:

We furnish you good, comfortable houses at 50 a room per month. We furnish you wood, coal and provisions laid at your door at market prices. Pacolet Mills houses are located on a hill and the place is noted for its health and free from all malarial diseases . . . We have good water, a splendid system of free schools, churches of different denominations . . . If you are a poor man there is no better location for you to select than Pacolet. It behooves every man to either educate his children or place them in a position to learn good trades.

The growth of mill villages led to two new classes of South Carolinians, the mill hands and mill tycoons. The mill hands came mainly from cotton farms and nearby mountains. Their political champion after 1900 was "Coley" Blease.

The early postwar industrialists usually came from the business world as merchants, bankers, realtors, and occasionally planters. A few, such as Dexter E. Converse and Henry P. Hammett, came up through the textile manufacturing ranks. Probably

This aerial photo of Calhoun Mills, a typical textile plant and village at Calhoun Falls, was taken circa 1926. In the right foreground are tennis courts and a house occupied by the factory manager. Behind the water tank is the company commissary (downstairs) and the recreation hall (upstairs). Just beyond is the mill church, used at that time by Baptist and Pentecostal Holiness congregations.

Sadie Pfiefer, an employee in the Lancaster Cotton Mill for six months, was photographed by Lewis Hine on November 30, 1908. Hine, noted for his photographs of industrial workers, was barred from taking pictures by several mill owners. Courtesy, Library of Congress

the most active promoter in North and South Carolina was Edgefield native Daniel Tompkins, who located in Charlotte. Under his leadership scores of cotton mills were built, and through speeches, letters, and news articles, Tompkins persuaded dozens of influential persons to become interested in textile manufacturing.

The development of cotton textiles, improved transportation and communication, and the natural increase of South Carolina's population between 1880 and 1920 led to marked growth in many of the state's cities and towns. Although Charleston and Columbia remained South Carolina's largest cities, increased development was most pronounced in the Piedmont region of the state. Greenville's population rose from 6,160 to 25,127; Spartanburg's from 3,253 to 22,638; and Anderson's from 1,850 to 10,570. Greenwood and Rock Hill were not far behind. The lowcountry towns of Florence, Sumter, and Orangeburg similarly kept pace.

Along with their growth, South Carolina's cities and towns underwent many changes between 1880 and World War I. The larger urban centers upgraded their police and fire departments, paved their main thoroughfares, modernized their water and sewer systems, installed electric lighting systems and telephone exchanges, and built street railways. Early streetcars were drawn by horses and mules, but

The South Island Ferry in Georgetown County operated between the island and the mainland. Courtesy, South Carolina Department of Highways and Public Transportation

Several seacoast villages fell victim to hurricanes, the worst occurring August 26-27, 1893. That storm swept away the Edingsville beach resort and killed an estimated 1,500 to 2,000 Beaufort County residents, most of whom were black. Some beach resorts continued to flourish elsewhere, especially as new modes of transport made them easier to reach.

In the meantime, hotels at Caesar's Head, Glenn Springs, and Table Rock continued to be patronized, and for the first two decades of the new century the Altamont Hotel flourished atop Paris Mountain. Several other antebellum watering places maintained local patronage.

At Camden and Aiken, around 1900, entrepreneurs built resort hotels, golf courses, and race tracks. The mild winter climate immediately began to lure tourists from the North. Both towns have continued to be centers of sports activity.

around the turn of the century, Charleston, Greenville, Columbia, Spartanburg, Anderson, Florence, and Rock Hill, and possibly one or two other towns, installed electric streetcars.

Also around the turn of the century, the state's cities and larger towns built recreation facilities: parks, bandstands, and playing fields. The cities and larger towns attracted fairs and circuses, built opera houses, and a few maintained zoos. Baseball became popular in the 1890s and a number of towns organized teams.

As in antebellum days, well-to-do families in town and country continued to visit beaches, mountains, and watering places during the summer. Meanwhile, changes had overtaken some pre-Civil War resorts.

In their recreation and celebrations, South Carolina towns exhibited a strong attachment to the past. They customarily held Confederate reunions, and nearly every courthouse town erected a monument to the Confederate heroes of its county.

In September 1870, as Thomas Green Clemson, the transplanted Pennsylvania scientist, surveyed the prospects for progress in South Carolina, he viewed the state's leadership critically. "Look at the late war," he wrote to his in-law James Edward Calhoun, "conceived in arrogance, matured in ignorance, and delivered in imbe-

The interior of the Orangeburg telephone exchange is pictured in 1917. Courtesy, Southern Bell Telephone

Prominent Greenville citizens gathered in 1891 to hold a fund-raising picnic for a hospital. Courtesy, Greenville News

cility." The state's intellectuals, he said, "are not educated to look to the future and take a comprehensive view of anything." In his own program for economic progress Clemson emphasized education. In fact, for four years he had looked in vain for financial support for a school to train young Carolinians in scientific agriculture and mechanic arts. In a moment of depression he wrote: "The people are too ignorant or too apathetic to understand and too short-sighted to venture a dollar to make thousands."

Clemson had no confidence in the Radical Republican regime then in control

of the South Carolina government. The Radicals did, however, lay the groundwork for free public education for all children of both races, and though they failed to appropriate sufficient funds to carry out the constitutional mandate, thousands of young whites and blacks received some schooling under their program. Their conscientious superintendent of education, carpetbagger Justus K. Jillson, admitted the deficiencies of the program. Nevertheless, he did his best to upgrade the system, sometimes at his own personal expense.

For several years after the Democrats regained control of South Carolina in

Right: This Confederate reunion took place in Hartsville, circa 1912. Major J.L. Coker is seated sixth from the right. Such reunions were held regularly throughout the former Confederate states while many veterans were still alive. Courtesy, Hartsville Museum

Right: Katherine Hammond and John S. Billings were married in this fashionable wedding at Redcliffe, former home of the bride's grandfather, on April 20, 1897. The home was located at Beech Island near Augusta. The shabby house was later renovated and is now part of a state park. Courtesy, South Caroliniana Library

Below: The railroad operated between Hagley on the Waccamaw and Pawley's Island from 1902 until 1906. Courtesy, Morgan Collection, Georgetown County Library

In this photo of an early Camden golf tournament, the Kirkwood Hotel, opened in 1903, is in the background. Note the sand "greens" and the ladies' fashions. Courtesy, Camden Archives

1877, there was little noticeable improvement. A reduction of the impoverished state's meager school appropriations threw the burden of education largely on individual school districts. As a consequence, some of the poorest were completely without schools in the 1880s.

Eventually the General Assembly offered some slight relief, but during the entire period of Conservative Democratic rule (1877-1890) the plight of the schools was terrible. Only in Charleston and a few towns did school terms run as long as eight months. In poorer counties and rural areas, the typical school operated two or three months in a one-room schoolhouse with one teacher who was paid from $15 to $35 per month.

In 1895 Ben Tillman's constitution provided for a state board of education for school districts between 9 and 49 square miles each, and for increased tax support. It was several years before improvement was visible. John Andrew Rice, writing about a rural Colleton County school in 1900, said: "The teacher was a country boy, himself just out of school, as touchy as a rattlesnake in spring, and scared. He had no imagination, his ignorance was profound, he needed money to go to college . . . these were his qualifications. He was, in fact, the average teacher of his day."

Gradually, as more money became available, the white schools were upgraded. In 1907 they received an annual average of eight dollars per enrollee, but the black schools, required by law, retrogressed. They received only $1.57 per enrollee, far below what they had received under the Conservative regime. In 1911 W.K. Tate, the state's first elementary rural school supervisor, reported: "The negro

school houses are miserable beyond description . . . Most of the teachers are absolutely untrained." Only in Charleston did schools for blacks compare favorably with those for whites. For years the city operated two grammar schools for blacks through the fifth grade and in 1911 added a black industrial school. Charleston employed only whites as teachers.

Most textile companies maintained grammar schools at their own expense for their workers' children. In many instances these schools were superior to the tax-supported public schools.

In 1907 the state began to establish public tax-supported high schools for whites. Prior to that time South Carolina high school students had to rely either on preparatory departments of colleges or attend tuition-charging private high schools. As the new program was initiated, every three-teacher grammar school that could possi-

The Jenkins Orphanage in Charleston was founded in 1891 by the Reverend D.J. Jenkins. He not only taught school there but organized a band that became well known for its travels over America and abroad. Courtesy, South Carolina Historical Society

bly round up the required minimum of 15 students for high school grades opened a high school.

Professor William H. Hand, state high school inspector in the early years, annually filed depressing reports of the inadequacies of the new high schools: poorly prepared teachers, a lack of scientific apparatus, severely restricted curricula, and instruction periods that were too brief. In fact, 58 so-called high schools in 26 counties were closed within 10 years of the new law. As for blacks, it was not until the 1920s that the state began to fund high schools for them. Prior to that time a few private black schools offered limited instruction on the secondary level.

In the realm of higher education South Carolina colleges were all but destroyed by the Civil War. Their students marched away to battle, while their administrators invested large portions of their slender resources in Confederate securities. During Reconstruction most schools made energetic efforts to raise funds and reopen. However, it was difficult for most institutions to operate with limited equipment, antiquated plants, and small staffs of usually no more than five or six professors.

It was also during Reconstruction that the first colleges for blacks were established in South Carolina. Claflin was founded in 1869 at Orangeburg by Methodist Episcopal clergy, and Benedict Institute (later Benedict College) was organized in 1871 at Columbia with Northern philanthropy to train Baptist ministers and teachers. Allen University, established in 1880, also in Columbia, had its roots in an earlier African Methodist Episcopal institute at Cokesbury. In the lean years of Reconstruction and after, the black colleges faced even more serious financial problems than their white counterparts.

Meanwhile, in 1866, historic South Carolina College was reorganized as a university; engineering, law, agriculture, and other practical subjects were added to the hitherto exclusively classical curriculum. With the admission of black students in 1873, faculty and white students departed in such numbers that the institution was left almost devoid of white patronage. With the end of Reconstruction the University was closed until 1880. The following year Governor Johnson Hagood breathed new life into the University when he advocated increased financial aid along with the reopening of The Citadel, which had been closed since the latter part of the Civil War.

Supporters of both schools cooperated; university appropriations were increased from a miserly $2,500 to $12,500 and rose steadily for several years afterward.

However, there was deep-seated antagonism to the University of South Carolina. Poverty-stricken denominational colleges were jealous of the University's tax-supported base and free tuition. The church schools could compete neither for professors nor students. When the Tillman movement got under way, the farmers clamored for a separate agricultural college, thus forcing the University to battle for its existence. Its supporters satisfied the clergy by agreeing in 1886 to an annual tuition charge of $40 for all students, except "competent and deserving" South Carolina youths unable to pay the same. On the other hand, the agrarians could no longer be held at bay when Thomas G. Clemson's will in 1888 provided adequate land and funds to establish a separate agricultural college.

While Tillman was governor, Winthrop College for women was also chartered. Under the energetic and Machiavellian David B. Johnson, Winthrop prospered. With the opening of two new state-supported colleges, partisans of the University feared its fate would soon be sealed. They were amazed that Governor Tillman supported continued operations of the University and The Citadel, the two "pets of aristocracy," as he called them. But he was willing to cut appropriations for the University, especially after the Panic of 1893 reduced state revenue.

When University partisans protested cuts in the school's funds, John Ashley, an illiterate legislator from Anderson County, retorted: "Let 'er die." Ashley was not without backing, for it became clear that the state could ill afford four colleges for whites as rivals for patronage. In addition, the legislature in 1896 established State A and M College for black students.

The University of South Carolina suffered further at the hands of Governor Blease. Blease was prejudiced against the University at least partly because of his expulsion years earlier for plagiarizing an essay. As governor, he sought to cut the school's annual appropriation, but, fortunately for the institution, its legislative supporters were able to minimize the governor's damage. Blease also attacked University president Samuel C. Mitchell on an unfair charge that Mitchell had caused Winthrop to lose $90,000 of Peabody funds, to be used instead for educating

"Old Main" at Lander College was built in 1904 when Williamstown Female College, founded in 1872 by the Reverend Samuel Lander, moved to Greenwood and came under control of the Methodist Episcopal Church, South. After World War II the church turned the college over to the County of Greenwood, which later turned it over to the state of South Carolina.

black teachers in other Southern states. Although innocent, the sensitive Mitchell eventually resigned rather than face continued onslaughts against his character.

Not only did the University suffer from Blease's wrath, but Thomas E. Miller, a former congressman and current president of State A and M, was forced from his position in 1911 for having openly supported Blease's rival in the governor's race of 1910. Miller said he had opposed Blease because the latter's "announced policy against the Negro was not founded upon justice and the best interest of the State."

At the turn of the century, a year's expense for a college student in South Carolina ranged from $100 to $150. Otherwise, admission requirements were far from stringent; Professor Hand reported in 1915 that "any high school pupil with 10 units to his credit can get into the freshman class of any college in the State, with the hope and expectation of being graduated in four years."

At best South Carolina colleges had one- and two-member departments, poor libraries, and few teachers of renown. Most of the professors and administrators who left their mark on the state were remembered more for their high moral principles and integrity than for their research, scholarship, or maintenance of high academic standards. Until the second decade of the twentieth century, many South Carolina college graduates were required to take additional undergraduate work before being admitted to graduate schools of renowned eastern universities.

For extracurricular activities the men's colleges devoted much time to literary societies, debating, and literary journals. Nine colleges participated in a much-publicized annual oratorical contest sponsored by the State Oratorical Association, organized in 1898. Forty-five contests were held before World War II disrupted the program, never to be resumed.

Male college students also turned their attention to intercollegiate athletics. In 1889 Wofford and Furman inaugurated intercollegiate football, and within a decade most men's colleges had taken up the sport. The first Carolina-Clemson football contest took place in 1896. The early football games were rough. Fights were not uncommon, there were endless disputes over the eligibility of players, and sometimes disputes terminated games prematurely. Most schools also added baseball, basketball, tennis, and track prior to World War I.

No women's college sponsored intercollegiate athletic competition in South Carolina. Rather, women participated in a host of intramural sports. Before World War I, college women were expected to leave campus only in the company of approved chaperones. Their lives were further regulated by afternoon "quiet" hours, "lights out" signals at night, punctuality at mealtime, and compulsory church atten-

The first faculty at South Carolina A. & M. College, now South Carolina State College, consisted of two men and seven women. Courtesy, South Carolina State College

The unveiling of this Confederate monument in Union took place in 1907. At the dedication MacBeth Young, mayor of Union, praised the Confederate women whose "tears and prayers hath saved the civilization of our beautiful Southland." This ceremony was repeated in many other South Carolina courthouse towns. Courtesy, Mrs. V. Randolph Hawkins

dance on Sundays. Some women's colleges placed restrictions on letter writing and on-campus visitors, while at Summerland College at Batesburg women could not make telephone calls without special permission. Of course, neither smoking nor drinking was tolerated.

Colleges for blacks were modeled after their white counterparts in both curricula and extracurricular activities. On paper their programs appeared to be impressive, but in practice their standards were poor. Their college departments were weak because of financial stringency, and most of their students did not measure up academically to the college level. Of the 956 students who graduated Claflin between 1880 and 1913, only 93 were listed as "college" graduates.

The rules for conduct for black students were similar to those imposed upon students in white institutions. There was one notable contrast between white and black colleges, however. The black schools,

because of financial necessity, were usually coeducational. Among white schools, only the University of South Carolina was coed. It enrolled its first woman student in 1895.

White schools and colleges, in addition to the standard curriculum, emphasized reverence for the Old South and the Confederacy. James McBride Dabbs, born in 1896 in the South Carolina "black belt," remembered that although no national flag floated over the schoolhouse, its inner walls were decorated with various Confederate banners, and on Fridays the students sang Confederate songs. When he was about 16, Dabbs heard his grandmother say she had never been reconstructed and never intended to be.

Out of the trauma of defeat, South Carolinians looked back fondly to a mythologized antebellum South of chivalrous gentlemen planters, lily-pure maids, contented slaves, and superior culture. The conviction that the officer in gray fought not to defend slavery but rather liberty and constitutional principles was unquestioned. In effect, South Carolinians (and other Southerners) made a religion of the Old South and the Lost Cause. These mythic memories were deeply embedded in the minds of Palmetto young people and greatly affected the lives of both races well into the twentieth century. Even many South Carolina clergy accepted the myth of the Lost Cause and felt no need to apologize for slavery.

In South Carolina the most active religious denominations during the postwar revival were the Baptists and Methodists, the strongest sects also before the war. During the early years of Reconstruction the Baptists set about raising a $200,000 endowment for Furman. Within a few years they had also established an orphanage, devoted money and attention to foreign missions, and gained thousands of converts in the new textile villages. Early in the new century they created a Board of Education, opened a hospital in Columbia, and adopted the weekly *Baptist Courier* as the official church organ. By 1916 there were 1,096 Baptist churches with 158,151 members in the state.

Methodist expansion followed similar lines. By 1916 there were two Methodist conferences with 851 churches and 105,306 members. By that time the church supported three four-year colleges, a junior college, two other schools, an orphanage, a weekly journal, and missions in seven foreign countries. Increased support of education, orphanages, and missions was common to all denominations whose memberships were was large enough to afford such efforts.

From time to time disputes over doctrine developed among Protestant sects. For example, the Presbyterian Synod of the state almost split in the 1880s over the question of evolution. Other controversies often arose over interpretation of the scriptures. As a consequence, the Pentecostal Holiness Church, the Church of God, and several smaller denominations were founded. Most of these churches, strongly fundamentalist in their theology, were in revolt against the growing liberalism of theological leaders in some of the older denominations. In some cases it was simply the poor wishing to withdraw from congregations that were dominated by the well-to-do. However, on the eve of World War I their membership was still small.

When the Civil War ended, all Protestant denominations tried to retain control of their black members. But the latter began to drift away as soon as they became aware that they would not be permitted to share in the management of church affairs. The Methodists and Baptists soon realized the futility of trying to hold their black members and willingly parted with them. In many cases they aided their black coreligionists in establishing new churches. The Presbyterians and Episcopalians were reluctant to part company with

their black members, but they too were unsuccessful in holding them.

All the while, Northern missionaries encouraged blacks to organize independent congregations, and they furnished financial support for church buildings and the establishment of colleges and institutes to educate black leaders. One of the most important social consequences of Reconstruction was the establishment of independent black churches.

The strongest black denominations were Methodist and Baptist. The latter organized a statewide convention as early as 1876, and by 1916 there were 1,353 black Baptist churches with 225,479 members. The independence of each black Baptist congregation from higher church authority was especially appealing to its members. Meanwhile, the black Methodists were divided among four main groups, the largest of which was the African Methodist Episcopal Church. The four groups maintained 1,325 churches with a combined membership of 173,548 in 1916. At that time black Baptists and Methodists were more numerous than their white counterparts.

As South Carolina's population was overwhelmingly rural, most churches, black and white, were located in the country. The average rural congregation was small, its minister poorly paid, and, except for Episcopalians and Presbyterians, often barely educated in theology. Many rural preachers of necessity worked at other jobs for a livelihood. In contrast to whites, black ministers were often political leaders in their communities, and their churches became places for political meetings.

Rural and small town churches of both races were social as well as religious institutions. There was much fraternizing before and after services, and picnic dinners were often held on the grounds. Many hardworking rural farm women, suffering more than their husbands from isolation, found the church the one significant social institution in their often drab lives.

Religion was also an important resource in a life of deprivation. South Carolina's one-crop economy created such lives for many. By 1900 approximately 55 percent of the state's farmers were tenants, mainly sharecroppers laboring on someone else's land. The tenancy rate for black farmers alone was close to 80 percent, and over half the black tenants produced less than $250 worth of crops annually. Because of low productivity (cotton was labor intensive), many tenants were never out of

Above: These officials of Bethel African Methodist Episcopal Church in Georgetown are pictured circa 1908. Courtesy, Morgan Collection, Georgetown County Library

Right: Construction of the "One Day Church" on South Church Street in Spartanburg took place on May 1, 1912. Services were held there the same evening. Officially named El Bethel Methodist Church, the structure was replaced in mid-century. Courtesy, B and B Studio, Spartanburg

debt, either to the landlord or to the furnishing merchant. Industrial workers fared somewhat better than farm tenants, but again, most were employed in low-wage cotton textile work. Seldom did a textile worker or farm tenant have a complete grammar school education.

Statistics also presented a gloomy picture of poor health for South Carolinians at the end of the nineteenth century. Sometimes poor health was due to poverty and ignorance. Sometimes it was caused by the climate that nurtured various parasites. Malaria, hookworm, and pellagra were common until World War I in spite of medical knowledge of how to control these diseases. Frequently, medical services were scarce or non-existent for poor people in rural areas.

Medical inspection of 415,000 schoolchildren in 413 counties throughout the Southern states found 43 percent infected with hookworm, with South Carolinians among the worst sufferers. Incidence of pellagra seemed to fluctuate with prosperity and depression, and malaria was endemic

wherever the mosquito thrived. Thanks also to ignorance, poverty, and poor medical services, South Carolina had an inordinately high rate of childbirth deaths and infant mortality.

Such distressing conditions did not respect race. However, blacks suffered in greater numbers. They also suffered something few whites did—discrimination. During the Conservative administration segregation was minimized, but with the advent of Ben Tillman discrimination became common. In 1900 the average black faced greater segregation, less justice, poorer schools, and less economic opportunity than he did at the end of Reconstruction. The Constitution of 1895 rendered blacks politically impotent. Jim Crow laws soon segregated the races in nearly every public walk of life. Blacks were furnished separate, but not equal, facilities in railroad trains, theaters, court rooms, public restrooms, and so on.

Blacks accused of serious crimes were on occasion summarily lynched rather than brought to trial. In South Carolina the number of lynchings reached a peak of 15 in 1898. This shameful activity received public encouragement from Governors Tillman and Blease. When arraigned and brought to trial by white officers, blacks, facing all-white juries and judges, stood little chance of acquittal if accused by a white witness. South Carolina's county prison (chain gang) population attested to that fact; in 1917 it consisted of 810 blacks and

69 whites. The all-pervasive discrimination against blacks changed little until after World War II.

Top: The dedication of St. Mary's Catholic Church in Georgetown took place on January 5, 1902. Courtesy, Morgan Collection, Georgetown County Library

Above: The "Tuesday Afternoon Club" was a social club for young black girls in Columbia in the early 1900s. Courtesy, South Caroliniana Library

Left: Convicts are pictured with their iron sleeping cages on a work detail near Society Hill, circa 1900. These cages were invented by W.S. King, Darlington County supervisor, to be used when work details were too distant from the jail for the inmates to return at night. Other counties used similar cages. Courtesy, South Caroliniana Library

Chapter IX

Two World Wars: 1914-1945

In the summer of 1914 prospects were bright for South Carolina cotton growers. A record crop was about to be harvested and prices were good, 12 to 13 cents a pound at the gin. On July 31 cotton exchanges closed in response to an expected outbreak of war in Europe. With that, panic gripped cotton growers over the entire cotton belt, and the federal government offered little in the way of relief. Some growers sold cotton as low as five and a half cents a pound before cotton exchanges reopened.

After the exchanges did reopen on November 16, cotton prices gradually rose and reached 20 cents in 1916. By the end of that year many South Carolina farmers were enjoying the greatest prosperity they had ever experienced. With American entry into the war in April 1917, cotton prices soared, reaching 43 cents in June 1919. Tobacco prices and those of other agricultural products also skyrocketed. The value of South Carolinian agricultural production rose from $166 million in 1913 to $446 million in 1918.

South Carolina industry—mainly textiles—likewise profited from the war. The value of industrial production jumped from $168 million in 1916 to $326 million in 1918. Urgent government demand for tents and uniforms strained the resources of the entire textile industry.

When Congress declared war against Germany in April 1917, the entire South Carolina delegation voted for the resolution except Fred H. Dominick, a law partner of Cole Blease. Dominick, a recently elected congressman from Newberry, had many constituents of German descent who believed Germany was no more responsible for the war than the Allied nations.

From the onset of America's entry, Dominick had support from Blease, as well

as John L. McLaurin, John G. Richards, and other Bleasites, who were determined to harass Governor Richard I. Manning. They organized a new "Reform" movement and accused the governor of trying to build up a personal political machine.

Blease personally led the attack. At a public meeting in July 1917, he declared that Manning was worse than the Reconstruction governors. He said: "They stole the money, but Manning is stealing the souls and bodies of your boys." Blease also denounced the Selective Service Act as unconstitutional and accused the "Manning faction" of using it unfairly to draft Reform party boys into service.

In 1918 Blease began to soften his criticism. He had failed to get the desired reaction and was anxious to win a Senate seat. He was likewise wary of the recently enacted federal sedition law, which had led to the indictment of W.P. Beard, one of his editor friends, and temporarily closed down the Charleston *American*, the newspaper of John P. Grace, another staunch supporter. His modified tactics availed him nothing. In the August Democratic primary, colorless Nat B. Dial swept the state, thus delivering one of the most ignominious defeats Blease ever suffered.

While the Bleasites publicly castigated Manning's administration, the governor marshaled the state's resources for war. He acted promptly to establish selective service machinery, to improve transportation and communication facilities, and to secure training camps for the state. Manning set up a state council of defense that promoted Liberty Loans, economy in food consumption, and increased food production, and that aided the Red Cross.

During the war Governor Manning did not forget reform. Having limited success in 1917 because of Bleasite opposition, in 1918 the governor fared better. The legis-

*Prime Minister Winston Churchill
and high-ranking officials observed
a military demonstration at Fort Jackson on June 24, 1942. Shown left
to right are: General George C. Marshall, chief of staff, U.S. Army;
Field Marshal Sir John Dill;
Prime Minister Churchill; U.S. Secretary of War Henry L. Stimson;
U.S. Major General R.L. Eichel-
berger; and General Sir Alan
Brooke, chief of Imperial Staff,
Great Britain. Courtesy, U.S.
Army*

lature was generous with appropriations for schools, colleges, and most agencies of public welfare. It broadened the use of the secret ballot for the Democratic primary to include all but rural precincts. Further, the legislature created an industrial school for girls and a training school for the mentally handicapped, and it fought off the farmers' attempt to kill the Tax Commission, then in the process of reassessing farm property. However, neither the governor nor the legislature supported the women's suffrage amendment proposed at that time.

While agricultural and industrial production soared, thousands of South Carolinians entered the armed services. Even as South Carolinians traveled to various camps across the country, the federal government began to establish training posts within South Carolina. The main army posts were Camp Jackson in Columbia, Camp Sevier in Greenville, and Camp Wadsworth in Spartanburg. Marines were trained at stations on Parris Island and in Charleston.

A typical story of an army training post in South Carolina is that of Camp Wadsworth. Spartanburg civic leaders conceived of the base and offered $200,000 to help persuade the War Department to locate a camp near the city.

A labor force of over 4,500, working at a feverish pace, had the camp ready for the first troops, arriving on July 27, 1917. Within two months 20,000 soldiers were in training at Wadsworth. Most of the trainees were members of the Twenty-Seventh Division, a New York national guard unit that boasted a number of celebrities, including Colonel Cornelius Vanderbilt. The train-

ing was rapid and rugged as foreign military veterans tried to instruct the American recruits for what they were to face in bitter trench warfare: machine guns, mortars, howitzers, barbed wire, poison gas, mud, and stench. Tents with little fuel made the training more rugged the following winter.

Spartanburg did its best to be hospitable to the soldiers. The city raised a special fund for camp activities. The Red Cross, the YMCA, the YWCA, the Chamber of Commerce, the civic and fraternal clubs, and the churches bestirred themselves to relieve the monotony of camp life.

The army itself made efforts to furnish recreation for the troops and their civilian visitors. Civilians were entertained with conducted tours of training areas and with parades, drills, teas, and band concerts. The audience always responded enthusiastically to the rousing strains of "Over There." Dances were held at various camp sites on Saturday nights. The camp also maintained a cafeteria for visitors. The soldiers themselves organized newspapers and clubs.

In September 1918 the camp was quarantined because of a diphtheria epidemic in Spartanburg, and the following month the worldwide influenza epidemic reached Spartanburg but was never severe among Camp Wadsworth soldiers. The quarantine ended five days before the armistice, November 11. On that occasion the camp and city, in common with the rest of America, went wild with joy. Whistles blew, bells rang, and guns were fired.

After the armistice the troops remaining at Camp Wadsworth suffered letdown. Gloom set in as the men thought only of getting home for Christmas. The camp, though receiving some convalescents at its hospital, was rapidly demobilized and officially closed on March 25, 1919.

Altogether, more than 64,000 South Carolinians joined the armed forces. Of that number, 2,085 died in service, 460 while in battle or of battle injuries.

The Forty-Second ("Rainbow") Division was the first outfit with South Carolina troops to reach France. The Eighty-First ("Wildcat" or "Stonewall") Division was trained at Camps Jackson and Sevier. One of its regiments, consisting largely of South Carolinians, aided in smashing the strongly defended Hindenburg Line south of Verdun near the close of the war.

South Carolina's star shone brightest in the exploits of its men in the Thirtieth ("Old Hickory") Division. Most of the division's South Carolinians were assigned to the 118th Infantry Regiment, commanded by Colonel Peter K. McCully of Anderson. "Old Hickory" reached France in May 1918, and after limited action it attacked the Hindenburg Line at Bellicourt on September 29. It broke the line, captured trenches and an important four-mile tunnel, and defeated two German divisions.

The Thirtieth won a disproportionate share of battle honors. Its members were awarded 12 Congressional Medals of Honor, 3 more than any other unit of like size. Of these 12 medals, South Carolinians of the 118th received 6. Only soldiers from New York and Illinois received more Medals of Honor than the South Carolinians. The state's six army heroes were Sergeant Gary Evans Foster, Inman; First Lieutenant James C. Dozier, Rock Hill; Sergeant Richmond H. Hilton, Westville; Sergeant Thomas Lee Hall, Fort Mill; Corporal James D. Heriot, Providence; and Corporal John C. Villepigue, Camden. Sergeant Hall and Corporal Heriot were killed in action. Besides the army heroes, Ensign Daniel Sullivan, Charleston, won a Medal of Honor for valiant service aboard the USS *Christabel*.

South Carolina came through the war with a broader outlook on world affairs; many South Carolinians had left the state for the first time in their lives. Agriculture

In 1918 Governor Richard I. Manning posed in front of the governor's mansion with a banner representing the military service of his five sons. Courtesy, Federal Security Savings, Columbia

Top: This Anderson automobile was built by the Anderson Motor Company in Rock Hill. Unable to compete with Detroit automakers, Anderson went into bankruptcy in 1926. Courtesy, Museum of York County

Above: South Carolinians began to take an interest in aviation in the 1920s. This photo shows daredevil aviator Elliott White Springs, a World War I ace, flying under the Buster Boyd Bridge on the Catawba River in 1923. Courtesy, Springs Industries, Inc.

and industry were prospering, and the future looked bright.

The postwar era was one of overall prosperity for America, but agriculture was among the weak spots in the nation's economy. Cotton prices dropped from 35 cents a pound in the fall of 1919 to as low as 13 cents at harvest time in 1920. Tobacco dipped from 39 cents to 21 cents a pound, while the cost of labor, feed, and fertilizer remained relatively high.

South Carolina cotton growers faced another serious problem, the boll weevil. This destructive insect, slowly moving east from Mexico for several years, reached the state in 1917. Two years later the pest devastated such a large part of the sea island cotton crop that the discouraged sea island planters ceased growing the staple.

To add to the farmers' troubles a nationwide depression struck in 1921. Congress made ineffectual efforts to meet the crisis, but neither new legislation, meetings, con-

ferences, nor efforts of the congressional farm bloc helped much. In South Carolina the state's political leaders seemed equally unable to alleviate the depressing agricultural conditions.

Although agricultural reformers called for farmers to diversify, a major problem continued to be a lack of reliable markets for vegetables, fruits, poultry, and dairy products. In the 1920s South Carolina agriculture was still dominated by small one- and two-mule farms. In 1930 the state had 157,931 farms with an average size of 65.8 acres. Tenancy had reached 65.1 percent. These small farmers' only sure means of a cash income was in growing cotton or, in the Pee Dee, tobacco.

There were exceptions. For many years a number of farmers on or near the lower South Carolina coast had engaged in growing truck crops for Northern markets, and in the 1920s several Greenville and Spartanburg county farmers tried commercial peach orchards. They developed a market system for shipping peaches north, and soon Piedmont county farmers from York to Oconee entered the business. A number of others in the midlands followed suit. During the 1930s South Carolina peach production averaged over 1.2 million bushels annually.

Although most South Carolina farmers grew either cotton or tobacco, a wide gap separated the richest and poorest. A 1925 to 1928 study of 369 farms in eastern South Carolina revealed that the top 25 percent averaged annual earnings of $3,916, while the lowest 25 percent averaged $285.

Meanwhile, the manufacture of cotton textiles expanded between 1920 and 1930 by almost $70 million in capital and 40,000 additional workers. By 1930 cotton textiles had overexpanded nationwide and faced cutthroat competition within its ranks. The industry also faced serious competition from synthetic fibers and foreign imports. As one textile executive announced, "King Cotton is sick!"

Along with these economic difficulties the state faced a number of other problems in the 1920s. One was concern over race relations. World War I had given many Southern blacks opportunities for better jobs and higher social positions than they had enjoyed previously. This was especially true for those who had served in the armed forces or who had migrated north to work in the war industry. At the war's end they did not want to surrender their newly acquired gains, and in the postwar readjust-

This group of blacks attended an undertakers meeting in Columbia, circa 1930. Not all blacks were impoverished; they developed their own professional class of morticians, lawyers, preachers, doctors, dentists, teachers, restaurant owners, hotel managers, and storekeepers. They had only blacks as clients, however, and the middle class segment of society they constituted remained almost unknown to whites. From this professional class came most of the civil rights leaders of later years. Courtesy, South Caroliniana Library

ment, race riots erupted in several Northern cities.

Fear of racial troubles in the South helped stimulate membership in a newly organized Ku Klux Klan. The Klan hoped to intimidate blacks as its predecessor had done during Reconstruction years. Hooded Klan parades and cross burnings became common events in many states, including South Carolina. The Klan not only intended "to keep the Negro in his place," but it was anti-Catholic, anti-Semitic, anti-foreigner, and anti-socialist. Despite the fears of many, no serious racial disturbances occurred in South Carolina. Segregation remained unchallenged.

The Klan, though never as strong in South Carolina as in other states, also hoped to reform society by discouraging "immorality." This appealed to people with fundamentalist religious beliefs, which were quite strong in most South Carolina denominations. South Carolina church folk also generally supported Prohibition. Enforcement of the law, however, proved to be difficult for state officials. Bootlegging flourished, witnesses were reluctant to testify in court, and convicted offenders were rapidly replaced by others eager to engage in the illegal traffic.

Closely associated with the prohibition of alcohol in the public's mind were the state's "blue laws," designed to prohibit public entertainment on Sunday. In 1927 Governor John G. Richards, the state's first chief executive to serve under the new constitutional provision of one four-year term, was determined to enforce the blue laws

vigorously, even to the point of prohibiting the sale of soft drinks. Within a few weeks rigid enforcement broke down in the face of hostile public opinion and adverse court decisions. The issue did not die, however, and public movies and many sporting events did not operate on Sundays over most of the state until the 1960s. Not until 1985 did it become legal to buy a shirt on Sunday.

One of the major issues in the state in the 1920s was that of public education. All the governors favored liberal support of the schools and wished to reduce some of the large discrepancies between financial support for white schools and for black schools. For instance, Charleston County annually spent $99.77 for each white pupil, while Hampton County spent only $2.29 for each black student.

In 1924 Governor Thomas G. McLeod enacted the "6-0-1" school law. By the terms

Governor John G. Richards, President Hoover, and North Carolina Governor O. Max Gardner are standing left to right in this photograph taken at the ceremony for the 150th anniversary of the battle of Kings Mountain in October 1930. Courtesy, Margaret Richards

Irvin Negro school, in Berkeley County, was in an area later flooded by Santee Cooper. The school is shown in December 1939. Courtesy, South Carolina State Museum

of this all-important law, the state would pay teachers' salaries for six months if local authorities would pay for the seventh month. The state also consolidated a number of small schools, bused rural white students, and established more high schools, including the first accredited high schools for blacks.

Nowhere under the 6-0-1 act did black schools become the equals of white institutions, however. In 1940 South Carolina spent an average of $46.80 per white pupil and $11.40 for each black. It is small wonder that almost two-thirds of South Carolina's adult blacks were functionally illiterate at that time.

In the 1920s South Carolina's institutions of higher learning were considerably upgraded. In 1921 the colleges raised entrance requirements, and all white colleges soon abandoned their preparatory departments. For advanced study the state supported a law school, a pharmacy school, and Ph.D. degrees in limited curricula at the University of South Carolina. Faculties were strengthened in nearly every institution and student enrollment climbed. By 1930, Carolina, Winthrop, Clemson, The Citadel, and State A and M had a combined enrollment of over 7,000 students. Nonetheless, when the General Assembly passed the 6-0-1 law for public schools, voters at the same time turned down a proposed

bond issue of $10 million to provide improvements at state-supported colleges.

Public education, although a thorny issue in South Carolina, did not create as much controversy as road building. Between 1917 and 1925 the number of registered motor vehicles in the state soared from about 40,000 to over 170,000, raising public demand for improved roads and bridges. The legislature levied gasoline taxes, motor vehicle taxes, and additional property taxes to support highway construction. Through federal legislation the national government also offered financial aid on a matching basis.

With the enactment of the "Pay-As-You-Go" Highway Act of 1924, the chief burden of financing and maintaining the roads was transferred from the counties to the State Highway Department. Immediately, the road improvement program speeded up, particularly with regard to hard surfacing. The pace was still too slow to please many South Carolinians who scrutinized the rapid development of North Carolina's paved highway system. In order to speed up South Carolina's road construction, Governor John G. Richards agreed to the sale of $65 million worth of bonds. In 1929 the legislature approved the road bond issue, but did not submit it to a popular referendum as required by the state constitution. The state supreme court, with circuit court judges also sitting and voting, ruled that the bond issue was legal without a popular referendum.

For the next six years South Carolinians argued about the bond issue. The chief opposition came from the upcountry, where roads were in better shape than those in the lowcountry. The opposition rallied around Olin D. Johnston of Spartanburg in the gubernatorial race of 1930. Johnston lost a close contest to Ibra C. Blackwood, whose enormous majority in Charleston furnished the margin of victory. Blackwood's victory enabled the State Highway Commission, under Ben Sawyer, to move ahead rapidly with the state's road building program. By June 30, 1933, there were 3,200 miles of hard-surfaced roads in South Carolina.

Although fraud was never proven in Governor Blackwood's election, many people continued to believe that Johnston had been cheated of victory. (Charleston ballots had been quickly destroyed after a Democratic Executive Committee hearing). In 1934, when Johnston again ran for governor, he easily defeated veteran politician Cole Blease. Johnston had boasted of his humble origins, thus wooing away many of the poor who had previously supported Blease.

Governor Johnston, unable to reverse the bond issue, sought to replace some

State Highway Commission members with his own partisans. Barred from such action by the courts, Johnston, in October 1935, called out the national guard, declared martial law, drove the commission from its offices, and seized highway funds from several Columbia banks. The legislature rebuked the governor for this high-handedness, and he was forced to yield when the courts opposed him.

In national affairs during the 1920s the Republican party was in firm control in Washington, and South Carolina political leaders had little voice in national councils. But with the stock market crash in 1929, followed by the Depression and the election of a Democratic president and Congress,

With the improvement of roads during the 1920s, Myrtle Beach began to flourish as a summer resort, and Greenville businessmen financed the luxurious Ocean Forest Hotel. The hotel was razed in the 1960s because it lacked central air conditioning and other modern amenities. Courtesy, South Carolina Department of Agriculture

The Prater Bridge across the Tugaloo River was one of several covered bridges in the state. Bridges were covered to prevent horses from becoming frightened. Prater was later burned, and the other bridges either met the same fate or were demolished to make way for modern structures. Photo by Lewis Moorhead

American hero Colonel Charles A. Lindbergh visited Spartanburg on October 12, 1927. Attending this "civic dinner" were Senator E.D. Smith, on Lindbergh's far right, and Governor John G. Richards, accompanied by Mrs. Richards, on his left. Courtesy, Philip Racine

South Carolina voices were heard once more in the national capital.

The worst depression in American history reached its lowest point in the winter of 1932-1933. A particularly heavy blow to the South Carolina economy occurred on January 2, 1932, when the People's State Bank's offices failed to open their doors. Thousands of people lost their savings. Meanwhile, cotton prices fell to five cents a pound, and many tenants were on the verge of starvation. At the same time, the textile industry was hit hard. Many mills shut down, and unskilled mill hands, if lucky enough to have jobs, commonly received 10 cents per hour.

During the Depression South Carolinians managed as best they could. Shoes and clothing were mended until they fell into tatters; houses remained unpainted and unrepaired. Many persons, both black and white, never saw a dentist and only in dire emergencies did they call on medical doctors, often as charity patients. Many lives were cut short for lack of proper food, shelter, and medical care.

For entertainment, people resorted to inexpensive pleasures: horseshoes, checkers, sandlot baseball and football, swimming at the old "wash hole," fishing, camping, singing, and dancing. Hillbilly bands came cheap, and "Chocolate" Brown's five-piece orchestra would travel 30 miles out of Greenwood for only $20 to play for a dance. Radio programs were free, and most towns had a movie house which offered 10-cent specials on certain days.

Governor Blackwood and the General Assembly were unable to cope with the economic crisis without federal relief funds. However, President Herbert Hoover was slow to comprehend the magnitude of the crisis, and his ineffective efforts led to Franklin D. Roosevelt's victory in 1932 with the promise of a "new deal."

For the farmers the federal government in 1933 offered the Agricultural Adjustment Act (AAA), which provided subsidies in seven basic commodities, including cotton and tobacco, to farmers who would agree to crop controls. The Commodity Credit Corporation (CCC) was established to advance loans to farmers with nonperishable crops as security. The Farm Credit Administration (FCA) reorganized farm credit agencies and supplied additional credit to the agrarians.

New Deal measures saved many landowners from bankruptcy but offered little benefit for South Carolina's 102,000 farm tenants. In fact, between 1929 and 1939 cotton acreage in America was reduced almost in half. In addition, landowners were increasingly turning to tractors and other mechanized equipment. Thus many landlords, contrary to the law, dismissed ten-

Above: The Tobacco Festival is held annually in the Pee Dee area. This was the Darlington County entry in 1938 at Florence. Courtesy, Darlington County Historical Commission

Left: This textile worker was employed in a Kershaw County mill in the 1930s. Courtesy, National Archives

Below: This was the home of a poor Indian "brass ankle" family and a cane grinder near Summerville in the 1930s. Courtesy, South Caroliniana Library

nants. During the 1930s more than 25,000 South Carolina tenant farmers gave up their farms to become day laborers or seek relief. But federal relief was meager—$10.49 a month in 1933 for white sharecropper families, $8.69 for blacks.

Meanwhile, the National Recovery Administration (NRA) aided the struggling textile industry to standardize wages at a minimum of 30 cents an hour and working hours at an average of 40 per week. The NRA likewise encouraged labor to unionize. Immediately the United Textile Workers (UTW) moved in and organized many mill workers in South Carolina and elsewhere. In September 1934 the UTW staged a nationwide strike that called for a 30-hour work week without a reduction in pay. The strike, the largest in South Carolina history, caused about two-thirds of the state's textile workers to walk off their jobs. Here and there workers organized "flying squadrons" to swoop down on plants still in op-

eration and try to intimidate workers loyal to management. Violence broke out occasionally, and Governor Blackwood called out the national guard to protect mill property and preserve order. At Honea Path six strikers were killed outside Chiquola Mill when mill guards fired into the crowd. After several weeks of futile negotiations the strike was broken, and its failure dealt the UTW a mortal blow. The South Carolina textile industry has remained largely nonunion to this day.

Other significant New Deal measures affecting South Carolina were the Civilian Conservation Corps, which employed young men; the Rural Electrification Administration, which brought electricity to thousands of rural homes; the Works Progress Administration, which created jobs for people of both races, and the Social Security Act. Additionally, the federal government financed the Santee Cooper hydroelectric power project at Pinopolis.

President Roosevelt, with his charming manner, his political savvy, and his magnetic "fireside chats" over the radio, became a great favorite among South Carolina voters during the early years of the New Deal. During his second term some of his followers became alarmed at his liberalism on racial matters, his support of organized labor, his efforts to "pack" the Supreme Court with pro-New Deal justices, and the growth of federal bureaucracy. Despite these differences, an overwhelming majority of the state's voters supported the president for reelection in 1936, 1940, and 1944.

This constancy came in the face of various changes on the political scene in

South Carolina. Colorful "Coley" Blease, who had served as governor from 1911 to 1915, was elected to the United States Senate in 1924 with the catchy slogan: "Roll up yer sleeves and say what cha' please; the man fer the office is Cole L. Blease." During his six years in Washington, Blease was still the showman. Yet in reality he offered little statesmanship and had no influence in national Democratic circles.

Blease's victory in 1924 was his last. In 1930 he lost his Senate seat to James F. Byrnes, the man he had defeated in a runoff primary in 1924. Nevertheless, the old demagogue never quit campaigning. In 1932 he tried to oust Ellison D. Smith from his Senate seat, and in both 1934 and 1938 he made futile bids for the governorship. By the time of his last race the elderly, white-haired Blease had lost most of his dash and fire; he calmly asked the voters to read their Bibles and "then think carefully and sanely" how they would vote. With Blease's death in 1942, there passed from the scene one of the most charismatic and controversial politicians in South Carolina's history.

Whereas Blease lost his last race in 1938, the unforgettable Ellison D. Smith won a notable victory. First elected to the Senate in 1908, Smith, who was better

known as "Cotton Ed," held his Senate position until his death on November 17, 1944.

In his first campaign "Cotton Ed" set the pattern for all his later political contests. He rode to speaking engagements atop a wagon load of cotton bales and wore a cotton boll in his coat lapel. He caressed the boll and loudly proclaimed: "My sweetheart, my sweetheart! Others may forget you, but you will always be my sweetheart!" For over 30 years his platform remained unchanged: states' rights, white supremacy, and a tariff for revenue only. Always an able and crafty stump speaker, "Cotton Ed" was seldom bested by hecklers. Without the benefit of a political machine, he served in the Senate longer than any other South Carolinian.

In his early years Senator Smith introduced measures beneficial to farmers, but later he seemed to be more interested in talk than in action. His nephew wrote of him:

He was an evangelical politician. The world-saving strain that ran through the family (ministers of the gospel) was used by him for his own ends, and the vocabulary was ready at hand. At some point in every speech the Lord's will got mixed up with the boys in grey storming an impregnable height, the purity of Southern womanhood, Yankees, the glorious past and still more glorious future.

Perhaps it was not altogether his fault, for as his nephew explained: "Sometimes he became serious, but they would not have it. A voice called from the crowd, 'Cut that out and tell us a story!' "

During the Depression, "Cotton Ed," as chairman of the Senate Committee on Agriculture and Forestry, spent most of his time fighting New Deal measures and defending white supremacy. He was sure that John C. Calhoun, looking down from his mansion in the sky, approved his walkout of the Democratic convention in Philadelphia in 1936 when a black man began to give the invocation. As *Time* magazine put it, Smith was "a conscientious objector to the 20th century."

Because of Smith's opposition to much of the New Deal, President Roosevelt tried to use his influence to unseat the crusty old spellbinder in the 1938 senatorial race. South Carolinians, however, resented the president's interference and refused to discard a colorful senator who embodied what many regarded as their independent heritage. Smith handily defeated his opponent, Governor Olin D. Johnston.

On election night "Cotton Ed" and his followers held a rousing rally in front of the statehouse. They were dressed in red shirts reminiscent of Wade Hampton's famous campaign of 1876. To the assembled crowd "Cotton Ed" shouted: "We are the sons of those who hurled defiance at the federal

Left: This snafu occurred on the last day that electric streetcars ran in Charleston, February 10, 1938. Other South Carolina cities also replaced their trollies with buses in the 1930s. Courtesy, W.D. Workman, Jr.

Below: President Roosevelt, Governor R.M. Jefferies, and Lieutenant General Ben Lear paused for this photo while inspecting military installations at Fort Jackson, Columbia, in 1942. Courtesy, U.S. Army

government in the 1860s and 1870s. Thank God, we have kept the faith."

With the outbreak of war in Europe in September 1939, American attention was largely diverted from politics. The nation began to rearm, and with this increased industrial activity the Depression, already waning, soon ended.

America gradually became drawn into the war by sending arms to friendly powers in Europe and restricting vital commerce with Japan. The nation's limited role came to an abrupt end on December 7, 1941, when Japanese planes bombed Pearl Harbor. It was all-out war thereafter.

Congress quickly extended the Selective Service Act, passed earlier, to conscript able-bodied males, ages 18 to 45 (later lowered to 38) for the duration. In time, approximately 170,000 South Carolina men saw action all over the world during World War II. Except for a few specialists needed in war production industries, there was hardly an able-bodied unmarried man in the state who did not enter some branch of the military service. In addition, some 2,500 South Carolina women served in the armed forces in noncombat roles.

South Carolinians served their country well. The Congressional Medal of Honor was awarded to five South Carolinians; Private First Class Thomas E. Atkins, Campobello; Private First Class William A. McWhorter, Liberty; Private Furman L.

Smith, Central; Lieutenant Colonel George L. Mabry, Jr., Sumter; and Sergeant Robert A. Owens, Greenville.

Meanwhile South Carolina became a vast training center for servicemen, mostly from Northern states. The state tried to provide recreation for them, but the crush of military personnel was too great for whatever the state had to offer. There was some grumbling among Northern servicemen, who came to regard South Carolina as an impoverished and backward state. Adverse criticism simply made South Carolinians defensive and resentful of Yankees.

During World War II many radio celebrities and Hollywood movie stars toured military camps in America and abroad to entertain service personnel. Among those who visited South Carolina were actors Bob Hope and John Payne and actress Jane Wyman. Pictured here are Payne and Wyman at a banquet in Greenville. Wyman is also remembered as the first wife of Ronald Reagan. Courtesy, Greenville County Library

During the war South Carolina textile mills turned mainly to government contracts and operated three shifts daily when workers could be procured. The Charleston Navy Yard mushroomed overnight into a city where teenagers, mothers, and elderly men became welders, riveters, machinists, carpenters, and mechanics. Some workers commuted daily from homes as far as 50 or 60 miles away. South Carolina farmers, also facing a labor shortage, continued to grow large quantities of cotton and food for the war effort.

Meanwhile the national government began to ration essential goods in short supply: meat, sugar, shoes, gasoline, and auto-

mobile tires. Men's three-piece suits were reduced to two pieces, and cuffs were omitted from pants. Senator Smith, still at war with the New Deal, strongly opposed rationing. Said he: "Why, they even tell me they're taking ruffles off ladies' lingerie. Who in hell expects to win a war that way?"

The government encouraged as many citizens as possible to become involved in war programs. Boy scouts and church organizations headed drives to collect scrap metal, paper, and rubber. Volunteers served as air raid wardens and air craft spotters, rolled bandages for the Red Cross, and attended first aid classes. A home guard was organized and trained for possible air at-

tacks or invasion. On the seacoast, a blackout was imposed to prevent shore lights from aiding enemy submarines in their search for American vessels. A volunteer shore patrol enforced blackout regulations.

Although politics took a back seat to war activity, it did not cease. Elections took place on schedule, and one South Carolina politico, James F. Byrnes, rose to a high position in the Roosevelt administration. Rewarded for valuable services to Roosevelt in the Senate by appointment to the Supreme Court in 1941, Byrnes resigned in 1942 to join Roosevelt's staff, and a few months later he was named director of the newly created Office of War Mobilization.

In 1944 Byrnes expected to become Roosevelt's running mate for the president's fourth try for the White House. Unfortunately for the South Carolinian, he had certain political liabilities that harmed his candidacy. He had been a Catholic but had left the church, was a racial segregationist, had supported measures that displeased organized labor, and his state had a small electoral vote. Roosevelt deserted Byrnes in favor of Senator Harry Truman of Missouri. The president's decision was

unpopular among South Carolinians and caused ill feelings against Truman.

South Carolinian Bernard Baruch also acted as an unofficial advisor to Roosevelt while holding an important wartime post in the government. Earlier he had also served as an unofficial adviser to President Woodrow Wilson. Baruch hosted Roosevelt on his plantation, "Hobcaw Barony," just east of Georgetown for several weeks in the spring of 1944.

That same year Olin D. Johnston, elected governor in 1942 for the second time, finally ousted Smith from his longheld Senate seat. Johnston, running hard on a racist platform, outbattled "Cotton Ed." The old senator was spared the pain of seeing his antagonist replace him, for he died shortly after the general election.

Although politics was relatively calm in South Carolina during the war years, change was in the offing, for the United States Supreme Court outlawed the Democratic party's white primary in Texas in 1944. Moreover, during the war segregation began to break down in the armed services and on common carriers. The state was on the verge of political and social turmoil at the end of the war.

President Roosevelt died suddenly in Warm Springs, Georgia, on April 12, 1945. When the train bearing his body passed through Clemson en route to Washington, Clemson College cadets stood at attention beside the railroad track. Courtesy, Pendleton District Historical and Recreational Commission

Reversing the Course of the Future, 1945-1970

World War II came to an end when the Japanese agreed to surrender unconditionally to the Allies on August 14, 1945. In Greenville word of the Japanese surrender came over the radio at 7:02 p.m., and the town "went slightly mad," in the words of the Greenville *News* the next morning. In Columbia fire sirens blared, and many families that owned automobiles used their precious gasoline to head to Main Street while blowing their horns. In Charleston the bells of St. Michael's pealed, sirens filled the night air, and flares and searchlights illuminated the skies over the harbor and the city.

As thousands of veterans began to return to the Palmetto State in the months that followed, home seemed strangely unchanged. In the upstate, mill whistles still regulated the life of the textile workers as they had for a half-century or more. A first-time visitor to Charleston, riding into town down Meeting Street north of Calhoun remarked, "The glory has departed." Black veterans, many who had seen the wide world beyond South Carolina for the first time, found the status quo of Jim Crow segregation stifling. They prepared to leave the farms and towns for better opportunities in Northern cities.

But appearances were deceiving. H. C. Nixon, a close observer of the region, commented that the South emerged from the war "with more social change and more unfinished business than any other part of the country." The wartime economic growth and social dislocation challenged the state to adjust to changing circumstances. Between 1945 and 1970 South Carolina would undergo more radical changes than it had in the century since the Civil War and Reconstruction.

For over 100 years the population of South Carolina had grown more slowly than the nation as a whole. Poverty and the migration of African Americans to the North were facts of life in the state. Trains headed north filled with blacks seeking greater opportunity, fed only with the brown sacks of fried chicken they carried with them, came to be known as "chicken bone expresses." By 1950 the state's population grew faster than the nation, at 11.4 percent, but the percentage of whites increased more, reflecting black out-migration. The number of people living in rural areas dropped below 75 percent for the first time, and many of those living in the country commuted by automobile on better roads to work in towns and cities. Over one-third of the people (36.7 percent) lived in urban areas.

As a whole, South Carolinians were living better. In 1929 the state was last in the United States in per capita income. By 1950 income was at 60 percent of the national average. But 24 of the 46 counties had incomes less than half of the rest of the nation. South Carolina was still a very poor state.

In agriculture the amount of land devoted to farming was dropping. In 1945 there were just over 11 million acres of land in farming (56.3 percent); by 1969 there were 6.9 million acres (36.1 percent). Cotton production dropped as well. In 1945 there were over 1 million acres planted; in 1970 only 300,000 acres. The greatest decline was in the piedmont counties of Anderson, Spartanburg, and Greenville. In the upstate, farmers turned to cattle and tree farming. In the Inner Coastal Plain, farmers planted soybeans. The average size of farms grew from 75

Longtime segregationist Senator Strom Thurmond greeted Harry Greenlee, a 1972 graduate of Daniel High School in Pickens County, before a picture of John C. Calhoun, giving South Carolina politics a new look. Courtesy, Pickens County Museum

Since World War II mechanical cotton picking machines have been used instead of manual picking throughout the cotton belt. This mechanical picker was at work in Spartanburg County, circa 1948. Courtesy, National Archives

acres in 1945 to 177 acres in 1969. The old ways of farming were changing as well. Tenants had begun to leave the farms before World War II, and mules began to disappear. Farmers turned to heavy farm machinery such as tractors and cotton pickers. But cotton pickers required modern cotton gins to clean the lint, and few new gins were built. By the 1950s the leading cotton states were Texas, Arizona, and California.

At the end of World War II textile manufacturing remained the largest indus-try in South Carolina. During the war years military demand required the mills to operate three shifts, and once peace was restored civilian markets drove even greater textile expansion. But changes in textiles came quickly. Mill companies resumed selling mill houses which had begun in the 1930s, and the old paternalis-tic system ended. Eventually a new generation of mill employees moved into the expanding suburbs of the towns and cities. When new textile mills were built, they were often located in the countryside,

Soybeans were grown at the Edisto Station's experimental farm in 1968. By the 1980s soybeans had become South Carolina's second most important crop, behind tobacco. Courtesy, Special Collections, Clemson University Library

Situated on a 670-acre site off I-85 in Spartanburg County, Hoechst Fibers Industries (now Trevira) began operations in 1967 as a joint venture between American and German firms. The plant employed as many as 2,200 operatives. It is an example of South Carolina's post-World War II industrial revolution. Courtesy, Hoechst Fibers Industries, a division of American Hoechst Corporation

The May Plant in Camden, owned by DuPont, opened in September 1950 to produce the new synthetic fiber, Orlon. Photo by by A. V. Huff, Jr.

and instead of mill villages they were surrounded with large parking lots. Modern machinery was operated by fewer, better educated workers, and conditions in the mills improved dramatically with the advent of mandated government standards. By 1955 the majority of the state's mills had come under the control of major corporations, such as J. P. Stevens, Dan River, Deering Milliken, and Lowenstein. Only a few independent companies were left, such as the Self Mills in Greenwood and Springs Industries with headquarters in Fort Mill. However, the day of the small, independent mill was over. New plants were constructed to produce synthetic fibers like rayon and nylon that were developed during World War II. The Celanese plant at Rock Hill was built at a cost of $60 million, and the DuPont plant near Camden cost $75 million.

In 1954 the legislature created the state Development Board to recruit new industry. The board, with such strong leadership as Francis W. Hipp of Liberty Life Insurance Company of Greenville, worked to diversify the state's industrial base so heavily invested in textiles. Crucial to developing this new vision was Charles E. Daniel, a Georgia native who grew up in Anderson. After World War I, he entered the construction business and in 1942 moved the new headquarters of the Daniel Construction Company to Greenville. He encouraged the state's governors and de-

Charles E. Daniel was the founder of Daniel Construction Company (now Fluor). At the time of Daniel's death in 1964, his company had built more than 400 plants in the South, about 250 in South Carolina alone. Courtesy, Special Collections, Clemson University Library

Sol Blatt of Barnwell served as Speaker of the South Carolina House of Representatives from 1937 to 1973 (with the exception of the years 1947–51). He was often called a member of the "Barnwell Ring.." Courtesy, South Caroliniana Library

velopment officials to join him on a series of industry-hunting trips to New York City which were highly successful. Daniel's own company prospered as he built hundreds of plants for these businesses.

To provide technical education to the workforce for the new industries coming into the state Governor Ernest F. Hollings appointed a legislative study committee chaired by state Senator John C. West of Kershaw. The committee recommended a program of special schools to provide immediate training and a series of permanent technical education centers across the state. The first permanent TEC School opened in Greenville in 1962, and a decade later there were 16.

Perhaps the most dramatic economic change in South Carolina came in 1950 when the Atomic Energy Commission decided to build a facility in the state to produce materials for nuclear weapons. An area of 310 square miles in Aiken, Barnwell, and Allendale counties was acquired, and some 6000 people were required to relocate. Entire communities were displaced, and many people built homes in New Ellenton. The DuPont Company built and managed the new facility which by 1952 was producing heavy water. The "bomb plant," as South Carolinians called it, cost over $1.4 billion and employed 8,500 workers. Aiken, North Augusta, and other nearby towns soon had large mobile home cities and increasing traffic problems.

Politically, South Carolina remained a legislative state; power resided primarily with the General Assembly, not the governor or the courts. Only rarely, as in the case of Ben Tillman, did the governor have

enough support among the people that he could control the legislature, and in Tillman's case a state constitutional convention, as well. Even county government was controlled by the legislature. The county budget, known as the supply bill, was passed by the legislature, and the state senator—who was given a veto over the supply bill in the Senate—was the most powerful figure in county government. Since local officials often remained in office for decades, the county delegation (the senator and House members) and other elected officials were sometime referred to as "the courthouse ring."

The legislature chose the judges and many state officials. It could stop the proposals of any governor, though in fact most governors had previously served in the legislature and had strong allies there. The Senate was the most powerful legislative body; it had fewer members; they were usually older than House members, and had served longer. The Senate had a seniority system, so that the senior senators had their choice of committee assignments. Most bills had to be approved by the Senate Judiciary or Finance Committee; the chairs of those committees could stop any legislation. Since the smaller, rural counties generally reelected their senators, a small group of senior rural senators controlled the legislature.

The most powerful members of the General Assembly from the 1930s to the 1970s were from Barnwell County. They

African Americans in Richland County waiting to register to vote in the August 1947 primary after Judge Waring declared the South Carolina white primary unconstitutional. Courtesy, South Caroliniana Library

included Senator Edgar A. Brown, chair of the Senate Finance Committee, and Sol Blatt, speaker of the House of Representatives. Earlier, Winchester Smith had been chair of the House Appropriations Committee, and J. Émile Harley had served as lieutenant governor and governor. Together they were known as "the Barnwell Ring."

At the heart of South Carolina's political system, as well as its social system, was racial segregation which was enshrined in the state constitution of 1895, and a series of legislative enactments. These were supported by U. S. Supreme Court decisions such as *Plessy v. Ferguson* in 1896. In 1944 the first crack in the system came when the Supreme Court ruled in *Smith v. Allwright* that the white primary in Texas (which excluded black voters) was unconstitutional. Plans were already afoot among South Carolina African American leaders to create a Progressive Democratic Party to encourage greater black political involvement. Fearing that the state's primary was in jeopardy, Governor Olin D. Johnston called a special session of the legislature to meet on April 14. "White supremacy will be maintained in our primaries," he told the General Assembly. "Let the chips fall where they may." In six days the legislature repealed all the laws regulating political parties, transforming them into private clubs.

In 1946 George Elmore, an African American from Richland County who was eligible to vote in the general election,

with the help of the NAACP, challenged the white primary. The case was heard by federal district judge and Charleston native J. Waites Waring. In July 1947 in the case of *Elmore v. Rice* Waring struck down the white primary in no uncertain terms: "It is time for South Carolina to rejoin the union. It is time to fall in step with the other states and to adopt the American way of conducting elections." Before the August primary, 35,000 blacks registered to vote.

The curious interplay of racial politics and progressive forces was played out in the career of Strom Thurmond of Edgefield as governor from 1947 to 1951. The first election for governor after World War II took place in 1946. There were 11 candidates in the Democratic primary, and the winner was Thurmond. Born in 1902, he had graduated from Clemson College and taught school briefly before he read law in his father's office. He served in the state Senate and was elected a circuit judge in 1938. Returning from the war, he ran as a reform candidate for governor. He urged progressive changes in the state constitution and attacked "the Barnwell Ring" in his speeches. As governor, Thurmond urged the creation of a pardon and parole board to curb the governor's pardon power, a power that had sometimes been misused. The Budget and Control Board centralized the finances of the state; it became the most powerful board in state government. A state development board began to recruit new industry. Thurmond

Pictured are Senator Olin D. Johnston (1896-1965) and elder statesman Bernard M. Baruch (1870-1965). The date of the photo is unknown. Courtesy, Anderson Independent

tested the limits of racism when he urged state parks for black citizens (separate, of course), an industrial school for African American girls, and vocational schools for black students. Even these modest steps earned Thurmond the epithet of a racial liberal.

By 1948 the National Democratic Party was identified with civil rights for black Americans. President Harry Truman's Civil Rights Committee called for an end to racial segregation in American, and Truman himself ordered the integration of the armed forces. When the party adopted a civil rights plank in its 1948 platform, white South Carolinians split on the issue. Edgar Brown, Sol Blatt, and by then U. S. Senator Olin D. Johnston remained loyal to the national party; Governor Thurmond did not.

While Thurmond did not walk out of the national party convention as other Southerners did, he attended a gathering of States Rights Democrats in Birmingham. Called Dixiecrats, they persuaded Thurmond to accept their nomination for president. In his acceptance speech Thurmond said forthrightly: "There's not enough troops in the army to force the southern people to break down segregation." In the subsequent election the Dixiecrats carried only Alabama, Louisiana, Mississippi, and South Carolina.

In 1950 Thurmond ran against Olin Johnston for the U. S. Senate. He accused Johnston of being "one kind of Democrat in South Carolina and another kind in Washington." The contest was the last of the old-time campaigns before the advent of television. The candidates shouted at one another and shook their fists in the air in the summer heat. In the end, Johnston defeated the governor by 25,000 votes, depending on his traditional base of support among the upstate textile workers.

In that same election James F. Byrnes, former U. S. house member and senator, supreme court justice, FDR's "assistant president, and secretary of state under Harry Truman, was elected governor. His inauguration in January 1952 was something of a homecoming for the state's most important national political leader since John C. Calhoun. Once in office Byrnes advocated a number of reforms, such as adequate funding for the State Hospital for the mentally ill. But his major focus was on the battle to maintain racial segregation.

In November 1950 Thurgood Marshall, chief legal counsel for the NAACP, presented the case of 20 African American parents from Clarendon County before the federal district court in Charleston, asking for equal state funding of schools for their children. The leading spirit behind the case, known as *Briggs v. Elliott*, was the Reverend Joseph A. Delaine, public school teacher and pastor of the Pine Grove circuit of the African Methodist Episcopal Church. Later he lost his teaching position, his house was burned, and he was forced to leave the state. The case was presented to a three-judge panel, including Judge Waring. The suit was denied, with only Judge Waring supporting the case. *Briggs* was appealed to the Supreme Court as part of *Brown v. Board of Education*.

Meanwhile, Governor Byrnes, knowing full well that the state could not defend its funding of black schools under the "separate but equal" doctrine of *Plessy v. Ferguson*, urged the General Assembly to support a massive effort to build African American schools that were equal to those for whites. Byrnes blamed "the politicians in Washington" and "Negro agitators in South Carolina" for the crisis. He warned that the state would "abandon the public schools" rather than submit to desegregation. The legislature adopted a three-cent sales tax and created the Educational Finance Commission that constructed new buildings, set up a statewide system of school buses and reduced the number of school districts. To improve instruction the legislature created a statewide system of educational television. But the General Assembly also created a special legislative committee, headed by Senator Marion Gressette of St. Matthews, to seek ways to maintain the status quo. The "Gressette Committee," as it came to be known, proposed an amendment to the state constitution permitting the state to close the public schools if necessary. Two years later, in 1952, Byrnes demonstrated his anger at the National Democratic Party by urging support for Republican candidate for president, Dwight D. Eisenhower. The governor invited Eisenhower to speak from the steps of the State House.

As South Carolina argued against the *Briggs* case (now *Brown v. Board of Education*) before the Supreme Court, black civil rights leaders in South Carolina were not cowed. James Hinton, state NAACP president, was clear about the future: "Negroes will not turn back. Whites and Negroes will have public schools in South Carolina after all of us have died and present officials are either dead or retired from public life." On May 17, 1954 the U. S. Supreme Court struck down the system of segregated schools and urged the states to comply with the ruling "with all deliberate speed." Governor Byrnes told the press that he was shocked. His feeling was shared by most white South Carolinians.

In November white citizens had a chance to express their discontent at the polls, though the election itself seemed to have little to do with race. On September 1, U. S. Senator Burnet R. Maybank died unexpectedly after winning renomination in the Democratic primary. Pressed for time,

the state Democratic Executive Committee decided to nominate a candidate to replace Maybank in the general election in November. Byrnes expressed some interest in returning to the Senate, but he was unacceptable because of his support for Eisenhower in 1952. The committee selected state senator Edgar Brown. Former governor Strom Thurmond announced as a write-in candidate and denounced "committee rule" in the campaign, continuing his long battle against "the Barnwell Ring." In the first write-in victory for a U. S. Senate seat in history, Thurmond was elected.

When George Bell Timmerman Jr. became governor in 1955—the first lieutenant governor in history to succeed to

The Civil Rights Acts of 1964 and 1965 followed a number of black demonstrations throughout the South. Black unrest continued, as in this strike by 300 hospital workers in Charleston in May 1969. About 900 people were arrested during the 100–day strike. Courtesy, Charleston News and Courier (now Post and Courier)

South Carolina House of Representatives in session with confederate flag over the podium. Courtesy, South Caroliniana Library

State Senator Edgar A. Brown, Governor E.F. Hollings, and Democratic presidential candidate John F. Kennedy were together in Columbia on October 10, 1960. Courtesy, Anderson Independent

Klan revived and held public rallies. Cities and towns formed white citizens' councils, organized like civic clubs, to promote segregation.

The voices of white moderates in the state were few, but attracted notice because they advocated a different approach to race relations. Dr. Chester Travelstead, dean of the College of Education of the University of South Carolina, publicly opposed the actions of the legislature, and he was forced to resign. The South Carolina Council on Human Relations replaced the older Interracial Cooperation Commission, and Alice Spearman, a native of Marion, became its executive secretary. Local councils provided opportunities for black and white citizens to meet together, as did YWCAs in a few communities. James McBride Dabbs of Mayesville, a former English professor at Coker College, became president of the Southern Regional Council in 1957, and published a series of books urging moderation. That same year a group of white ministers published a compilation of statements by leading citizens of the state urging better race relations. Entitled *South Carolinians Speak: A Moderate Approach to Race Relations,* the book was denounced by Governor Timmerman.

the governorship—he strongly supported the state's opposition to integration. The emergence of Martin Luther King Jr. as leader of the bus boycott in Montgomery, Alabama in late 1955 raised racial tensions in South Carolina even higher. The legislative session of 1956 was dubbed the "segregation session" because of the laws it passed. One required labeling of blood by the race of the donor in blood banks in the state; another banned NAACP members from state employment. In September 1957 when President Eisenhower ordered National Guard troops to protect black students attending Central High School in Little Rock, Arkansas under court order, Timmerman denounced the president as a dictator and a promoter of communism. On the local level, whites joined in the protest against integration. The Ku Klux

Among the state's political leaders a more moderate view of race relations emerged, beginning in 1958 with the election of Ernest F. (Fritz) Hollings as governor. Hollings belonged to a new generation and was the first of what journalists called "New South governors."

Hollings was particularly attuned to the emerging business leadership in the state. To be sure, racial progress was not even, and there was violence at times, but change was in the wind.

Hollings was born in 1922 in Charleston, graduated from The Citadel and fought in World War II. He went to law school at the University of South Carolina after the war and was elected to the legislature. In 1954 he was elected lieutenant governor. An enthusiastic recruiter of new business, he worked aggressively with Charles Daniel and the State Development Board.

Like governors before him, Hollings defended segregation in his inaugural address in January 1959, but within a year the civil rights movement threatened to disrupt the relative calm in the state. In October black baseball star Jackie

Harvey Gantt entered Clemson College in February 1963 without incident after a long court battle. This was the first instance of racial desegregation of a public educational institution in South Carolina in the twentieth century. Courtesy, Pendleton District Historical and Recreational Commission

Robinson was in Greenville to address the state conference of the NAACP. At the Greenville Municipal Airport Robinson was ordered out of the white waiting room. In response, the NAACP sponsored a march of some 250 African Americans to the airport on January 1, 1960—Emancipation Day. On February 12 in Rock Hill some 100 students from Friendship Junior College staged a sit-in at two downtown stores. Other sit-ins followed across the state. There were efforts to desegregate public libraries. Business leaders in Columbia and Greenville set up biracial committees to work out peaceful ways to integrate public facilities.

In the spring of 1961 Harvey Gantt, a black student, applied for admission to the architecture school at Clemson. Working quietly behind the scenes, Hollings, Edgar Brown, Charles Daniel of Greenville, and John K. Cauthen, executive of the S. C. Textile Manufacturers Association, determined that the state could no longer defy the law without violence, and violence would harm economic growth.

A clue that things were going to be different came in a speech that Daniel made in July at the Watermelon Festival in Hampton. He put the matter forthrightly: "The desegregation issue cannot continue to be hidden behind the door . . . We must handle this ourselves more realistically than heretofore, or it will be forced upon us in the harshest way. Either we act on our own terms or we forfeit the right to act."

When riots began at the University of Mississippi in September in the wake of court-ordered integration, Edgar Brown, who was a life trustee of Clemson as well as a leader in the state Senate, declared that South Carolina would "not tolerate violence on the Clemson campus." Dr. Robert Edwards, president of Clemson, worked both with state officials and campus leaders to guarantee "integration with dignity," as one journalist described it.

Hollings delivered his final address to the legislature in January 1963: "This General Assembly must make clear South Carolina's choice, a government of laws rather than of men. We must move on with dignity. It must be done with law and order." Harvey Gantt enrolled at Clemson without incident on January 28, less than two weeks after Hollings left the governor's office.

Hollings was succeeded by Donald S. Russell, born in 1908 in Mississippi but reared in Chester. He graduated from the University of South Carolina and the USC law school, and soon joined the firm in Spartanburg of which James F. Byrnes was a member. Russell eventually joined Byrnes in Washington and served as his assistant in the White House and in the State Department. He served as president of his alma mater (1951–57), resigning to run for governor. He was defeated by Hollings, but was elected four years later. After his inauguration Russell hosted a barbeque on the grounds of the Governor's Mansion to which all citizens were invited—black and white. Within months the federal court ordered the integration of the University of South Carolina, and there was limited integration of the public schools in Charleston, Columbia, and Greenville.

The summer of 1963 was especially difficult in Charleston as hundreds of local black citizens and students took to the streets to demonstrate for equal employment and equal treatment in local businesses. Martin Luther King Jr. spoke in Charleston to support the movement. Governor Russell ordered 130 members of the highway patrol to assist city and county police. Eventually Mayor Palmer Gaillard secured promises from 87 business owners to meet the demands of African Americans.

When Senator Olin D. Johnston died in 1965, Russell resigned as governor, and he was succeeded by Lieutenant Governor Robert E. McNair. McNair immediately appointed Russell to Johnston's seat in the Senate. Born in Cades in 1923, McNair grew up in Berkeley County. He served in World War II and returned to the University of South Carolina and the USC law school. He first practiced in Moncks Corner before moving to Allendale, where he was elected to the state House of Representatives, serving until he was elected lieutenant governor.

Perhaps the nadir of the civil rights era in the state occurred in Orangeburg during McNair's administration. Beginning on January 29, 1968 black students from S. C. State and others attempted to integrate an all-white bowling alley near the campus. Tensions escalated, and on February 8, after a series of protests, Governor McNair ordered 250 members of the National Guard and additional highway patrolmen to aid city police and the local patrol. A large crowd of students gathered at the edge of the campus, shouting at the officers and throwing things. Eventually the students were fired on. Three students

Republican presidential candidate Dwight D. Eisenhower, Governor James F. Byrnes, and Mrs. Byrnes are pictured in Columbia on September 22, 1952. Before World War II presidential candidates of both major parties rarely, if ever, campaigned in South Carolina. Courtesy, Anderson Independent

were killed, and 26 were wounded. The next day McNair called the incident "one of the saddest days in the history of South Carolina." The press called it "the Orangeburg massacre." Nine patrolmen were later tried but acquitted; only Cleveland Sellers, a civil rights worker, served time in prison.

The following year McNair was faced with a strike by black hospital workers protesting racism at the Medical University of South Carolina in Charleston. From March until June 1969 the city was the scene of marches, some led by Coretta Scott King, the widow of Martin Luther King Jr. McNair ordered 500 members of the National Guard to patrol the streets. Finally, the federal government threatened to cut off funds from the hospital for civil rights violations, and the strike was settled.

In 1968 the courts had ruled that school districts had to eliminate their dual school systems; the old freedom-of-choice plans would no longer work. Greenville and Darlington counties were ordered to desegregate immediately. Governor McNair worked to head off the violence that had occurred in other states. He appointed a citizens group to work with business and local leaders. On television the governor made his position clear: "I will oppose any attempt to close down the public schools. . .When we run out of courts and time, we must adjust to the circumstances." In February 1970, in the middle of the academic year, the Greenville school district closed its separate schools one week and with the help of community volunteers reopened a unitary system the next. There were public protests and

bomb threats, but the transition occurred without violence. In Darlington County, however, the story was different. At first 3,000 white students boycotted the schools; then in March an angry mob in Lamar overturned two school buses. The state highway patrol and members of the State Law Enforcement Division restored order. In September 1971, when schools opened again, every district in the state had changed to a unitary system.

Thousands of whites refused to send their children to racially integrated schools. Local churches and community groups established private schools that remained all white. Many of these schools were located in counties where a large majority of the school-age population was African American. As white students enrolled in private schools in those areas, the students in the public schools were mostly African American and many of them came from very poor families. Between 1964 and the mid-1970s there were nearly 200 new private schools opened in South Carolina.

Meanwhile changes were taking place in the political sphere. A new Republican Party was growing in South Carolina as dissatisfaction grew with the pro-civil rights position of the national Democratic Party. Increasingly, the growing business community in the state began to identify with Republican economic policies. Thurmond's Dixiecrat candidacy for president in 1948, and James F. Byrnes's support for Eisenhower in 1952 and 1956 and Nixon in 1960 garnered support for Republican candidates in presidential races. Then in 1964 Strom Thurmond switched parties when Republicans nominated conservative Barry Goldwater for president. Though Goldwater was decisively defeated by Lyndon Johnson nationally, he carried South Carolina in a landslide—a first since Reconstruction. A year later Congressman Albert Watson switched parties. In 1968 Thurmond became a key figure in Richard Nixon's "Southern strategy" to win the White House.

At home in South Carolina a small, committed group of Republicans began to build a statewide party. The leader of the group was J. Drake Edens, Jr. of Columbia. He was strongly supported by textile magnate Roger Milliken of Spartanburg. Bob Jones University, an avowedly fundamentalist institution that had moved to Greenville from Tennessee in 1947 became a force in Republican politics in the upstate. In 1961 Charles E. Boineau

James F. Byrnes, Republican presidential candidate Richard Nixon, and evangelist Billy Graham are shown on the State House steps on November 3, 1960. Courtesy, Sumter Daily Item

Jr. of Columbia became the first Republican elected to the state legislature since 1902. By 1970 there were five.

The year 1970 was a turning point in state politics. At the same time that the Republican Party was growing, African Americans, who became a component of the Democratic Party in the state, were gaining political power. Over 200,000 blacks registered to vote under the Voting Rights Act of 1962. Albert Watson, the Republican candidate for governor in 1970, forthrightly supported white supremacy and was defeated by moderate Democrat John C. West by 28,000 votes. Thurmond, who had supported Watson, began to moderate his position and work more closely with black citizens. White Democrats, like Marion Gressette, who had once championed segregation, began to court African American voters. Never again would blatant racism be a political issue in the state.

Also in 1970, South Carolina celebrated the tricentennial of the first permanent English settlement in Charleston. For many Carolinians the highlight of the celebration came on April 25 when the opera *Porgy and Bess* was performed in Charleston. A major modern American classic set in Charleston, written by composer George Gershwin and Charleston author, DuBose Heyward, it had been performed around the world but never before in South Carolina because it required blacks and whites to appear on the same stage. The performances were sold out, and local audiences were thrilled. In the words of native journalist Jack Bass, *Porgy* had come home.

A month after the general election in 1970, Governor McNair commented on the changes that had occurred in the state: "The single most important aspect of the last ten years in South Carolina is the fact that we reversed the course of the future."

Chapter XI

Building a New South Carolina: From 1970 to the Present

When Governor McNair reflected on the election in 1970 in South Carolina, he spoke of reversing the future: "We have turned ourselves around. We proved to ourselves and to the people of South Carolina that there is reason to hope—that there is reason to believe that we have the capability of providing a better destiny for our citizens." What inspired those words was the election of yet another "New South governor," John C. West of Camden over an openly segregationist candidate.

West entered the governor's office with vast legislative experience. Born in Camden in 1922, he served in World War II after graduation from The Citadel. As a veteran, he completed USC law school and began the practice of law. After serving as a member of the state highway commission, he won a seat in the state Senate in 1954 and remained there until he was elected lieutenant governor in 1966. In his campaign for governor in 1970, West applauded the state's progress in race relations and promised that he would work on the problems "that have for so long shackled us"—poverty, illiteracy, and ignorance. In his inaugural address West pledged a state government that was "color blind."

With race no longer the single most important political issue in the life of the state and the campaign to attract industry increasingly successful, there were other factors as well that forecast a better future. In the last three decades of the 20th century the state's population outstripped the growth of the U. S. population. The decade of the 1970s saw the greatest growth—20.5 percent—while the nation as whole grew 11.5 percent. People from other parts of the country and foreign born people relocated to South Carolina, many to work, many retirees seeking a milder climate. For the first time since 1880 the non-white population began to grow—up from 30.7 percent in 1970 to 31.2 a decade later. By 2000 the percentage of non-whites was 32.8 percent. Many young African Americans who would have left the state in the decade and a half after World War II remained at home where there were jobs and good living conditions. Older blacks who had left the state earlier began to return "home" to retire. At the end of the century there was an influx of Asians and even more Hispanics, reflecting a national trend.

The rural population continued to drop; in 1980 over half of the population—54.1 percent to be exact—lived in urban areas for the first time in the state's history. But fewer rural people were involved in agriculture; they commuted to work in nearby towns and cities. The urban growth did not reflect a major expansion of the state's cities which remained about the same size, but the growth of sprawling suburban areas. After the 2000 census, the federal government designated ten areas in South Carolina as Metropolitan Statistical areas, indicating where the major urban growth was located: Anderson, Augusta-Richmond County, GA-SC (including Aiken and Edgefield counties), Charleston-North Charleston, Charlotte-Gastonia-Concord, NC-SC (including York County), Columbia, Florence, Greenville, Myrtle Beach-Conway-North Myrtle Beach, Spartanburg, and Sumter. Not included was the Beaufort-Hilton Head area, a rapidly growing retirement and vacation destination.

Agriculture continued to decline. In 1969 there were 6.9 million acres in farming; in 2000 4.8 million acres. At the same time, the average farm size grew from 177 acres in 1969 to 197 acres in 2006. Cotton production continued to decline after 1970, reaching a low of 53,000 bales in 1983. Soybeans, planted as a cash crop first in the 1940s, increased as cotton

A physicist, Ronald E. McNair of Lake City joined the national space program in 1978. The second African American in space, he was killed aboard the space shuttle Challenger *on January 28, 1986 when it exploded shortly after launch at Cape Kennedy. Other South Carolinians in space were Charles Duke of Lancaster, who landed on the moon, and Charles Bolden Jr. of Columbia, the pilot of two space missions in 1986 and 1990. Courtesy NASA*

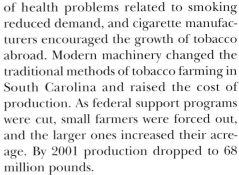

A Hispanic Festival on Main Street in Greenville. The growing population included an influx of thousands of Hispanic people into the state through the 1990s and later. Hispanic communities are sponsoring Spanish language radio stations, restaurants, and festivals. Courtesy, Greenville News

The South Carolina Cotton Museum is located in Bishopville in Lee County, just off I-20. With a series of artifacts and media presentations, the museum presents the history of cotton production and its importance to the history of South Carolina. Photo by A. V. Huff, Jr.

declined. However, they reached their peak in 1982 with 1.6 million acres in production. Increased costs and falling prices of soybeans resulted in fewer acres in production—450,000 acres in 2000. A corresponding rise in demand for cotton and better prices led to a revival of the cotton culture in the state in the 1990s. By 2000 South Carolina produced 379,000 bales, mostly in the Inner Coastal Plain.

Perhaps the greatest change in agriculture after 1970 was in tobacco production. After World War II tobacco had flourished in the Pee Dee region because of federal support programs. In 1955 growth reached an all-time high of 197 million pounds. By the 1970s published reports

of health problems related to smoking reduced demand, and cigarette manufacturers encouraged the growth of tobacco abroad. Modern machinery changed the traditional methods of tobacco farming in South Carolina and raised the cost of production. As federal support programs were cut, small farmers were forced out, and the larger ones increased their acreage. By 2001 production dropped to 68 million pounds.

Peaches have been grown commercially in South Carolina since 1870 when Colonel R. B. Watson began production in the Ridge in what is now Saluda County. By the 1920s peaches were grown in three areas of the state—the Piedmont, the Ridge east of Columbia, and the Coastal Plain. In the 1980s unusual drought conditions caused some farmers to reduce or abandon peach farming. But in 2000 South Carolina was the second largest producer of peaches in the nation behind California and ahead of Georgia that for many years had advertised itself as the "Peach State."

In 2005 field crops in terms of their value were cotton ($99 million), corn ($69 million), tobacco ($62 million), hay ($49 million), soybeans ($48 million), and wheat ($28 million). But, agricultural production is much more diverse than traditional field crops. The top ten commodities by rank were broilers (31 percent), flowers and nursery plants (16 percent), cattle (9.3 percent), turkeys (7.3 percent), cotton (4.8 percent), soybeans (3.5 percent), eggs (3.4 percent), tobacco (3.4 percent), hogs (3.0), corn (3.0), other crops (9.4), and other livestock (6.0). The total value of agricultural products sold in 2005 was $1,818,729,000.

In the last quarter of the 20th century new industry continued to come into the state. While most of the new operations located in the upstate, there was a strong effort to recruit businesses elsewhere. In Dillon County, for example, 19 industrial plants of various sizes opened between 1950 and 1977. Many of the new companies that located in South Carolina were international. In 1973 Spartanburg County had 24 foreign corporations employing 4,000 workers. Michelin, the French tire maker, built two plants in the upstate, and Interstate 85 had so many companies flying the flags of European nations it was sometime referred to as the *autobahn*. Michelin moved its North American headquarters to Greenville in 1985

and Bowater in 1993. The next year BMW, the German car maker, opened its first total automobile manufacturing facility outside Germany in Greer.

According to the State Development Board, $14.3 billion was invested in new industry from 1975 to 1985. In that decade chemicals and related products accounted for 26.4 percent, metalworking 26.6 percent, paper and printing 17.3 percent, and textiles 13.9 percent. By 2007 per capita income in South Carolina had risen to 82 per cent of the national average, up from 50 percent in 1950.

But the textile industry was in difficulty. Just as Southern textiles had profited from lower costs and cheap labor at the expense of New England for nearly a century, now developing nations were producing textiles at a much lower cost with cheaper labor. Many textile companies began to invest in plants in other countries and close their plants in South Carolina. Some developed more narrowly focused product lines and scaled back their operations. Under the leadership of Roger Milliken, Milliken and Company transformed itself into a technologically innovative business with a major emphasis on research and development. With operations in six states and 12 foreign countries, it became perhaps the largest

textile company in the United States. After 1970 Springs Industries continued its niche business of producing bedding, but in 2006 it merged with a Brazilian company. It changed its name to Springs Global and transferred its production facilities overseas, gradually closing its plants in South Carolina. Some older mill buildings across the state were razed, some remodeled for other purposes, such as condominiums, and others used as warehouses. A number of empty mills burned to the ground. Clearly, the era of textile dominance in South Carolina was over.

In the 1980s the Savannah River plant, such a boon to the state's economy earlier in the century, became problematical. Since the 1950s the plant had produced tritium and plutonium in sizeable quantities—both necessary for the nation's nuclear weapons. In the aftermath of the Cold War, South Carolina leaders were concerned that the Savannah River site would become a major dumping ground for the nation's nuclear waste. In 1986 Governor Richard Riley announced an agreement with the Department of Energy that the state would be dropped from the list of potential storage facility and shipments of waste would cease after 1992. Plutonium production ended in 1988, and the DuPont Company announced that

North American Michelin headquarters in Greenville near I-85. In 1985 after building two plants in South Carolina, Michelin, the French tire maker, moved its North American headquarters to the state. Courtesy, Michelin

Charles H. Townes, a native of Greenville and a graduate of Furman University, was awarded the Nobel Prize in physics in 1964 for his work on developing the maser and the laser. Two other South Carolinians have since won the Noble prize—Joseph L. Goldstein of Sumter and Kary B. Mullis of Columbia. Courtesy, Furman University

Top right: As many as 350,000 people visit Myrtle Beach on a summer weekend. Courtesy, Myrtle Beach Chamber of Commerce

Bottom right: Harbour Pointe Villas in Hilton Head were completed in 1984. Many villas and condominiums have been erected on the island. Courtesy, Lee McCleskey, and Miller, Hilton Head

it would cease operating the plant. The following year the site was placed on the National Priority List for cleanup, and it was regulated by the Environmental Protection Agency. Yet the production of tritium was still crucial to the nation's stockpile of nuclear weapons, and Savannah River remained an important facility for the Department of Energy. A major focus of work there became the cleanup of nuclear waste. Increasingly important was the research conducted by the Savannah River National Laboratory related to waste disposal and other technological problems.

Another adjustment to the state's economy was the retrenchment in military spending. Until his death in 1970, Congressmen L. Mendel Rivers, first elected to the House of Representatives in 1940 and eventually chairman of the Armed Services Committee, used his position to insure federal spending on military installations in the low country. But the collapse of the Soviet Union brought major cuts in military appropriations. In the late 1980s the Myrtle Beach Air Force Base had over 4,000 military and civilian personnel, but the base was closed in 1993. Likewise, the Charleston Naval Shipyard had provided an economic boost for the Charleston area for much of the 20th century. But the shipyard was also closed in 1995, bringing with it a temporary shock to the local economy.

A growing component in the state's economy in the latter decades of the 20th century was tourism. Although visitors had come to Charleston in great numbers since the 1920s and the state had been an important stop for highway

travelers on their way to Florida, the construction of the interstate highway system in the 1950s brought ever larger numbers of visitors to Myrtle Beach, Charleston, and Hilton Head. By 2000 South Carolina attracted 30 million tourists annually. In 2005 spending on tourism reached $16 billion and accounted for 11.2 percent of the state's workforce. Hotels, air travel, and leisure activities accounted for the vast majority of the tourism dollars.

In 1993 the state Development Board became the state Department of Commerce, and governors have used the department to support the creation of modern knowledge-based industries. The Department of Parks, Recreation, and Tourism, created in 1967, not only oversees state parks and welcome centers but also coordinates a wide variety of economic development and leisure programs.

South Carolinians enjoy baseball and basketball (though textile leagues have

long been disbanded), football, golf, tennis, track, bowling, softball, volleyball, fishing, swimming, and hunting. Most of the hunting is done on private preserves. Many former rice plantations were converted into hunting clubs by Northern money early in the 20th century.

Several new sports have become prominent in South Carolina since World War II. The development of powerful out-board motors has led to the rise of water-skiing. Soccer, inaugurated in the 1960s by Clemson University with a group of international student players, has become an important intercollegiate and interscholastic sport throughout the state. Stock car racing has become a third important sport. There are numerous small racetracks in the state, but the largest and most prestigious is located at Darlington. The first NASCAR race was held on Labor Day, 1950, and since 1960 two NASCAR races have attracted from 50,000 to 75,000 fans.

Since the 1920s communities have sponsored festivals highlighting their uniqueness. There are azalea, cotton, tobacco, and watermelon festivals with parades and dances. There is the Chittlin' Strut in Salley and the Pumpkin Festival in Pumpkintown. More recently arts festivals are held in a number of the cities. The most notable is Spoleto, founded by composer Gian Carlo Menotti in 1977 in Charleston as a counterpart of the European festival in Italy. It has become an international event offering more than 120 performances over 17 days. It has given rise to two other festivals in Charleston, Piccolo Spoleto showcasing local talent, and the Moja Arts festival focusing on Caribbean and African American arts and music.

Increasingly the state has celebrated its heritage with active historical societies on the state and county levels, and some 50 museums, including the State Museum in Columbia opened in 1988. Over 1,300

Dance is an integral part of the Spoleto USA Festival in Charleston each spring and summer. International in scope, it is the best-known arts festival in the state. Photo by William Struhs

Middle: An NCAA soccer playoff match between Clemson and South Florida took place before 5,500 spectators at Clemson University on November 16, 1975. In 1984 and 1987 Clemson won the NCAA soccer championship. Courtesy, Pickens County Museum

Bottom: The pits at the Darlington Raceway are pictured circa 1960. Courtesy, Bill Kiser

South Carolina's only National Park was established as a national monument in 1976 and declared a national park in 2003. It contains 22,200 acres of the largest remaining old-growth bottom land forest in the nation and borders the Congaree River southeast of Columbia. Photo by A. V. Huff, Jr.

the island along with restaurants, hotels, and other businesses. In 1972 the Sea Pines Company developed Wild Dunes on the Isle of Palms. Two years later the Kiawah Island Company began to build a similar resort. In subsequent decades the coast between Myrtle Beach and the Savannah River filled with developments, and thousands of people bought retirement homes or vacation homes on the South Carolina coast. Unfortunately so much development spawned ecological problems and displaced or segregated whole communities of African Americans. But resort communities now dot the entire state.

In politics, major changes in the way the legislature controlled state government occurred as the result of both constitutional revision and federal court decisions. Discussion of the revision of the Constitution of 1895 had occupied much of the 20th century. A major flaw in the constitution was the requirement that the limit on the bonded indebtedness of local governments could only be raised by constitutional amendment. By 1966 such amendments made the South Carolina constitution one of the longest in the nation. Not until 1968 was the provision on indebtedness changed.

Meanwhile a committee was appointed by the legislature in 1966 to study revision. Known as the West Committee, it was chaired by later governor John C. West. Eventually the committee recommended article-by-article revision. Five articles were approved by the voters in 1970 and ratified the following year. Complete revision of Article III dealing with the legislature failed, but a new Article V paved the way for a unified court system and additional modifications in the 1980s.

Changes in the General Assembly came, not by revision but by federal court decision. In 1964 the U. S. Supreme Court ruled that each senator or representative must represent an equal number of persons. In 1967 the legislature, faced with the growing urbanization of the state, failed to reach agreement on reapportioning the Senate, the power base of the rural counties. In 1983 after a series of attempts to guarantee every county at least one senator, the Senate was divided into 46 single member districts; no longer would counties have automatic representation. Meanwhile, in 1974 House districts were redrawn into single-member districts.

sites are now on the National Register of Historic Places. State and national parks celebrate the natural history and major events in South Carolina's past. In 2003 Congress created the Congaree National Park, southeast of Columbia, to preserve 22,000 acres of the nation's largest tract of old growth bottomland hardwood forest.

The development of tourism and the state's mild climate provided the impetus for a new kind of total resort community that is more sensitive to the environment. The pioneer development began on Hilton Head Island when Charles Fraser developed the Sea Pines resort in the late 1950s and 60s. Its golf and tennis facilities attracted nationwide attention. Outside Sea Pines, gated communities grew up on

Small, rural counties no longer controlled the General Assembly. Gradually the old power brokers began to step down. In the Senate, Edgar Brown retired in 1972 after a political career of a half-century. "The Bishop of Barnwell," as he was called, died in 1975.at the age of 86. In the House, Sol Blatt of Barnwell remained speaker until 1973, though he kept his seat in the legislature. When he died in 1986 he was the longest serving legislator in the United States. For a few years the old barons still held power in the Senate. Marion Gressette of St. Matthews, a member of the Senate since 1937, succeeded Brown as chairman of the Judiciary Committee and president pro tem until his death in 1984 at the age of 82. Gressette was succeeded by Rembert Dennis of Moncks Corner, but Dennis was forced to retire because of ill health in 1988. The old era was dying.

The lack of county representation in the legislature required a new system of local governance. No longer was legislative control of city and county government feasible, and the new urban representatives were more favorable to change. The Local Government Act of 1975 provided uniform home rule for cities and counties, though each local entity could define what services it provided. There were two important exceptions to the law, however. Special service districts, such as fire and sewer districts, and school districts, were exempt.

In the wake of the civil rights movement and federal court decisions, African Americans slowly began to win election to political offices. In 1970 three African Americans were elected to the House of Representatives—Herbert Fielding and James Felder of Charleston County and I. S. Leevy Johnson of Richland County. But not until house districts became single member in 1974 were 13 blacks elected. This group organized the Black Legislative Caucus the following year and began to win some symbolic battles. The first portrait of an African American—Mary McLeod Bethune—was hung in the State House, and Martin Luther King Jr.'s birthday was recognized though not yet made a state holiday.

In 1983 in a special election the Reverend I. DeQuincey Newman, a major civil rights activist in the 1960s, was elected to a seat in the state Senate; his district was 64 percent white. He was warmly welcomed by fellow senators, including Marion Gressette of St. Matthews who had once chaired the legislative segregation committee. Ill health forced Newman to resign his seat two years later. In 1996 the number of African Americans in the state legislature reached its greatest number in the modern era—26 in the House and eight in the Senate.

In 1992 James E. Clyburn was elected to Congress, the first African American elected from South Carolina since 1897. Born in 1940, he graduated from South Carolina State University, and in 1974 Governor West appointed him state human affairs commissioner. In January 2007 Clyburn was elected House Majority Whip.

Two South Carolina African Americans became pioneer judges. In 1979 Matthew Perry, who had been appointed to the U. S. Military Court of Appeals in 1976, was appointed a federal district judge. In 1994 Ernest A. Finney, Jr. was elected the first black chief justice of the South Carolina Supreme Court. Born in 1931, he was a graduate of Claflin College and the South Carolina State University law school. In 1972 he was elected to the state House, and in 1976 he was elected the first black circuit judge in South Carolina. He became an associate justice of the state Supreme Court in 1985.

Women began to take a greater role in public life at the end of the 20th century. Before the middle of the century only one woman had served in the General Assembly—Senator Mary Gordon Ellis of Jasper County, who was elected in 1928. By 1984, 27 women had served in the legislature. In 1974 Juanita Goggins of York County was the first African American woman elected to the state House, serving for six years. In 1979 Nancy Stevenson of Charleston was elected lieutenant governor of South Carolina, after serving two terms in the state House. In 1986 Elizabeth J. Patterson of Spartanburg was the first woman elected to a full term in Congress, after serving in the state Senate (1979–86). The daughter of U. S. Senator Olin Johnston, she remained in Congress until 1993.

Three South Carolina women have served in high judicial positions. In 1988 after serving in the state House (1975–88) Jean H. Toal was the first woman elected to the state Supreme Court. In 2000 she was elected chief justice, succeeding the retiring Chief Justice Ernest Finney. Jean Galloway Bissell served on the U. S. Court of Appeals for the Federal District from 1984 to her death in 1990, and Karen J. Williams

In 1983 the Reverend I. DeQuincy Newman, longtime civil rights activist, was elected to the South Carolina Senate; he was the first black to sit in that body since 1888. Courtesy, I. DeQuincy Newman

of Orangeburg was appointed to the U. S. Fourth Circuit Court of Appeals in 1992.

Republican growth in South Carolina seemed stalled in 1970. In that year Republicans held only five seats in the House and three in the Senate. That year also saw the disastrous defeat of Albert Watson in his racist campaign for governor. Shortly thereafter Strom Thurmond signaled a change in the political climate by employing his first African American staff member, working closely with black officeholders, and responding to the needs of the black community for federal assistance. While Thurmond helped Watson secure appointment as a federal administrative law judge for the Social Security Administration, he also recommended the nomination of black civil rights attorney Matthew J. Perry to the U. S. Military Court of Appeals in 1976.

South Carolina Republicans achieved a milestone in 1974 with the election of James B. Edwards as governor, the first Republican since 1877. The outcome of the election itself was the result of unusual circumstances. Born in 1927 in Florida, but reared in Charleston from an early age, Edwards graduated from the College of Charleston, served in World War II in the maritime service, and attended the University of Louisville School of Dentistry. In 1960 he opened an oral-surgery practice in Mount Pleasant. Attracted to Barry Goldwater's conservative philosophy, he became active in the Republican Party in Charleston County. Losing a special election to Congress in 1971, he won a state Senate seat the next year. He quickly won the respect of colleagues

of both parties. In the first statewide Republican primary for governor in 1974, Edwards challenged South Carolina favorite son, General William C. Westmoreland, former commander of American troops in Viet Nam, and won what many considered an upset victory.

Meanwhile, the Democrats were having problems of their own. Charles (Pug) Ravenel of Charleston was disqualified by the state Supreme Court for not meeting the residency requirement. Congressman Bryan Dorn was selected to replace Ravenel. Edwards campaigned as a reform candidate with the slogan "No Debts and No Deals." He won the election by 18,500 votes. He was a popular governor and worked well with the Democratically-controlled legislature. Edwards was a pioneer who paved the way for future GOP candidates for statewide office.

A major achievement of the Edwards administration was the passage of educational finance reform. When lawsuits challenging unequal school funding in other states received national attention, South Carolina leaders proposed the Education Finance Act of 1977, with the full support of the governor. The law attempted to equalize funding of schools by establishing a minimum level for every district and making additional grants to poorer districts. Disparities remained, but the EFA was a major step forward in school funding.

The governor's office returned to the Democrats with the election of Richard W. Riley in 1978. Born in 1933 in Greenville, Riley was a graduate of Furman University, served in the Navy in World War II, attended USC law school, and in 1960 began the practice of law. He was elected to the state House of Representative in 1962 and served until he was elected to the state Senate in 1966. For a decade he was one of the "Young Turks," in the Senate, challenging the old power structure. In 1978 he was elected governor with 61 percent of the vote, and after the state constitution was changed to allow the governor a second four-year term, he was reelected with 70 percent of the vote. Riley's second term focused on educational reform in the state and resulted in the passage of the Education Improvement Act.

After the legislature rejected his first effort at reform in 1983, Riley set about harnessing grass roots support. With business and education leaders at the forefront, thousands of citizens attended open forums across the state. A comprehensive program of basic skills tests, merit pay for teachers, and accountability at every level—all funded by a one cent increase in the sales tax—was passed in 1984. The EIA was hailed as a national model for state educational reform.

Politically, the election of Governor Edwards in 1974 and the "Southern strategy" of the National Republican Party developed during Richard Nixon's campaigns for the presidency strengthened the hands of state Republicans in their bid for election. Democrats failed to develop a disciplined party structure—leaving candidates to raise their own funds and develop individual campaigns, while Republicans were better organized and funded. Democrats could reliably count on the African American vote in the state—about 25 percent of the total vote statewide—and 25 percent of the white vote scattered throughout the state. The "one man-one vote" court decision that shifted power to the growing urban areas favored Republicans, and the creation of single member districts in the legislature permitted the election of more black Democrats but fewer white Democrats. From 1970 to 1994 Republicans gained additional seats in the General Assembly, as well as offices on the county and local levels. After the 1994 election, Republicans gained control of the House of Representatives; in the 2000 election Republican control of the Senate was assured.

Of key importance to Republican control of the legislature was the election of David H. Wilkins speaker of the House in 1994. Born in Greenville in 1946, he graduated from Clemson and the USC law school. Elected to the state House in 1980, he was highly respected by Democrats and Republicans alike. He rose to chair the Judiciary committee and was elected Speaker pro tem while Republicans were still in the minority. When the Republicans became the majority party in 1994, Wilkins was elected speaker, a position he held for 11 years until appointed ambassador to Canada in 2005. As speaker, he was regarded as fair and even handed, working with members of both parties and a succession of governors to ensure the adoption of progressive legislation while maintaining the fiscal conservatism typical of South Carolina state government.

In many ways, the administration of Carroll A. Campbell Jr. (1987–1995) was a

high water mark of the new Republican hegemony in South Carolina. Born in Greenville in 1940, Campbell went into business soon after graduating from the McCallie School to help support his siblings. He completed a degree from American University only after his election to Congress. In 1971 Campbell was elected to the state House of Representatives but was unsuccessful as the Republican candidate for lieutenant governor in 1974. He became executive assistant to Governor Edwards and subsequently was elected to the state Senate and then to Congress in 1978. In 1986 he was elected governor with

In 1984 Governor Richard W. Riley signed the Education Improvement Act on the grounds of the Governor's Mansion. It was the key legislation in reforming education in South Carolina and became a national model for state reform. Riley served as Secretary of Education in the Clinton administration. Courtesy, Richard W. Riley

David H. Wilkins of Greenville was elected first Republican Speaker of the House of Representatives in the twentieth century. Known for his fairness and ability to work with members of both parties, he served for 11 years. In 2005 Wilkins was appointed ambassador to Canada. Courtesy, Greenville News

51 percent of the vote and reelected in 1990 with more than 69 percent.

A series of events during Campbell's tenure allowed him to strengthen the power of the governor. First, he increased the governor's control over the budget-making process in 1988. Traditionally, the state budget was prepared by the state Budget and Control Board and submitted to the legislature. On his own, Campbell prepared and sent an executive budget to the Budget and Control Board for the first time. The law was subsequently revised to empower the governor to submit a proposed budget to the board.

The next year Campbell had another opportunity to strengthen the governor's office. In September 1989 Hurricane Hugo, the most destructive storm in the state's history, killed 17 people, left 65,000 people homeless, and cut a $5 billion swath of destruction along the coast from Charleston to Myrtle Beach and inland through Holly Hill, Sumter, and Rock Hill. The governor coordinated federal, state, and local relief efforts. This action established the governor's role in crisis management.

Operation Lost Trust began in April 1989 when Ron Cobb, a lobbyist and former member of the legislature, was arrested as part of an FBI investigation of bribery involving members of the General Assembly. Eventually, 17 members of the legislature, seven lobbyists, and three other people were convicted for bribery, extortion, or drug use. In May 1990, Dr. James Holderman, president of the University of South Carolina, resigned after charges were made that he had used university funds for private benefit. These scandals provided Governor Campbell the opportunity to revive the momentum for reorganizing state government. In 1991 he created a panel of citizens to make recommendations. In 1993 the legislature adopted a compromise plan that consolidated 145 agencies. Thirteen of the agency heads were henceforth appointed by the governor, and could be removed by him. These executives reported directly to the governor and with their appointment it was the first step toward the creation of a cabinet.

Campbell also spent a great deal of time and energy in strengthening the state Republican Party. He solidified state support for Ronald Reagan and George H. W. Bush by playing a major role in their presidential campaigns. As governor, Campbell helped create a viable party structure, raised funds, recruited candidates, and encouraged Democratic officeholders to switch parties. When he left office in

1995, the party was firmly established.

Even so, the Republican majority elected David M. Beasley governor in 1994 by only 50.4 percent. Born in Lamar in 1957, he attended Clemson and graduated from the University of South Carolina and USC law school. He served in the state House (1979–1994) first as a Democrat, then switching to the Republican Party in 1991. When Beasley was inaugurated governor in 1995, he was widely regarded as a figure of great promise in the Republican Party nationally.

In 1998 the legislature passed the Education Accountability Act which required school readiness tests, academic standards for each grade level, and testing to gauge achievement. Beginning in 2001 report cards for each school and district were to assess the level of success or failure. For all of the state's efforts to improve education, the graduation rate rose very slowly as did student scores on the Scholastic Aptitude Test. Clearly progress, especially in the poorer areas of South Carolina, was going to require a sustained commitment over a very long period of time. There was no quick fix for decades of neglect.

Two issues brought Beasley's reelection in 1998 into question—the controversy over the Confederate flag and the debate over video poker and a state lottery.

Since 1961, as part of the state Civil War Centennial and while white South Carolinians were still resisting the civil rights movement, the Confederate battle flag had flown over the dome of the State House. There had been periodic calls for its removal by African American groups. Various proposals had been made, and in 1994 Governor Campbell supported a compromise that failed. In a referendum that same year 75 percent of voters in the Republican primary supported keeping the flag in place. In 1997 Beasley, influenced by the business community and a rash of racial incidents across the state in 1996, supported a compromise worked out by senators on both sides of the controversy. The proposal called for removal of the flag from the State House, relocating it beside the Confederate Soldiers monument, granting protection of Confederate monuments in the state by statute, and erection of a monument commemorating African American history on the grounds of the State House. Many of Beasley's supporters were enraged, and in his campaign for a second term Beasley retreated from his initial position in support of the compromise.

At the same time a debate arose over the legalization of video poker and a proposal to increase state revenue by creating a lottery. Beasley was opposed to both.

Despite the state's prohibition against gambling, a little noticed amendment to the Appropriations Bill in 1986 permitted a burgeoning video poker industry to develop much to the chagrin of a majority of South Carolinians. When Governor Beasley promised to use his influence to stop legalized gambling, the industry began to pour contributions into his opponent's campaign chest.

Beasley's Democratic opponent,

One of the key parts of the compromise legislation to remove the Confederate flag from the State House in July 2000 was the erection of a monument on the capital grounds honoring the history of African Americans. This panel recounts the emancipation of enslaved people in the state. Photo by A. V. Huff, Jr

James H. Hodges of Lancaster, strongly supported a flag compromise and also a state lottery—but only if the proceeds were used to support funding for public schools and higher education. In the election the Democrats mounted a well-organized effort to turn out voters, and Hodges defeated Beasley with more than 53 percent of the vote.

Born in 1956, the new governor was a Phi Beta Kappa graduate of the University of South Carolina and the USC law school. In 1986 he was elected to the state House, where he chaired the Judiciary Committee, and in 1994 when the Republicans won a majority he became minority leader. As governor, Hodges used his influence to support the Confederate flag compromise, and on July 1, 2000, the flag finally came down from the State House dome. On the explosive video poker issue, the legislature punted by ordering a referendum on the issue in 2000 and adopted taxes on the games if the referendum upheld them. But the state Supreme Court intervened on October 15, 1999, and declared the referendum unconstitutional and ordered all video poker machines shut down by July 1, 2000.

The issue of a state lottery to benefit education was hotly debated across the state. Hodges and the pro-lottery supporters in the legislature faced the combined forces of the religious communities—both conservative and moderate. The legislature adopted a constitutional amendment permitting a lottery and submitted it to the voters in November 2000. It was approved by a large majority. Once legislation implementing the lottery was passed, millions of dollars began to flow into school programs, scholarships for college students, and chairs for university faculty. In addition to the lottery, Hodges championed First Steps, a preschool program to prepare children better for first grade. However, a slowing economy and declining state funding provided Hodges little opportunity for promoting major programs.

In the 2002 campaign, Hodges faced Marshall (Mark) C. Sanford, Jr. of Sullivan's Island, who had defeated the incumbent lieutenant governor in the Republican primary. In a carefully orchestrated campaign, Sanford defeated Hodges by 53.9 percent. Born in 1960 in Florida, Sanford moved to Beaufort with his family before his senior year in high school. A graduate of Furman University, he earned a graduate degree in business from the University of Virginia. With no prior experience in political office, he was elected to Congress in 1994 and served three terms. He was the first governor since Donald Russell who had not served in the General Assembly. Sanford was elected to a second term in 2006 by 55.1 percent.

The year 1970 was a turning point in the history of South Carolina. For 300 years, since the beginning of English colonization in Charles Town, the determination of white Carolinians to dominate African Americans—through slavery and segregation—had been a major factor in the history of the state. The election of 1970 signaled that a new era had begun. Racism still persists, but increasingly South Carolinians are learning to live in an inclusive society. There are difficult problems facing the state, to be sure, including poverty, education, threats to the environment, and integrity in public life. But they are no longer addressed within a structure of legal racial discrimination. In 1983 Governor Richard Riley envisioned a bright future for the state: "An old South Carolina in dying. A new South Carolina is struggling to be born. We will not build the new South Carolina with bricks and mortar. We will build it with minds. The power of knowledge and skills is our hope for survival in this new age."

James H. Hodges of Lancaster was governor from 1999 to 2003. During his term of office a compromise over the Confederate flag compromise was adopted, video poker was banned, and the state Education Lottery was created. In addition, First Steps, a program of pre-school children began. Courtesy, Governor's Office

*Construction of St. Michael's Anglican (Episcopal)
Church in Charleston began in 1752. The first services
were held in February 1761. Three years later the clock and
eight bells were istalled. Photo by A. V. Huff, Jr.*

These houses on East Battery in Charleston were built by wealthy planters and merchants before the Civil War. The citizens of the city watched the bombardment of Fort Sumter in April 1861 from the rooftops. Photo by A. V. Huff, Jr.

Opposite page: The main house at Arcadia Plantation near Georgetown was built about 1794 by Joseph Allston on his rice plantation, Prospect Hill. Prior to the Civil War it was owned by Joshua J. Ward, the largest rice producer on the Waccamaw River. In 1906 it was purchased and remodeled by Isaac Emerson, who made a fortune in Bromo-Seltzer. It was inherited by his son-in-law George Vanderbilt and remains in the family. Photo by A. V. Huff, Jr.

Charles Towne Landing State Historic Site contains the reconstructed earthworks built by the early English settlers to protect Charles Town from attack by the Spanish in Florida. The park is located on the original site of the settlement (1670–1680) on Town Creek off the Ashley River. Photo by A. V. Huff, Jr.

The Miles Brewton House on King Street in Charleston was constructed by the wealthy merchant and slave trader between about 1765 and 1769. It is generally considered the center of the finest Georgian townhouse, outbuildings, and gardens in America. It is listed as a National Historic Landmark. Photo by A. V. Huff, Jr.

Pegasus is one of the major pieces of sculpture by Anna Hyatt Huntingdon at Brookgreen Gardens near Pawley's Island. In 1931 Huntington and her husband, railroad heir Archer M. Huntington, created the sculpture gardens out of four former rice plantations. They presented it to the state the next year. Some 200,000 people visit Brookgreen annually. Photo by A. V. Huff, Jr.

This photograph taken on Fripp Island shows the palmettos, grasses, and dunes native to the barrier islands on the South Carolina coast. Photo by A. V. Huff, Jr.

All Saints, Waccamaw was one of the richest rice growing areas in the nation prior to the Civil War. Today the old rice fields still line the banks of the Waccamaw River. At Litchfield Plantation the old fields are clearly visible. Photo by A. V. Huff, Jr.

This boat dock on Hilton Head Island on the Intracoastal Waterway is a familiar scene on the streams and rivers fronting the newly constructed resorts that now stretch along the South Carolina coast and on the barrier islands. Photo by A. V. Huff, Jr.

On Saturdays in the fall the highways of the state are filled with cars and vans traveling to intercollegiate football games. At Paladin Stadium in Greenville the Furman football team is always a contender in the Southern Conference. The winner of one national championship, the Paladins regularly play in post-season contests. Courtesy, Furman University

Many of the houses on Pawley's Island were built by antebellum rice planters to escape the humid, malaria-prone plantations further inland. Pawley's has been a favorite vacation area for South Carolinians ever since. Many families have stayed in the same houses for generations. Pawley's has its own ghost, the Gray Man, who warns the residents of storms and hurricane. Photo by A. V. Huff, Jr.

Charleston is South Carolina's busiest port, serving as the fourth largest container port in the United States. This is the Columbus Street Pier on the Cooper River. The other ports in the state are Georgetown and Port Royal. Photo by A. V. Huff, Jr.

African American artist and Florence native William H. Johnson (1901–1970) studied in New York and worked there as well as in France and Scandinavia. In his later career he painted scenes of black life in South Carolina from his childhood. This painting is on display at the Greenville County Museum of Art. Art museums in Charleston, Florence, and Columbia, as well as the Smithsonian in Washington, D. C., display his work. Courtesy, Greenville County Museum of Art

In 1977 composer Gian Carlo Menotti, with the support of the National Endowment for the Arts, established the Spoleto USA Festival in Charleston. Each year the opening ceremony before the City Hall begins 17 days of artistic performances that draw thousands to the events. Photo by William Struhs

Chapter XII

Chronicles of Leadership

Accommodation and adaptation are key words in the economic history of South Carolina. The state's economy has flourished for a number of reasons, not the least of which has been the willingness of South Carolinians to be receptive to new ideas, to new industries and businesses, and to new people.

To this openness and receptivity South Carolina has been able to add a stable work force, a pleasant climate, state and local governments mindful of the needs of industry, and a flexible, progressive banking and financial system.

South Carolina's tradition of accommodation to new industry dates back to the early 1800s, when canny New England textile mill owners realized that South Carolina, more than any other part of the South, had water power. Many of them came south, and for many of these the move was successful. South Carolina supplied raw materials and a labor force. The New Englanders brought capital, management skills, and a burgeoning technology. The combination was strong enough to overcome technical and financial upheavals as well as the ravages of a terrible war.

As the decades passed, more industries and businesses located in South Carolina. At first these were exclusively American firms, but recently many foreign firms have branched into South Carolina.

The state has become practiced at adapting to meet new conditions as technical, financial, and managerial requirements of industry change. When trained or retrained workers are needed, the state's educational system can supply the demand. When innovative, imaginative financing arrangements are needed, the state's financial system can respond. When reasonable governmental action is needed, that can be realized also.

The result is a strong, diversified, and stable economy. In one plant in South Carolina, cotton cloth is produced using methods that have not fundamentally changed for hundreds of years. Just down the road another South Carolina industry uses space age technology to shape superhard metal to infinitely small tolerances. South Carolina industry today is a happy combination of traditional and contemporary industries and businesses, not dependent on the health of any single factor in the American economy.

South Carolinians were and continue to be practical, pragmatic people who know the value of work and the value of money. For example, they saw the advantages of water-power as quickly as the New Englanders did. Side-by-side with entrepreneurs from Boston and Providence, South Carolinians built their own textile mills and established family-owned enterprises that still exist and prosper.

Furthermore, when trees and inexpensive labor were all they had, South Carolinians built paper mills. Then when paper mills struggled for markets, one builder converted the process to make paper cones for textile mills and prospered mightily. In addition, South Carolinians looked at the infant industry of over-the-road trucking and found ways to supply insurance at rates the truckers could afford.

Such entrepreneurial citizens are the heart and soul of the accommodation and adaptation that have bolstered South Carolina's economy.

The organizations whose histories are detailed on the following pages have chosen to support this important literary and civic project. They illustrate the variety of ways in which individuals and their organizations have shaped the state, making South Carolina an excellent place to live and work.

In addition, many of South Carolina's fine institutions of higher education which are helping shape its future, are specially showcased here.

Cotton awaits shipment at the railroad wharf in Georgetown, circa 1900. Courtesy, Georgetown County Library

BENEDICT COLLEGE

In 1865 in the South, liberated African American people and recently emancipated African American citizens had difficulty in securing an education. Thus, private schools were established by religious organizations. In South Carolina in 1865, a majority of the nearly 10,000 free Negroes could read and write, and about 5 percent of the slaves could do likewise.

Benedict College was founded in 1870 in Columbia, South Carolina by Mrs. Bathsheba A. Barber Benedict of Pawtucket, Rhode Island. She was an abolitionist and a staunch member of the American Baptist Home Mission Society. On December 5, 1870 classes began under the see of President Timothy Dodge on an 80-acre plantation which had been purchased and named the Benedict Institute. Located in historic Waverly, with its main campus bordered by Harden, Taylor, Laurel, and Oak Streets, the present main campus is in Columbia.

The investors'—Mrs. Benedict and the Baptist Home Mission Society— long-term goal was to educate recently emancipated African Americans and produce citizens that would become "a power for good in society." From 10 students in 1870 to 2,533 in 2007, Benedict College has grown into an accredited institution with a faculty and staff of 471 members and a curriculum of 28 major programs.

In 1891, with 243 students, Benedict had a superior teacher education program whereby its students were hired in the public schools before they graduated because they made the highest grade on the County Examinations. The demand for college educated teachers was high. Today, Benedict has nationally accredited programs in Teacher Education, Environmental and Health Sciences, and Social Work. Also, Benedict is ranked second in the United States by the American Institute of Physics for producing African American students with a bachelor's degree in Physics.

The Benedict campus has grown from a worn down plantation mansion to a total of 37 buildings located on the main campus as well as on nearby sites. The campus has extended from ap-

Mrs. Bathsheba Barber Benedict

proximately 20 acres in 1994 to approximately 100 acres in 2007. In 1988, the National Register of Historic Places named five buildings as "Historic:" Morgan Hall–1895, Pratt Hall–1902, Duckett Hall–1925, Antisdel Chapel–1932, and Starks College Center–1938.

Many significant developments have taken place over the years, including the merging of Mather School of Beaufort, South Carolina under the presidency of Dr. Benjamin F. Payton; creating a Community Development Program that helped to restore the nearby Black community, creating a business incubator for new entrepreneurs, creating strategic planning for the college, returning football on May 31, 1995, and opening the Charlie W. Johnson Football Stadium (a state-of-the-art edifice) in 2006. All of the latter was accomplished under President David H. Swinton.

The Division of Community Development was inspired by Dr. Swinton,

who, for four years, headed the Urban Institute, a "think tank" located in Washington, D.C., focusing on racial disparities and social policy programs. With his training in economics and public policy at New York University and Harvard University, he brought to Benedict College an emphasis on community change, especially those areas that surround the college and the citizens who would be affected in positive ways.

The Division of Community Development (DCD) became a reality in 1997. It focused on issues affecting children and families, business and economic development, democracy and government, and educational excellence through research, public service, and teaching. The Benedict-Allen Community Development Corporation, a part of DCD, has the mission of promoting the revitalization of nearby communities—building new affordable houses and renovating older structures. Today, 20 new brick houses have been built and/or renovated and 20 more are planned for new construction under the corporation.

The programs operating (past and current) under DCD are:
- Credit Smart Program
- Design For The Education and Equity of African American Students
- Upward Bound Program
- Project Re-Connect For Non-Custodial Parents
- Transportation: Highway Construction & Commercial Driving
- Youthbuild Program
- The Child Development Center (109 Children, age 0-5)
- Technical Assistance Program For 35 Black South Carolina Mayors
- Gear-Up Program
- Teen Power Program
- Outreach To Rural Communities

- The Housing Assistance Program

In 2002, under the Division of Community Development, the Business Development Center was built to develop and implement a business entrepreneurial program and to create a business incubator. The incubator houses 14 businesses. Training, educational seminars, clerical assistance, and a revolving loan fund are provided for the 12 entrepreneurs in the training program.

In 2006 DCD created a Center of Excellence For Community Technology, focusing on research, development, and project implementation to serve public and community interests. Areas now under design are community networking, community and public broadband, smart/green building for affordable housing, e-commerce for small businesses, and community portals.

During the summer months DCD has operated more than 25 programs for children and teens, including Pre-Calculus Workshop, Challenge Learning Center, Mathematics Enrichment Program, Language Arts Camp, NAACP Youth Entrepreneurial Institute, Young People's Christian Assembly, Youth Summer Sports Camp, and Benedict College Fun Camp.

Dr. Charlie W. Johnson, for whom the new football stadium is named, was elected to the Benedict College Board of Trustees in 2000, becoming its chairman in 2001. Beyond serving in this capacity, he has made notable contributions to the college. Providing full scholarships for 25 students from Louisville, Kentucky where his businesses are located, he gives opportunity to young people who could not afford the financial requirements of college matriculation.

When the athletic programs needed buses, Dr. Johnson donated two charter/tour buses. Additionally, he presented all football players and coaches with college leather jackets. Once the college decided to purchase 61 acres in the City of Columbia for its athletic programs of football, track, baseball, and tennis, it faced the task of raising funds to build the football stadium. Dr. Johnson and his wife, Betty, became the first major

Dr. David H. Swinton

contributors with a $2 million contribution.

The stadium, dedicated September 2006, is a $12 million state-of-the-art facility that seats 15,000 fans. Housed in the LeRoy T. Walker Health and Wellness complex, it is a premiere arena among other sporting facilities in the SIAC Conference.

On February 7, 2007, Dr. Johnson announced at a press conference at Benedict College a new program created by CWJohnson Xpress Company, with a unit based at Benedict: "Driving For Inner City Development." The program emphasizes truck-driving training for young men and women. It will empower them, especially low-income African American adults as well as ex-offenders, in obtaining a marketable skill and learning how to become entrepreneurs. Upon satisfactory completion of the program, graduates are offered full-

time employment with CWJohnson Xpress.

Dr. Johnson brings to Benedict College years of experience in professional football and in the world of business. For six years he played football for the San Francisco 49ers and for the Baltimore Colts where he won a Super Bowl ring. Then, in 1987, he opened Active Transportation, Inc. in Louisville. By 1990 the company employed 3,000 workers across the United States. In 2000 Active Transportation had revenues in excess of $500 million. With his wife— Betty Johnson, also a business expert—by his side, they formed another trucking business. Committed to the maintenance of historical Black colleges and universities (HBCUs), they give at least $800,000 annually to the United Negro College Fund.

Benedict College leadership has had a local, state, national, and international presence in civic and educational affairs for many years. Most recently, however, the following roles are significant: Chairman, The Columbia Chamber of Commerce; author, *Status of African Americans In South Carolina: Fifty Years After Brown vs. Board of Education*; Chairman, The Columbia Urban League Board; founder, Broadband In The Cities and Towns, a national summit to move broadband technology to support community and economic development; founder, the Evening College, especially designed for working adults; producer, The South Carolina Educational Television and Public Broadcasting System Black History Teleconference in 50 USA states and 177 foreign countries.

The Black History Teleconference, titled "The Struggle Continues," began in 1987 as an in-state program during the month of February in celebration of Black History Month. Under the auspices of South Carolina Educational Television (SCETV), one of America's highest rated systems, the program opened in three in-state sites: Columbia, Sumter, and Charleston. Distinguished South Carolina African Americans interacted with senior high school students. Within three years, the program moved its operation to Columbia, the headquarters of SCETV.

Each year, six senior high schools are involved, with forty seniors per school seated as audience. Coupled with Benedict students, the audience is "treated" to lessons in African American history through discussions of the theme by distinguished African Americans. The annual theme comes from the Association for The Study of African American Life and History, founded by Dr. Carter G. Woodson in 1916. It is based in Washington, D. C.

Across the 20 years of its existence, the Teleconference has involved 188 senior South Carolina high schools and 174 distinguished African American guest speakers. Among the past guest speakers are: Dr. Benjamin S. Carson, Johns Hopkins Hospital; Dr. E. Ernest Guile, Dean of the College of Dentistry, King Saud University, Saudi, Arabia; Dr. Mae Jemison, medical doctor and astronaut; Four-star General Lloyd Newton, U. S. Air Force; Hon. Alan Page of the Supreme Court, St. Paul, Minnesota; Bishop John Hurst Adams, The A.M.E. Church; Hon. Wellington Webb, Mayor, Denver, Colorado; Nate Archibald, The Boston (Massachusetts) Celtics Basketball Team; Brig. General Clara Adams-Ender, U. S. Army; Hon. J. Gary Cooper, U. S. Ambassador to Jamaica; Roy Roberts, Senior Vice President, General Motors, Inc.; Captain Shirley Tyus, Pilot, United Airlines; Dr. Aubrey Manley, President, Spelman College, Atlanta, GA; Miss Mary Wilson of "The Supremes"; Dr. Jennifer Beckwith, Superintendent of DODD Schools in Italy; Dr. Beverly Malone, President, Royal College of Nursing, London, England; Mrs. Toba Garret International Cake Designer, New York City; Dr. Jonathan D. Farley, young (32) mathematical genius, Professor of Mathematics at M.I.T. and at Harvard

University; Dr. Oral Moses, International Baritone, Opera Performer; and Attorney Randall Kennedy, Professor of Law, Harvard University.

Local sponsors of the teleconference have included African American churches, community groups, and local Greek organizations. Nationally, sponsors of the program included groups such as the Tuskegee Airmen, National Association of Firefighters, Scottish Rite Masons, National Society of Black Engineers, National Dental Association, and all Black Greek-letter sororities and fraternities.

Today, the program airs annually in February. It goes out to all 50 United

The Swinton Center—Benedict College

Administration Building—Benedict College

States as well as to 177 foreign countries. Additionally, the DODD (Department of Defense Dependent) High Schools connect the program to their school satellite systems, located in Spain, Italy, Germany, and England, mainly through the Armed Forces Network. In Africa, through various cable networks, the program goes to many schools and colleges, including African University, an institution of the United Methodist Church.

Today, the thrust of Benedict College, a Baptist-related institution, has not changed since its founding: "A Power For Good In The Society." The dedication of its faculty, staff, and administration undergirds the success of the college, with 65 percent of them holding doctorate or terminal degrees,

with a School of Honors where over one-third of the students enter graduate or professional schools upon graduation from Benedict, and with many faculty and staff members involved in community improvement projects and civic programs. The college is indeed a successful institution in the broader community. Among the many success stories at the college are two that stand out: the graduation of its first group of engineers in 2007 and its graduation of many first-time generation family members.

Benedict's future is akin to its past: serving as one of America's premiere institutions of higher learning and proudly holding high the banner of one of America's HBCU's—Historically Black Colleges and Universities.

BOB JONES UNIVERSITY

Within the cultural and academic soil of liberal arts education, Bob Jones University exists to grow Christlike character that is Scripturally disciplined; others-serving; God-loving; Christ-proclaiming; and focused Above. —Mission statement of Bob Jones University

Bob Jones University was begun in 1927 by the evangelist Dr. Bob Jones Sr., who saw the need for a Christian institution of higher learning. During his travels as an evangelist, he came to see that for many, their faith in God had been shaken during their time in college. He envisioned an institution that could uphold the tenets of the Bible, provide a place of learning and moral guidance, and instill a deep appreciation of the arts while building leadership for future generations.

Ground was broken on December 1, 1926 in Bay County, Florida, the original site of the university. By the following fall, the first class of 88 was enrolled at Bob Jones College, studying and attending daily chapel services. Degrees were available in Bible, music, and speech, and students participated in a variety of spiritual and artistic endeavors. The school survived the onset of the Great Depression, but as the nation's

Dr. Stephen Jones was installed as the fourth-generation president of Bob Jones University at Convocation, May, 2005.

Dr Bob Jones Sr. (seated) founded Bob Jones College in 1927 and served as its first president. Dr. Bob Jones Jr. (left) became president in 1947 and Dr. Bob Jones III in 1971. Circa 1961.

financial disaster wore on, the college was forced to move from its Florida home.

While this difficulty may have thwarted others, the leaders at the school viewed it as an opportunity to look toward faith for an answer. In 1933 a new home was found for the college farther north, but still at home in the South. The new campus in Cleveland, Tennessee, proved to be well situated to help financially challenged students attain local employment. In addition, the school instituted a work scholarship program which helped students financially. The cultural community of the college expanded as well, with intramural sports and arts programs. By this time, even though the Depression was still raging, enrollment was steadily on the rise.

The school continued its expansion and after World War II, doubled its enrollment, thanks in large part to the newly adopted GI Bill. Relocation was once again imminent, but this time it was due to a happier circumstance: the school population was burgeoning and the college needed room to grow.

It was at this time that the school found its permanent home in the Palmetto State. Construction for the new Greenville, South Carolina campus began in September of 1946. The expansion extended to the university's academic offerings as well; three new schools were added, bringing the total to six. In 1947 the new school opened and was officially renamed Bob Jones University. That year, Dr. Bob Jones Jr. was elected by the school's board of trustees to follow in his father's footsteps as university president and continue the work of leading young Christians toward academic success and future leadership grounded in the teachings of the Scriptures.

On the first day of classes for the fall 1947 semester, 2,500 students walked through the doors of the school's original 18 buildings. Soon, the Greenville campus had added media and communications facilities, with its own radio station, WMUU, as well as a Christian film department named Unusual Films. During this time, Dr. Bob Jones Jr. also began a notable collection of religious art, the BJU Museum & Gallery, which today is the most extensive of the great Italian Baroque collections in the United States.

Daily chapel services in the Founder's Memorial Amphitorium play a key role in achieving BJU's objective of strenthening each student's belief in the truths of God's Word.

The Bob Jones University campus occupies 210 acres just inside the city limits of Greenville.

In 1964 Dr. Bob Jones Jr. also became the university's chairman of the board, and Dr. Bob Jones III was elected vice president of the university. A few short years later, the founder of the school, Dr. Bob Jones Sr., passed away. Though this was a great loss to the university community, his legacy was carried forward under the leadership of Dr. Bob Jones Jr., who was named university chancellor in 1971. During the 1970s, the chancellor and the school's newly named president, Dr. Bob Jones III, led the way to create meaningful curriculum choices for Christian educators and home schoolers by forming the Bob Jones University Press. This extension of the university's educational service has continued through the years, most notably with the launch of BJ LINC and BJ HomeSat satellite programs, which benefit thousands of students from home school families and Christian schools every day by providing interactive lessons that engage and educate home-schooled children around the world.

In 1997, Dr. Bob Jones Jr. passed away. He is well remembered for his passion and zealous preaching of the Gospel. To remember this fine leader, educator, and preacher, the university built the Bob Jones Jr. Memorial Seminary and Evangelism Center.

Today, Bob Jones University still stands as a full-spectrum liberal arts school focused on building the faith and integrity of the future leaders of the community through a deep understand-

ing of the Scriptures, personal responsibility, and a deep appreciation of the arts. The university emphasizes a philosophy of community and service that teaches young men and women the beauty and benefit of living, and leading, a life based on the teachings of Christ.

The school's educational philosophy is threefold. On the most fundamental level, the school is founded on the literal, error-free position of the Scriptures, that it is truth. Students take a class in Bible studies each semester to continually learn and understand the foundational precepts from which they can grow in faith. Secondly, the liberal arts focus addresses the desire to educate the whole person. Third, the school focuses on the fine arts. In teaching these different elements, Bob Jones University seeks to prepare young men and women for not only a life of learning and ongoing intellectual curiosity, but also to instill a deep

sense of service and community central to the teachings of Christ.

In this manner, students are encouraged to reach out into the community in meaningful ways, and they are always ready and willing to lend a hand when needed. The university works with the city and county when a large-scale, all-hands type effort is needed. Students can be relied on to be there for both huge drives as well as more intimate, personal volunteering. More than 50 percent of the student body volunteers on a weekly basis, reaching out to others in nursing homes or helping with children. Recently, the university adopted a nearby elementary school. In cooperation with, and at the request of the principal and faculty there, BJU students help the children

With over 100 undergraduate majors and 70 graduate programs, BJU has a strong reputation for academic excellence with a biblical worldview.

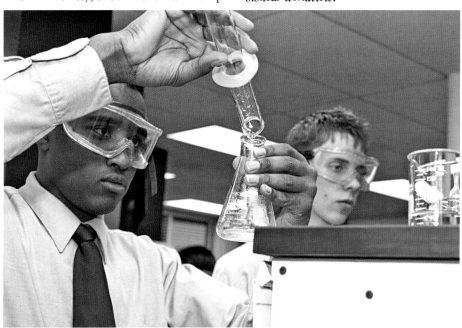

in the ways their educators feel they need guidance most.

"We feel blessed to be in South Carolina," says BJU President Stephen Jones. "We benefit from being here, but we also try to be a benefit to the state by contributing to the state and making it a better place to live."

Bob Jones University offers both undergraduate and graduate degrees in a wide range of majors, with over 100 undergraduate and 70 graduate programs. The university's ministry-focused majors are very popular courses of study, as are the offerings of the college of Arts and Science, including English, humanities, pre-law, and the sciences. The university was recently accredited by the Transnational Association of Christian Colleges and Schools (TRACS) and is currently polishing its wide roster of degree offerings, which includes majors such as Accounting, Bible Evangelism, Electrical Engineering, Music Education, Pastoral Studies, Voice Performance, and Youth Ministries among over 100 other undergraduate academic choices alone. Graduate degrees focus primarily in areas of divinity and ministry, education, and fine arts.

There are over 4,000 students enrolled in both programs each year, with 3,000 housed on campus in 10 residence halls fully equipped for modern student life. The campus also sports a 7,000-seat amphitorium, as well as a 2,600-seat auditorium and 3,300-seat dining common.

BJU awards over 900 graduate and undergraduate degrees each year.

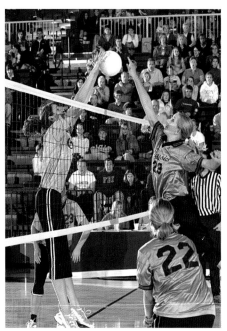

BJU students participate in intramural sports through literary societies similar to fraternities or sororities. Each society fields sports teams and participates in community projects, intra-scholastic competition, and debate.

Summer and night programs are available to accommodate graduate students who may work or have children, or both. All 50 states are represented in the student body, along with approximately 50 foreign countries. The university occupies a sprawling 210 acres in Greenville, 100 miles southwest of Charlotte, North Carolina and 150 miles northeast of Atlanta, Georgia.

Students also participate in an active campus life, with activities ranging from faith-based groups, a business association, and many fine and performing arts clubs. The campus has active communications activities as well, with a school newspaper, radio station, and television station. Sports are also a very popular campus activity. Though the school does not participate in intercollegiate sports activities, its approach to intramural sports is designed to maximize participation and give all students the

opportunity to take on active leadership roles.

The school's 45 societies, which are similar to traditional fraternities and sororities, are the focus of much of the interpersonal, ministry, and social activity for the students. Through the societies, students can participate in highly integrated sports competition. The 21 men's and 24 women's societies are divided into four leagues, two each for men and women. This makes it possible for an exceptionally high number of students to participate in sports such as soccer, basketball, softball, volleyball, and table tennis. The university's scholastic bowl is another intramural school activity that students in the various societies can participate in and grow in knowledge and camaraderie.

After 34 years as president, Dr. Bob Jones III retired from that position in 2005 and was appointed chancellor of Bob Jones University. Now, his son, Dr. Stephen Jones, the great-grandson of the founder of the university, carries on the family legacy of teaching and Christian leadership as the fourth president of the school. When asked about the family legacy, Dr. Stephen Jones is extremely modest and notes that there is no requirement in the school charter that the Jones family head the university. He attributes the handing over of the reigns through the Jones family line to the grace of God, the wisdom of the board of trustees, and the strong Jones family belief in teaching, education and Christian leadership.

When asked about the future of the university, Dr. Stephen Jones acknowledges that despite further secularization of the United States, "it is important for the school to remain true to the mission and goals set forth by the school's founder. While the university must endeavor to remain relevant and in touch with its students and community, this cannot come at a deterioration of the values the school has stood for since its inception." To this end, Bob Jones University remains steadfastly committed to providing the best liberal arts education possible while remaining true to its values of Christian spirit and leadership.

PRESBYTERIAN COLLEGE

Presbyterian College was born of the dreams of a humble pastor determined to restore a territory plundered by the Civil War. Only 22, the Reverend William Plumer Jacobs arrived in Clinton in 1864 to serve as pastor of First Presbyterian Church. Eight years later Jacobs and the church founded the Clinton High School Association to provide the young people of Laurens County a place to receive a Christian-based, liberal arts education. Educator and Presbyterian William States Lee became the school's first principal and teacher. Students met in a renovated pre-war academy building in south Clinton.

By 1880 South Carolina had reestablished its public school system, and Clinton no longer had need of a private academy. That same year on October 11 the Clinton High School Association became the Clinton College Association, an occasion noted in the session minutes of First Presbyterian Church by the simple statement: "The College of Clinton, to be under Presbyterian influence and control, was organized today."

The original college classes, with two faculty members and 15 students, were held in a white-framed building measuring 30 by 50 feet. Students paid $36 per year for instruction, and an additional $12 per month for room and board. Coeducational instruction occurred from the start. Young men and women entered the school on equal footing and took the same classes; the members of the first graduating class were all women. Most female students

William Plumer Jacobs, the founder of Presbyterian College.

came from the local community, as female students could not live in college housing. Women did not live on campus until 1965 when the college became fully coeducational.

Although affiliated with the Presbyterian Church, the college was non-denominational. Its mission was to promote a pure morality, a high standard of religious culture, and faithful study of God's word. Enrollment rose quickly, and by 1882 the college was home to 45 students. Classes met in a downtown building until 1886 when the college purchased land on South Broad Street and constructed Recitation Hall, which sat on the present-day campus of the Thornwell Home.

In 1890, R.N.S. Young and J.N. Copeland donated 16 acres of land that

served as the nucleus of the present campus and included what is now known as the West Plaza. Clinton College became the Presbyterian College of South Carolina and began to draw students from beyond Clinton. The following year the Alumni Association built Alumni Hall, a three-story dormitory with accommodations for 32 students. A dining hall and a dormitory for professors were added in 1892.

The Presbyterian Synod of South Carolina took over the governship of the college in 1905 and debated moving the college to a different site with a bid process. Bennettsville, Sumter, Chester, Yorkville (now York), and Clinton presented bids. Clinton's $40,000 bid was not the highest, but the community acted quickly and raised additional funds to preserve their college.

New president William G. Neville built a central building to house classrooms and offices. The Administration Building designed by Charles Coker Wilson opened in 1907 and was later renamed Neville Hall in William Neville's honor. This lovely domed Georgian building still stands as the centerpiece of the campus.

In 1912 President Davison McDowell Douglas hired Charles Leavitt, an engineer from New York, to lay out the horseshoe-shaped West Plaza anchored on the east by Neville Hall. In keeping with its goal to produce graduates of high moral character, Presbyterian College adopted an honor code, a student-run system still flourishing today, to govern students' academic and social lives. Enrollment passed 200; Leroy Springs Gymnasium and Smyth Dormitory were added to the campus.

In 1921 the Synod of South Carolina hoped to increase enrollment at Columbia's all-female Chicora College and asked the college to accept no female students for a decade. The college complied. Enrollment continued to grow, however, and in 1926 when Dr. Douglas left PC to become president of the University of South Carolina, the size of PC's faculty and student body had tripled, 15 acres had been added to the campus, and four major buildings had been built.

The campus in 1908, from left to right: Judd Dining hall, Neville Hall, and Laurens Dormitory.

New president The Reverend John McSween launched an ambitious fundraising campaign, adding Bailey Stadium, and an indoor swimming pool to Springs Gymnasium. His leadership took the college safely through the Great Depression, a time when colleges suffered decreased enrollment and revenues. PC faculty salaries were reduced four times between 1928 and 1935; operating budgets languished and financial aid took significant amounts of student fees.

William P. Jacobs II, grandson of the college's founder, became president in 1935. Pushing to boost enrollment and clear the college's debt, he refused a salary his first two years in office.

Dr. John V. Griffith, *current president of Presbyterian College, working on the Habitat House.*

Contributions from churches and individuals grew. Jacobs added unusual programs to the curriculum, including classes in radio broadcasting and aeronautics. He emphasized PC's intercollegiate tennis program, bringing national recognition to the college for years.

Presbyterian College accelerated its academic programming during World War II. Students could earn degrees and graduate as officers in three years. The campus also hosted a separate pre-flight training program for those entering the Army Air Force. More than 1,000 PC

Neville Hall today.

graduates served in World War II. Mrs. Lillian Brown, wife of Dean Marshall Brown, took on a special project to support the troops. Her newsletter, affectionately called the "Bee-Mail" by those who received it, enabled PC soldiers to keep in touch with the college and receive news of classmates throughout the war.

As veterans returned, the college experienced dramatic growth. The 99 students on campus in February 1945 became 400 the following fall. Dean Marshall W. Brown became the college's new president as the country's economy improved and college enrollment surged.

Brown instituted a long-range plan, raising funds for endowment and new buildings. College assets tripled, the endowment rose 627 percent, and church support quintupled. By 1963 the student body numbered 540 and the number of faculty had doubled.

President Marc C. Weersing arrived in 1964. He shepherded PC through full coeducation and the end of racial segregation. The college restructured its curriculum, enrollment surged, and the size of the faculty doubled yet again. In 1979 president Dr. Kenneth B. Orr continued the college's growth, increas-

Christmas at Presbyterian College.

ing enrollment, staff, and endowment assets. Ten new buildings graced the campus by his retirement in 1997.

Presbyterian College arrived in the 21st century under the leadership of Dr. John V. Griffith (1998–) and a period heralded by significant additions to the college's academic programs, faculty, students, and facilities. A new strategic plan, developed under his leadership, continues to chart the college's growth. A general education curriculum whose highlights include international programs, internships, and unique cultural and arts opportunities has resulted in record enrollment. A $160 million Promise and Challenge campaign has produced new facilities for living (Senior Hall and Carol International House), athletic play (new Bailey Memorial Stadium, Martin Soccer Stadium), study (Lassiter Science Hall, the Arnold Archives and Thomason Library), and infrastructure support (information technology) that benefit the PC and Clinton community alike. New professorships have strengthened the already strong faculty, and increased financial aid resources insure that qualified students have access to a PC education.

Presbyterian College holds fast to its core mission and high standards of

South Carolina Professor of the Year Robert Hudson conducts a biology lab.

integrity. The college motto: "Dum Vivimus Servimus," ("While we live, we serve"), continues to endure the test of time. Students and faculty serve their community through Student Volunteer Services, started in 1969. SVS opportunities include tutoring programs, work with the elderly, spring break work projects, the Special Olympics and Habitat for Humanity. In 1994 college faculty and students began a partnership with local businesses, churches, and schools to mentor local students who show academic and personal potential but fall short of their capabilities. The C.H.A.M.P.S., or Communities, Helping, Assisting, and Motivating Promising

The football team takes the field at Bailey Stadium.

Students program runs year-round, and includes a two week residential summer camp at the college.

Presbyterian College provides the community a rich cultural life through lectures, art exhibits, concerts and theatrical performances. The college's library and intramural facilities serve local residents, while college faculty and staff serve on many local boards. The college is involved in local economic development, spearheading a downtown bookstore and a fine downtown restaurant.

From its modest beginning, Presbyterian College has been transformed into an institution with a 240-acre campus and a national reputation for academic excellence. Its 1,200 students represent 30 states and 11 foreign countries. Its international study programs include China, Oxford, Spain, and Cuba. In 2007 PC's long tradition of excellence in intercollegiate athletics culminated in a move into NCAA Division I athletics. The distinguished sons and daughters of Presbyterian College have become outstanding leaders in the Presbyterian Church, in business and industry, education, athletics, journalism, medicine, the military, and public service. Perhaps most importantly, Presbyterian College continues to live its motto, producing servant leaders for the world today.

CLEMSON UNIVERSITY

Clemson University is one of the nation's top-ranked public academic institutions, a school with a small-college campus life and atmosphere but high tech research, technology, and engineering power. Combined with a nationally recognized sports program, Clemson is an institution that consistently delivers all-around educational opportunities for its students.

Thomas Green Clemson created the idea of the Clemson Agricultural College when he signed and sealed his will on November 6, 1886 and the terms became public when he died April 6, 1888.

Clemson was a scholarly young man, excelling in the sciences and learning a great deal in his studies abroad. He studied agriculture, chemistry and geology while in preparatory school in Vermont. His earliest agricultural essay was published in the late 1920s. He earned his diploma as an assayer, testing ores and minerals for their chemical composition. It was through his studies and early career as a mining engineer that he developed a deep respect for higher learning and the advantages of scientific thinking and processes.

Clemson was born in Philadelphia but moved to the South upon his marriage to the daughter of John C. Calhoun, South Carolina's famous statesman, opening his eyes to both

Clemson College opened as an all-male military institution with 446 students. This photograph is one of the college's first groups of Officer Cadets.

Standing high atop Bowman Field in the center of campus, Tillman Hall, with its clock tower that still tolls across its landscape, was the first building raised. Built in 1890, this historical facility is home today to the Eugene T. Moore School of Education.

politics and agricultural science. During Clemson's years in the South, he saw how the Civil War ravaged the Southern landscape and left little of the former glory enjoyed by Southern farmers.

Clemson took it upon himself to help resolve the problem in his will in 1888: ". . . believing that there can be no permanent improvement in agriculture without a knowledge of those sciences which pertain particularly thereto, I . . . devote the bulk of my property to the establishment of an agricultural college upon the Fort Hill place."

Yet as with many things after the Civil War, the founding of the university was not quite that simple. It took active lobbying of the state legislature to accept the generous gift; in the end, the resolution passed by a single vote. The year after Clemson's death, the governor of South Carolina signed the bill that officially established what was then known as Clemson Agricultural College.

When the college opened in July 1893 there were 446 young men enrolled in what was then an all-male military school. In 1955 the first women were enrolled as full-time, degree-seeking students. In 1955 Clemson also changed from a four-year uniformed cadet membership and fulfilled its land-grant obligation by requiring all males to enroll in basic ROTC for the first two years with an option to continue. That obligation was not removed until the U.S. Congress amended the land grant act in the 1970s. In 1964, in recognition of its growth, continued expansion of academic offerings and research work, the state legislature renamed the school Clemson University.

The antebellum plantation home of John C. Calhoun, the 19th century South Carolina statesman, and later of his daughter and son-in-law Thomas Green Clemson, sits on its original site in the center of the Clemson University campus. Restored, named a national treasure, and furnished mostly with family artifacts, the university honors Clemson's vision that "the preservation of the home . . . shall always be open for the inspection of visitors."

Clemson achieved "integration with dignity" when its first black student, Harvey B. Gantt, enrolled. Gantt graduated in 1965 with honors in architecture and later served two terms as mayor of Charlotte, N.C.

More than a century later, the university founded by Thomas G. Clemson has retained its strong traditions while quickly moving to the forefront of public university academics. Clemson is now a thriving, public university that enrolls over 17,000 students from all 50 states and approximately 90 countries around the world every year. The university includes five colleges: Agriculture, Forestry and Life Sciences; Architecture, Arts and Humanities; Business and Behavioral Science; Engineering and Science; and Health, Education and Human Development. Within these colleges, over 70 undergraduate and 100 graduate degrees are available, from accounting to zoology. Over 1,200 full-time faculty members attend to the higher education of this diverse student body, and the university strives not only to provide a fertile environment for students, but for faculty as well, affording grounds for professional development for this dynamic group of scholars and educators.

As delineated by Thomas Clemson's will, the school is governed by a board of 13 members, six of whom are selected by the South Carolina State Legislature and seven of whom are life members. Clemson University is accredited by the Commission on Colleges of the Southern Association of Colleges and Schools to award bachelor's, master's, specialist, and doctorate degrees.

The Clemson campus is one of unique Southern beauty. It rests along the foothills of the Blue Ridge Mountains and is situated on the banks of Lake Hartwell, providing picturesque views of the classic South Carolina landscape. Both Fort Hill, the manor home where John C. Calhoun resided, as well as the Hanover House, which was built in the early 1700s but moved to the Clemson campus in the 1940s, have been designated on the National Register for Historic Places. Located on university grounds is the South Carolina Botanical Garden, 295 acres of cultivated woodland preserve, where nature and culture converge through educational programs, garden tours, and art exhibits.

The university has very high academic standards. Its freshman SAT scores are the 14th highest among the nation's 164 national public universities. Nearly half of the freshmen were in the top 10 percent of their high school graduating classes. And, two-thirds of incoming freshmen proudly represent the state of South Carolina.

Clemson University is also home to unique honors programs, including the Calhoun Scholars Program, University Honors Program and The National Scholars Program. They and all of the other students on campus can stretch their minds and hone their learning skills at Cooper Library, which boasts an immense catalog of materials, over 1.5 million items, including the papers of John C. Calhoun, Thomas Green Clemson, James Byrnes and Strom Thurmond.

This state-of-the-art physics class gives example to the classroom experience Clemson students encounter. As one of the country's top public research universities, Clemson strives to create a smaller classroom environment with an overall 14/1 student to faculty ratio.

Unmatched in excitement and enthusiasm, the traditional "run down the hill" before every football game in Clemson's "Death Valley," Memorial Stadium brings more that 80,000 fans to their feet as the Tigers take the field.

In addition to on-campus learning activities, students at Clemson have a host of interesting opportunities to explore in the real world. This includes the opportunity to study abroad. Students can travel to far-off locales such as Africa, South America, or Europe on their summer breaks, or spend a semester or year immersed in studies around the globe, from Japan to Russia to Australia. Students can also take advantage of internship programs closer to home, but directly in line with the students' future plans. These types of off-campus opportunities give students the chance to explore the world beyond their college experiences.

Clemson's contribution to its community and society as a whole goes far beyond its rigorous academic training of students. Clemson University is also on the forefront of research in a number of fields, and offers comprehensive research facilities to support these scientific endeavors, including the

Godley-Snell Research Center, the Center for Optical Materials Science and Engineering Technologies (COMSET), the Advanced Materials Research Lab (AMRL), the Clemson University International Center for Automotive Research (CU-ICAR) and the Biosystems Research Complex. In keeping with the original intent of founder Thomas Clemson, the school's Research Farm Services stay on the cutting edge of agricultural and farm sciences, dedicated to developing and disseminating knowledge for sustainable production methods in the Southern region and beyond. From the 240-acre Musser Fruit Farm to centers for all manner of farm animals (dairy cows, swine, poultry), Clemson University continues the legacy of its founder in researching and developing meaningful ways to bolster agricultural methods.

Clemson's prominent and well-respected athletic program, with 19 varsity Clemson Tigers teams that compete in the Atlantic Division of the Atlantic Coast Conference of the NCAA Division I, is supported by energetic and spirited fans. The university's football season is kicked off each year in grand fashion with the annual First Friday Parade. On the Friday afternoon before the team's first home game, floats created by the school's fraternities, sororities, and other campus organizations roll through the main street of the town of Clemson, progressing straight onto the campus and into the university's amphitheater where the first pep rally of the year is kicked off.

Clemson sports give students, parents, alumni, and community members the perfect opportunity to interact and get caught up in Clemson spirit. Clemson Memorial Stadium was affectionately dubbed "Death Valley" by Lonnie McMillian, a former coach at a rival school who so named it because it was where his team always got killed when they came to play Clemson. At each Clemson home game, the 80,000-plus crowd gets fired up right from the start

Continuing the long tradition of excellence in ACC sports, Clemson basketball offers some of the best athletic abilities to the sport.

by the Tigers' traditional entrance, running down the hill into the stadium. After their warm-up, they exit to the locker room and a few minutes before kickoff, board two buses, ride around behind the north stands to the east end zone, and to the top of the hill where they each rub Howard's Rock, a large rock brought by a Clemson fan from Death Valley, California, to former head coach Frank Howard, which now sits sentry to the stadium affixed to a pedestal. Since 1966 Howard's Rock has been a vital part of Clemson tradition, thought to be imbued with good luck, and serving as a focal point of inspiration for the Tigers. With fanfare that includes cannon blasts and the Clemson marching band playing a rousing version of the "Tiger Rag," the crowd goes wild as the team runs down the hill, ready to take on the opposition.

While football is an important part of Clemson's sports identity, there are many other teams that carry on the Tiger spirit, as well. Men and women's teams include basketball, cross country, soccer, swimming and diving, tennis, and track and field. Many national titles over the years have emanated from Clemson's impressive track and field, men's soccer and golf lineup. Men's sports also include baseball, while women have varsity volleyball and rowing teams. The campus is ideally equipped for sports with Littlejohn Coliseum for men's and women's basketball, a championship John E. Walker Sr. Golf Course, Riggs Field, home of the men's and women's nationally ranked soccer programs, an indoor track, tennis facilities, swimming facilities and Doug Kingsmore Stadium, a national caliber baseball stadium. Intramural athletics and over 40 club sports are also offered so that all Clemson students may enjoy the fun and competition.

There are plenty of other activities for students, as well. Clemson has an active Greek community, with approximately 30 fraternities and sororities. There are six student-run media outlets including *The Tiger*, the campus newspaper, and WSBF, the Clemson University student radio station.

The school's original military character has not been lost over the years. There are both Army and Air Force ROTC detachments as well, which include specialized sub-organization. These are: Company C-4 Pershing Rifles, K-7 Scabbard and Blade, Maj. Rudolph Anderson Jr. Squadron Arnold Air Society, Maj. Dennis H. Satler Chapter Silver Wings, Clemson Rangers, and Tiger Platoon.

Clemson notable alumni include: David Wilkins '68, U.S. Ambassador to Canada; Christie Kenny '77, U.S. Ambassador to the Philippines; Strom Thurmond '23, former U.S. Senator and former South Carolina governor; and Harvey Gantt '65, the first African American mayor of Charlotte.

Clemson's athletic program has also produced Olympic medalists and professional athletes in a variety of disciplines. In the summer of 1988, Mike Milchin pitched the United States Olympic baseball team to a gold-medal victory—all while on summer break from his studies at Clemson! Mark McCoy and Gigi Fernandez carried on the Clemson spirit in 1992, each earning gold in the

An example of the nationally recognized initiative to develop a culture of curiosity, this student-centered research project in the Culinary Lab engages students in the Food Science and Human Nutrition Department.

One of many research labs on campus, this robotics laboratory offers students a fully equipped lab to investigate a full spectrum of control issues—from material handling to high speed magnetic bearings.

110 hurdles and tennis, respectively. Clemson students and alumni brought home 6 medals in 1996, including golds for Kim Graham and Carlton Chambers, each in the 4x100 relay. The Olympic tradition carried on into the 21st Century, with Shawn Crawford bringing home both silver and gold, the latter in a solo performance in the 200 meters.

Notable pro athletes who cultivated their talent at Clemson include NBA stars Elden Campbell, Larry Nance, and Wayne "Tree" Rollins. NFL footballers from Clemson include Philadelphia Eagles linebacker Keith Adams, six-time pro bowler Michael Dean Perry, and famed defensive lineman William "The Refrigerator" Perry.

Clemson University has no plans to slow down any time soon. The school is actively working to be ranked in the Top 20 public universities in the very near future, buoyed by the university's steadfast adherence to the ideals of the school's founder as the highest mission of the institution. By continuing to fulfill the covenant between its founder and the people of South Carolina to establish a "high seminary of learning" through its historical land-grant responsibilities of teaching, research and extended public service, Clemson University bridges its most time-tested traditions with a vision for the future.

CONVERSE COLLEGE

Founded upon the conviction that "the well-being of any country depends much upon the culture of her women" and compelled by the vision to "enable students to see clearly, decide wisely and act justly," Converse has been a pioneer in women's education for more than a century. Throughout her history, the Spartanburg, South Carolina college has offered a liberal arts education within a residential environment—purposefully keeping class sizes small and ensuring that every student has a faculty advisor. Today, innovative programs for graduate and advanced study complement the undergraduate program.

Converse believes that the Founder's Ideal is a call to arms to develop engaged leaders who think critically and creatively and affect positive change in the world. Since the college's founding, graduates have used their Converse experience as launching pads for successful careers and active citizenship. Among Converse alumnae are a Pulitzer Prize winner, a renowned heart researcher, a Texas Supreme Court Justice, a prominent civil rights attorney, Broadway performers, the deputy crew commander for Titan IV Rocket launches at Cape Canaveral, and the first female circuit court judge in South Carolina.

Although the doors of Converse opened October 1, 1890, the first step towards the founding of the college was taken in 1889 when a prominent attorney assembled a group of Spartanburg citizens to discuss the project. Among

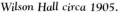

Wilson Hall circa 1905.

Members of The Class of 1916 at The Crows Nest.

the 13 men was Dexter Edgar Converse, a native of Vermont who had settled in Spartanburg before the Civil War and had become a successful pioneer in the cotton mill industry.

Mr. Converse was especially interested in establishing a college for women because his daughter, Marie, was approaching college age and he wanted her to have every possible educational advantage. His initial and subsequent contributions to the cause were so valuable that the college was given his name.

Initially, the college was operated as a stockholders company and Mr. Converse headed the first board of directors, comprised entirely of Spartanburg citizens. They elected the Reverend Benjamin F. Wilson as the first president. The first faculty roster was comprised of sixteen members and the student body numbered 168.

On January 2, 1892 the main building was destroyed by fire, but was immediately reconstructed and enlarged. The work of the college hardly suffered interruption. In 1896, by the voluntary act of the stockholders, Converse College was incorporated under the laws of the state of South Carolina and a self-perpetuating board of trustees was established. This meant that Converse was converted into a permanent gift to the cause of higher education for women.

Beginning in the 1900s, Converse matured into one of the leading colleges for women in the South. Academic requirements were strengthened, the ablest teachers supplemented the faculty and new buildings were constructed. It was during this period that the college's School of Music received a national rating as a professional school of music. Converse became a charter member of the National Association of Schools of Music, which is recognized by the U.S. Department of Education as the accrediting agency for music curricula.

In 1964 Converse introduced graduate programs, including the Master of Art in Teaching (MAT) program, the first degree of its kind in South Carolina. The graduate program would later become the School of Education and Graduate Studies and offer a wide range of degrees in fields such as music, education, the liberal arts, and marriage and family therapy.

In 1983 the college introduced Converse II to fit the schedules and ambitions of adult women, whether they are a few semesters shy of a bachelor's degree or a freshman taking college-level courses for the first time.

In 2003 the college completed the most successful capital campaign in its history with $82.5 million in private gifts. The campaign led to the establishment of the Nisbet Honors Program, the Chapman Study Abroad Experience endowment, and an endowment to fund faculty initiatives for innovative teaching and scholarly achievement; renovation of residence halls and the Montgomery Student Center; and construction of The Sally Abney Rose Physical Activity Complex, the Justine V. R. "Nita" Milliken Addition of Milliken Fine Arts Building and Phifer Science Hall.

Momentum continues today as Converse focuses on providing distinct educational experiences that enable creativity and develop the adaptive capacity necessary for students to succeed in the ever-changing word.

- Converse Model Programs (Arab League, NATO, and UN) are national leaders having defeated such institutions as Harvard, UC–Berkley, Northeastern, Ohio State, and all three U.S. military academies. Converse is home to

Converse faculty and student research in Phifer Science Hall.

the Southeast Region Model Arab League competition, headquarters of the Carolinas Committee on U.S.-Arab Relations, and helped establish and run a high school Model Arab League program in Amman, Jordan.
- The Daniels Center for Leadership and Service is a partnership between academic affairs and student affairs to provide leadership development training and opportunities to learn, serve and lead on campus and in the community.
- In 2006 Converse became the first women's college to attain the

prestigious All-Steinway School distinction.
- The curriculum supports 51 undergraduate degrees and 33 majors including South Carolina's only Master's in gifted education program and first Bachelor of Fine Arts in creative and professional writing, and the Upstate's first undergraduate music therapy degree program.
- A member of Conference Carolinas, Converse competes in NCAA Division II—the highest level of any women's college.
- In 2007 Converse and Clemson University joined forces to increase the number of women entering science fields through a new dual degree program in engineering.

Converse College is committed to developing adaptable individuals for the 21st century who are equipped with the character, knowledge, skills and perspective to transform the world around them.

NCAA Division II soccer.

FURMAN UNIVERSITY

Furman University's colonial roots stretch back to 1751, when Oliver Hart, a Baptist pastor in Charleston, South Carolina, created an education fund to train young ministers. After the American Revolution, his successor, Richard Furman, envisioned a college in the nation's capital and preparatory academies in every region. Shortly before he died, Furman established a convention of South Carolina Baptist churches to sponsor a Southern academy. In 1826 the Furman Academy and Theological Institution was chartered and named in his memory

By 1820 the tiny frontier village of Greenville was a summer resort for South Carolina's low country planters. They encouraged residents to build academies, one for boys and one for girls. In 1823 William Bullein Johnson, a Baptist minister, became principal of the Female Academy, which soon enrolled about 100 girls.

The Furman Academy opened in Edgefield in 1827 with three "indigent and pious" young men as students and W.B. Johnson as chairman of its Board of Agents. But the school was not especially successful and moved several times, first to the High Hills of the Santee near Sumter, then to Winnsboro.

In 1850 the state Baptist Convention voted to transform the struggling institution into a liberal arts college and locate it in Greenville, with its healthy climate, low cost of living and abundance of Baptists. Within a few years the college had a 50-acre campus with an impressive Italianate main building, an

The front gate and spectacular fountain have welcomed visitors to Furman for nearly 50 years.

The main building on the Furman University campus in downtown Greenville was Richard Furman Hall, an Italian Renaissance structure completed in 1854.

enrollment of approximately 60 students, a new president (James Clement Furman, son of the founder), and a new name: The Furman University.

In 1854 the South Carolina Baptist Convention chartered Greenville Baptist Female College, and the Academy's land, buildings and trust were conveyed to Furman's trustees. In 1858 Furman's theology department became the Southern Baptist Theological Seminary, which eventually moved to Louisville, Kentucky.

When the Civil War began, most Furman faculty and students enlisted. The university closed in the fall of 1861, but the Female College stayed open. Many of its students joined the Ladies Association in Aid of Confederate Vol-

unteers, using the old male academy building as a soldiers' rest home. Charles Judson, Furman's treasurer, became president.

After reopening in 1866 Furman struggled financially for the next 30 years, as did the Female College. But as the 19th century drew to a close and Greenville grew prosperous through textiles, Furman began to emerge from the shadow of poverty and mediocrity. A.P. Montague became president of Furman in 1897, and he and his successor, Edwin McNeill Poteat, expanded the physical facilities and raised academic standards.

The Female College, under the direction of "Lady Principal" Mary Camilla Judson, began a library and expanded its offerings to include elocution and calisthenics. The college became independent from Furman in 1909, and in 1914 President David Ramsay changed its name to the Greenville Woman's College.

In the early 1920s, Furman president William McGlothlin assembled a strong faculty, but the school once again suffered from financial problems. Then, in December 1924, Furman learned that it was a beneficiary of The Duke Endowment, established by James Buchanan Duke to provide support for children, health and education in the two Carolinas. Since that time Furman has received more than $100 million in grants from The Endowment, which is one of the nation's leading philanthropic foundations.

Support from The Duke Endowment helped Furman survive the Great Depression, but the Woman's College faced bankruptcy and had only one choice: coordination with Furman. Between 1932 and 1937 the schools were gradu-

ally merged, and GWC became the Woman's College of Furman University. When the United States entered World War II, many Furman faculty and most male students enlisted. During the war Furman was almost entirely female, and the men's campus became a military training center.

After the war, the influx of veterans swelled enrollment to 1,400 and led to a decision to unite the two campuses. Trustees purchased 1,100 acres on the outskirts of Greenville and erected buildings designed by the architectural firm of Perry, Shaw, Hepburn, Kehoe and Dean, which had restored Colonial Williamsburg. Under the direction of President John Plyler, men moved to the new campus in 1958 and women in 1961.

When Gordon Blackwell became president in 1965, Furman became the

The Bell Tower with carillon sits adjacent to Furman Lake under the shadow of Paris Mountain.

first private college in South Carolina to admit African American students. A more demanding curriculum was adopted and an extensive study abroad program instituted. In 1973 Furman was granted a chapter by Phi Beta Kappa, the nation's most prestigious academic honor society.

John E. Johns was appointed president in 1976. Under his leadership, the

A long-standing tradition is rekindled each September as the Paladins hit the gridiron. Furman is a highly successful member of the Southern Conference.

Furman's internationally recognized and ambitious conservatory-style music program presents nearly 200 open-to-the-public concerts each year.

university's endowment grew tenfold, the campus made great strides in its use and acquisition of technology, and both the faculty and the student body grew stronger and more diverse.

Furman's formal ties with the South Carolina Baptist Convention ended in May 1992, and the Board of Trustees reaffirmed the university's mission as a liberal arts college within the Christian tradition. In the same year, Mrs. Charles Daniel bequeathed $24 million to Furman.

David E. Shi became Furman's 10th president in 1994. New construction, expanded emphasis on international studies, and a renewed commitment to experiential education (engaged learning) have marked his presidency.

Furman today consists of 2,600 undergraduates representing more than 40 states and 15 countries. Most are attracted to the school by its national reputation for academic excellence and its emphasis on a well-rounded college experience. The campus, considered one of the most beautiful in the nation, features more than 30 major buildings, a 30-acre lake, a formal rose garden and a golf course.

LIMESTONE COLLEGE

Limestone College has always been a pioneer in providing access to higher education for those who otherwise might not have enjoyed that access. In 1845, when higher education was only a dream for young women, Limestone was founded as the first women's college in South Carolina and one of the first in the United States. In the early 1900s, when young men from the local area sought higher education, but could not afford to attend distant universities, Limestone admitted them as daytime commuting students.

In the 1970s, when most colleges and universities had no interest in educating working adults, Limestone established the Block Program, one of the pioneer programs for non-traditional students. The Block Program allowed students to complete their bachelor's degrees entirely through evening classes, using a novel one-course-at-a-time accelerated format. In the mid 1990s, through the establishment of the Virtual Campus, Limestone emerged as a national leader in applying computer technology to teach students who could not utilize traditional classroom settings. In 2005 the Block Program and the

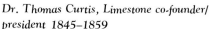

Dr. Thomas Curtis, Limestone co-founder/ president 1845–1859

Virtual Campus were combined into the Extended Campus Program. Providing higher education access to those needing it the most has been a proud theme throughout the history of Limestone College.

Limestone College is an accredited, independent, coeducational, four-year liberal arts institution, and a non-denominational Christian college. Limestone's main campus is located in Gaffney, nestled among the rolling hills in the Piedmont region of the state. The county seat of Cherokee County, Gaffney, and its suburbs have a population of approximately 25,000, and are within an hour's drive of the Greenville/ Spartanburg and Charlotte metropolitan areas. Limestone also offers its Extended Campus Classroom Program at ten sites throughout South Carolina. Today, Limestone is truly a statewide college.

The institution that became Limestone College was founded by Dr. Thomas Curtis and his son, Dr. William Curtis, distinguished Baptist ministers and scholars who were born in England and emigrated to the United States in 1833. Dr. Thomas Curtis served churches in Maine, Georgia, and South Carolina, including the Wentworth Street Baptist Church in Charleston, while Dr. William Curtis was pastor of the First Baptist Church in Columbia.

The Curtis Administration Building is the college's most recognizable building.

For much of the 20th century, Dr. Montague McMillan was a highly respected professor and deeply revered alumna (Class of 1911) at Limestone. Known by generations of students as "Dr. Mac," she served her alma mater from 1917 to 1971 and was author of a comprehensive history of the college (1970).

Cooper-Limestone Institute, circa 1888

In 1845 Dr. Thomas Curtis was able to fulfill his dream of establishing an institution of higher learning for young women by purchasing a magnificent building at Limestone Springs, which had been constructed in the 1830s as a resort hotel. The village of Limestone Springs, now a part of Gaffney, had developed adjacent to mineral water springs, which attracted families from the Midlands and Lowcountry who wished to avail themselves of the supposed medicinal value of the spring water and avoid the oppressive summer heat of their home regions.

Originally named the Limestone Springs Female High School, the new institution attracted the daughters of the most influential families of South Carolina, who sought the finest liberal arts education available in the antebellum period. On November 6, 1845, 67 young women began their classes at Limestone.

Dr. Thomas Curtis assumed an active role in education beyond the confines of his own school. He was instrumental in organizing the South Carolina Teachers Association and founding the Southern Baptist Theological Seminary, which eventually moved from Greenville, South Carolina to Louisville, Kentucky.

Tragedy struck Limestone in 1859, when Dr. Thomas Curtis, returning from a visit to the North, perished in a shipboard fire on Chesapeake Bay. Leadership of the college passed to his son, Dr. William Curtis. During the War Between the States, William was an ardent supporter of the Confederate cause. He was a signer of the South Carolina Ordinance of Secession and loaned a large sum of money to the Confederate government. When the South was defeated, there was no hope of repayment and the wealthy planters who had sent their daughters to Limestone were now destitute.

Despite these difficult times, Limestone managed to survive. Peter Cooper, prominent industrialist and inventor, briefly considered the possibility of transforming Limestone into a Southern version of his famed Cooper Union in New York City. While his plans for Limestone did not materialize, in 1881 the school became known as Cooper-Limestone Institute. In 1898 it became Limestone College.

During the late 19th and early 20th

Capt. John H. Montgomery (left), chairman of the board of trustees, 1888–1902; Dr. Wylie Cicero Hamrick (right), chairman of the board of trustees, 1921–1935.

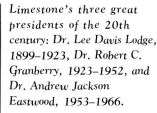

Limestone's three great presidents of the 20th century: Dr. Lee Davis Lodge, 1899–1923, Dr. Robert C. Granberry, 1923–1952, and Dr. Andrew Jackson Eastwood, 1953–1966.

centuries Limestone was fortunate to have trustee leadership from two of the leaders of the textile industry in Upstate South Carolina, Captain John Montgomery of Spartan Mills and Dr. Wylie Cicero Hamrick of Hamrick Mills. Captain Montgomery served as chairman of the board of trustees from 1888 until his death in 1902. Under his leadership and through his personal generosity, Limestone regained its stability and reputation. Dr. Hamrick served as a member of the board of trustees from

1899 until his death in 1935 and oversaw Limestone during its golden years of expansion. His descendants have played prominent leadership roles at Limestone down to the present day.

During the 67 year period, 1899–1966, Limestone College was led by three of the most influential presidents in the long history of the institution—Dr. Lee Davis Lodge (1899–1923), Dr. Robert C. Granberry (1923–1952), and Dr. Andrew Jackson Eastwood (1953–1966). Each of these three leaders is memorialized through the naming of major campus buildings in their honor—Dixie Lodge, Granberry Gymnasium, and Eastwood Library.

One of Dr. Lodge's first endeavors was the construction of the Winnie Davis Hall of History. This unique structure, one of the most architecturally splendid buildings on any college campus, was occupied in 1904 and named in honor of the daughter of Confederate President Jefferson Davis and Varina Howell Davis. The new building was to be used to promote the study of Southern history and Southern literature. Dr. Lodge proposed to make Limestone a great center of historical study, where the rich materials of the South could be collected, preserved, organized, and interpreted. Visiting scholars would share their knowledge with Limestone students.

For the next 40 years, Limestone students who completed a prescribed sequence of history courses received a special diploma from the Winnie Davis School of History in addition to their Limestone diploma.

Limestone College has always been deeply involved with improving educational opportunities in Gaffney and Cherokee County. In the late 1890s, shortly after the creation of Cherokee as a separate county, Limestone administrators supported the efforts of local citizens to establish a public school system. When the new system opened its doors, every teacher was a Limestone graduate. More than a century later, Limestone provides a large percentage of teachers to Cherokee County and the Upstate.

During World War I Limestone continued its outreach efforts to the local

Winnie Davis Hall of History, opened in 1904, was considered the "jewel of the campus" and is now the focus of a $4 million restoration campaign.

community. Under the leadership of Professor Eunice Ford, later dean of the college, Limestone established evening classes to assist local citizens gain the necessary literacy skills to serve their country both in the military and in critical civilian occupations.

In 1923 Dr. Lodge was succeeded by Dr. Robert C. Granberry. Many of the buildings on Limestone's front campus date from his presidency. Both the Hamrick Hall of Science, a gift from Dr. Hamrick who was then serving as chairman of the board of trustees, and the Carroll School of Fine Arts, a gift from longtime benefactor James A. Carroll, were completed in 1925.

From 1921 until 1941 Limestone was formally affiliated with the South Carolina Baptist Convention, a relationship which ended amicably when control of the institution passed to a self-governing board of trustees. In 1928 Limestone College received regional accreditation from the Southern Association of Colleges and Schools (SACS), an accreditation which has been continuously maintained since that date.

In 1953 Dr. Andrew Jackson Eastwood, longtime professor of history, ascended to the presidency of Limestone. During his tenure, student enrollment increased, admission standards were

raised, and the relationship between the college and the local community was strengthened.

The Fullerton Auditorium, completed in 1964 and seating nearly 1,000, provides one of the finest performance venues in the Southeast. Limestone's priceless Aeolian-Skinner organ, constructed by G. Donald Harrison, who also built the organ for the Mormon Tabernacle in Salt Lake City, was moved into the new auditorium.

Following the passing of Dr. Eastwood in 1966, Limestone College experienced many of the challenges facing other higher education institutions during those turbulent years. During the next twenty-six years Limestone had eight presidents, three of them serving on an interim basis.

Male commuting students had been allowed on campus in the early 20th century, but there were no residence halls for men until the late 1960s when Limestone became a coeducational, liberal arts college. With desegregation occurring throughout the nation, African American students were admitted to the college for the first time. In recent years, Limestone has been cited for the diversity of its student body.

In the 1970s Limestone developed a novel, accelerated approach to education for working adults. The Block Program, which has served as a national model for successful evening programs, gave working adults the opportunity to complete their baccalaureate degrees without sacrificing their jobs.

Limestone's intercollegiate athletics program began during the 1972–1973 academic year with four sports—men's basketball, men's tennis, men's golf, and women's volleyball. Blue, old gold, and white were selected as the school colors. The nickname for the athletic teams was "Saints," and a Saint Bernard dog was chosen as the Limestone mascot. Facilities for intercollegiate athletics improved dramatically in 1976 with the opening of the Timken Physical Education Center, which contained a 1,500-seat basketball arena and an aquatic center. In 1984 the men's golf team brought home Limestone's first national title, winning the National Association of

Independent Athletics (NAIA) Championship. Limestone added a men's baseball program in 1987 and selected as its first coach former major league pitcher and future Hall of Fame member Gaylord Perry.

In 1991 Limestone secured membership in NCAA Division II, and in 1998 joined the Carolinas-Virginia Athletic Conference (CVAC). In 2007 the name was changed to Conference Carolinas.

In recent years the men's and women's lacrosse teams have enjoyed particular success at the national level. The men's team won NCAA Division II national championships in 2000 and 2002, while finishing second in 2001, 2003, 2004, and 2005. The women's team finished third nationally in 2004 and 2006.

In October 2005 Limestone dedicated a new Physical Education Center containing a state-of-the-art Fitness Center and athletic training facilities, a wrestling practice area, locker rooms, classrooms, and offices. Today, Limestone College sponsors nine sports for men and nine for women. More than 50 percent of Limestone's day students participate in intercollegiate athletics.

Dr. Walt Griffin became president of Limestone College in 1992, at a time when the institution was experiencing dwindling enrollment, major financial deficits, and deteriorating buildings. However, Limestone not only recovered from the hard times of the 1980s, but has flourished during the 15 years of Dr. Griffin's presidency and is now enjoying an era of growth, stability, and renewal.

Day Program enrollment has increased each year and is now 750. The Extended Campus enrollment has tripled, aided by the establishment in 1996 of the Virtual Campus Internet Program. With a total enrollment approaching 3,500, Limestone is one of the largest private colleges in South Carolina.

Limestone College is committed to the liberal arts and sciences and to educating men and women for leadership, service, and professional responsibility in the 21st century. While receiving a

Limestone President Dr. Walt Griffin, 1992-present.

strong foundation in the liberal arts, Limestone students generally major in fields directly related to career preparation—business administration, education, computer science, social work and physical education.

Limestone is privileged to have a distinguished and dedicated faculty, with 75 percent possessing the Ph.D. or other terminal degree in their academic disciplines. The student-faculty ratio is 12:1. At a time when many higher education institutions are increasingly relying on the services of part-time faculty, more than 90 percent of the daytime classes at Limestone are taught by full-time faculty and staff.

Limestone students are active in campus and community life through social, service, and athletic organizations. The Honors Program challenges those with exceptional intellectual ability; the Christian Education and Leadership Program serves those interested in deepening their religious commitment; and the Program for Alternative Learning Styles fosters academic success for those with documented learning disabilities.

Increased enrollments in recent years have produced financial recovery and growth. Limestone has had a balanced operating budget with a year-end surplus annually since 1992. This financial stability has allowed Limestone to complete major renovations of most campus buildings. Ten of the buildings on Limestone's front campus are on the National Register of Historic Places, along with the old quarry (now a lake) adjacent to the campus. Soon, the college will renovate Winnie Davis Hall of History, returning what was once the "jewel of the campus" to her former glory, with museum space for Southern history exhibits and classrooms for the rapidly expanding student population.

Dr. Madison Sarratt, Class of 1906, was Limestone's first male graduate and later served as vice chancellor of Vanderbilt University. Dr. Sarratt eloquently expressed the feelings of many whose lives have been touched by Limestone College when he wrote:

We like to think of education as a stream that flows from small beginnings to deep and wide and powerful rivers. If I should apply this to my own education, I would say that Limestone was the spring where my small river originated. I hope it is still flowing.

After 162 years, the spring of education continues to flow at Limestone College.

The men's lacrosse team celebrates their 2000 NCAA Division II National Title.

MORRIS COLLEGE

In 1874, in the years following the abolition of slavery, a group of African American men, united by their religious beliefs and faith, sought to create an organization that could assist in improving the condition of African American people. They received a charter from the State of South Carolina in 1877 to organize under the name of the Baptist Educational, Missionary and Sunday School Convention of South Carolina. The charter stated:

The object of this convention shall be to promote the cause of Christ, especially in South Carolina by establishing a Theological and Literary Institute for the training of young men for the ministry, and also for the education of our sons and daughters.

Even with the charter in hand, it would take 28 years, until 1905, for the organization, now known as the Baptist Educational and Missionary Convention of South Carolina, to find firm footing. Leaders met in Beaufort, South Carolina, and appointed a Committee of Twenty-Four to seek a location and build a college. The next year Dr. J. J. Durham was appointed educational secretary of the convention. He went on to become chairman and the leading voice in the work of the Committee of

Twenty-Four. In addressing the convention, he drew an analogy between the birth of a child and the birth of the proposed Baptist College. He summarized:

The conception has taken place. The idea has developed. The time of delivery is at hand. The woman is in travail. The birth pains are already severe. The doctor has been sent for. The midwife has done all she could do. The baby must be born, nourished, and nurtured. The time is now.

The Committee voted to name the new institution Morris College in honor of Reverend Frank Morris, a pioneer leader of the Rocky River Association. It then began to seek out the best location for the new school. The Committee considered several different options in Anderson, Gaffney, and Sumter, and initially voted to secure a 10-acre site in Anderson. However, when the Committee began its negotiation with trustees of the property in Anderson, there were differences that could not be resolved, and the Committee decided instead to accept an offer from the Wateree Upper Division for a 12-acre site in the City of Sumter. The Convention was then offered a favorable property trade, and thus Morris College finally found its permanent home on a 33-acre site adjacent to North Main Street. The school lies approximately 50 miles east of Columbia in the very center of the state of South Carolina.

In 1906 the Baptist Educational and Missionary Convention of South Carolina granted the authority to move

Partial view of campus in 1915.

forward with haste. By 1908 Morris College was finally established "for the Christian and Intellectual Training of Negro youth." This undertaking represented a heroic venture in higher education for members of society who previously had little or no opportunity to further their formal education. The majority of the "founding fathers" of Morris College were poor and without any formal learning, but they possessed an "unfaltering faith in God and a zeal to provide for others the educational opportunities they themselves were denied."

On April 12, 1911 the college received a certificate of incorporation from the state of South Carolina. Initially, Morris College provided schooling on the elementary, high school, and college levels. The college curriculum included programs in liberal arts, in "normal" education for the certification of teachers, and a theological program. In 1915 the bachelor of arts degree was conferred on the first two graduates. The institution discontinued its "normal" program in 1929, its elementary school in 1930, and its high school in 1946.

During 1930–1932, the school operated only as a junior college, but it resumed its full four-year program in 1933. The word "Negro" appearing in the original certificate of incorporation was eliminated on August 14, 1961, thereby opening the doors of Morris to students of all ethnic groups.

Morris College has more than justified the faith, the labors, and the sacrifices of its founding fathers. The services it has rendered have been extensive and beyond value. In the early decades of its history, Morris College provided elementary and high school training for Negro youth at a time when such opportunities were meager or nonexistent in many communities. From its beginning the college has been a center for training ministers and teachers for the pulpits and schools of the state and of the nation. The college is a historically Black institution offering educational opportunities to many low-income students who might not have the resources to attend college but are aided by the college's policy of maintaining some of the lowest tuition rates among all of the private colleges in South Carolina.

Morris operates as an accredited four-year college offering twenty-one academic degree programs. Presently, the college offers programs of study leading to the baccalaureate degree with major programs or major combination programs in a wide variety of subjects. The most prestigious and popular programs at the college include Business Administration, Biology, Criminal Justice, Mass Communications, Health Science, Organizational Management, Sociology, and Teacher Education. The Teacher Education program is rigorous; though many students declare this major in their first year, a challenging examination at the end of the sophomore year must be passed in order to continue in this program. In keeping with the school's original purpose, there is also a strong Pastoral Ministry program, which offers bachelor's degrees in both Pastoral Ministry and Christian Education. Students augment their Morris College education with real-world experience through the school's cooperative education program, which offers juniors and seniors paid internships at a variety of businesses and institutions.

In the 70th year of its history, on December 13, 1978, Morris College achieved the goal of full accreditation by the Commission on Colleges of the Southern Association of Colleges and Schools. On January 1, 1982 Morris College became the 42nd member of the United Negro College Fund, the

Dr. Luns C. Richardson, college president (left), with Dr. Bobby L. Brisbon during the college's special event to dedicate the Bobby Leroy Brisbon Curriculum Resource Room.

Graduates from the Class of 2007. Center is Tegan T. Foster, 2007 senior class president.

nation's largest and most successful black fund-raising organization. The college has embarked upon a new era of institutional improvements that has moved it further into the mainstream of American higher education and that has enabled it to render even better service to its students and to the community.

The school has a current enrollment of 1,000 with 700 students residing on campus. Students enjoy a rich cultural life at Morris College, with a wide offering of extracurricular activities in student government, sports, music, the arts, as well as active Greek-letter organizations. The school also offers an accelerated evening program for adult students, giving working adults who have already earned at least sixty college credits the opportunity to earn a bachelor's degree in as little as 18 months.

As an organization the college has made many important contributions to the local Sumter community. In 2006 the college received a grant of $600,000 from the U.S. Department of Housing and Urban Development to construct several new houses and to rehabilitate a number of existing houses in the North Sumter neighborhood adjacent to the college. Morris offers an active Service Learning program in which students from various classes engage in community service activities relating to the classes in which they are enrolled, and it places a number of its students to serve

Students from the Morris College Management Institute-Advance Program at the college's 96th Annual Baccalaureate Commencement Convocation held on May 5, 2007.

as interns in local businesses and agencies and as tutors in local public schools. The school also operates an annual Upward Bound Program that helps students in the public schools improve their learning skills and thus reduce dropout rates. It schedules a Middle School Visitation Day and a High School Visitation Day to encourage public school students to start thinking about and planning to pursue a college education.

The college sponsors a non-degree continuing theological education program for ministers at 14 sites throughout South Carolina. It provides one of its on-campus facilities free of charge for the use of the local Head Start program, and it makes other facilities available to local organizations, conventions and other groups to hold their meetings and conferences. It has carried out various health and wellness programs for residents of the community, and it operates a residential summer camp for children from across the state and another residential summer camp for teenage boys. It sponsors an annual three-day Christmas Holiday Basketball Tournament in which sixteen high school teams from across the state and beyond participate.

Morris College has had nine presidents in its history, and all have made distinctive contributions to the growth and development of the institution. However, two presidents of the college stand out above all others for both the length of their service to the college and for the significance of their accomplishments in promoting growth in programs, enrollment and facilities.

Dr. Odell R. Reuben came to the presidency in 1948 at the age of 30, the youngest chief executive the college has ever had. He was also notable for being the first African American to have earned a doctorate degree in religion from Duke University. As president, he expanded the curriculum, promoted faculty development, and established an affiliated School of Religion for the training of ministers. During his tenure, the college constructed a new Science Building, a general classroom building, a gymnasium, two new residence halls, a dining facility, and a Student Center. His death in 1970 ended 22 years of distinguished service to the college.

Dr. Luns C. Richardson became president in 1974, a position he continues to serve in to this day (2007). Dr. Richardson's period of service has seen some of the school's most significant accomplishments, including a doubling of the college's enrollment, the addition of many new academic programs, the achievement of accreditation by the Commission on Colleges of the Southern Association of Colleges and Schools, and the achieving of membership for the college in the United Negro College Fund. Another remarkable achievement of the Richardson era has been the addition of 212,625 square feet of newly constructed facilities to a campus that

The Adams-Daniels-McLester-Sanders Women's Residence Hall.

Morris College participates in the Hurricane Katrina relief effort.

contained only 154,369 square feet of facilities at the beginning of the era. With regard to this accomplishment, it has been said that Morris College is the newest 100-year-old college in the United States.

The growth of the college has been particularly helped since 1965 through funds received from the U.S. Department of Education under the Higher Education Act, student financial aid received from the federal and state governments, major contributions from member churches and associations of the Baptist Educational and Missionary Convention of South Carolina, funds received from the United Negro College Fund, and funds contributed by Morris College alumni.

One major obstacle that the college had to overcome in order to grow and prosper was to achieve regional accreditation. However, the standards of the accrediting agency were such that accreditation could not be achieved until the college replaced its inadequate library with a new facility at a cost of $2.5 million. Through the cooperative efforts of churches, alumni, and government agencies, the funds were raised, construction of the facility was initiated

and the college was awarded regional accreditation in 1978.

A second major obstacle was the product of Hurricane Hugo, which hit in September 1989, and was at that time the largest and most destructive hurricane ever to hit the United States. It struck the coast of South Carolina and moved in a direct line to Sumter where it tore the roof off of one residence hall, completely destroyed the gymnasium, and damaged so many other buildings that the college had to send all students home while massive efforts were made to get the school functioning again before the entire fall semester would be lost. By moving quickly to bring in a

number of temporary classroom buildings and clean up the campus, students were called back to the college only two weeks after they departed. The students returned with even greater resolve to make their college experience more meaningful, and they proudly wore new T-shirts that read, "I survived Hugo." With the scheduling of missed classes on Saturdays, the fall semester was fully saved, and no student failed to graduate on time because of the storm.

Indeed, Morris College has a longstanding tradition of overcoming obstacles. It has educated thousands of students who have carried out the college's motto: "Enter to Learn; Depart to Serve." They have served in numerous professional careers as lawyers, teachers, ministers, social workers, community action workers, health service workers, business persons, civil service administrators, military officers, accountants, college professors and more, and they are rendering service throughout South Carolina and the nation. During the 2007–2008 academic year, the college celebrates its 100th year of operation, and its legacy of service, leadership and excellence will continue to define the institution as it moves ahead to educate new generations of students.

Teacher Education candidate reads to students at the Wateree Head Start program in the Learning Resources Center during the college's observation of National Library Week and Week of the Young Child.

SOUTH CAROLINA STATE UNIVERSITY

Right in the heart of South Carolina, there is a thriving institution that has a long history of nurturing the leaders and teachers of the next generation. Committed to providing the highest order of undergraduate and graduate education that is affordable and accessible to every student, South Carolina State University continues a legacy of excellence in education that has spanned over a century.

South Carolina State University was founded in 1896 as the only public university for black students under the second Morrill Land Grant Act of 1890. Since that time, generations of young black students were given agricultural and mechanical training to help better both themselves and the South Carolina community. The commitment to education and teaching did not stop at the campus borders, however. Through the school's extension program, agents were sent to homes and farms to provide knowledge to families without the means to journey to the school.

As the school grew into the 20th century, academic offerings and facilities expanded. But, the school was not immune to the Great Depression, which caused the demise of different sections of the university. Nevertheless, the school weathered some of the hardest

The graduating class of 1913 and Reverend Bollie Levister sit on the steps of Morrill Hall.

times seen in the history of the nation, helped in part by New Deal programs, which aided in the creation of Wilkinson Hall, the university's first freestanding library building.

As a black university in the heart of the South, the school holds a unique place in the historic development of equal rights, often at the cost of the additional weight of ongoing adversity. In 1947 the U.S. Army created an

ROTC detachment at South Carolina State University, and enrollment was mandatory for all male students up until 1969. At the end of World War II, there was a boom in enrollment, thanks in part to the GI Bill. Though the expansion was positive, the school's graduate and law school programs were actually created in an effort to prevent black students from enrolling at the University of South Carolina and expand the institutional separate but equal agenda. The law program eventually closed in 1966 after the end of segregation at the University of South Carolina.

An unfortunate tragedy in 1968 underscored the continuing tension in

Left: Nine members of the early faculty of the college, circa 1901–1903. Shown are, from left to right (top row) Eugene F. Mikell, instructor in band and orchestra, employed 1897; at his elbow, Alice B. McCloud, instructor in English, employed in 1900; Lillian C. Mack, instructor in English, employed in 1901; and Johnson C. Whittaker, employed in 1900 as professor of mathematics and Commandant, providing instruction in military science, a state function of the land grant title of the school. Whittaker a native of Camden, had been among the first American of African descent to attend West Point Military Academy from 1877 to 1881, but had been wrongfully expelled and was posthumously awarded his commission in 1995 by President Bill Clinton. Shown on the bottom row, from left to right are Otis Cecil Davenport Council, assistant teacher (Model School), employed in 1896; Lousie B. Forham Holmes, instructor in art, employed in 1896; Julia A. McClain Douglass, instructor in kindergarten methods, employed in 1896; and Olive Saspostas. Sasportas had been admitted to the college as a senior on the first day of its opening and soon after her admission became an assistant instructor in English. Ms. Sasportas was the first person to receive a bachelor of arts degree from the Colored Normal, Industrial, Agricultural and Mechanical College of South Carolina.

the community. Four years after the Civil Rights Act of 1964, most public institutions and businesses had been desegregated. However, the Orangeburg All Star bowling alley still enforced segregation, spurring SC State students to stage a protest in front of the establishment. The first protest went without incident; the second night, however, 15 students were arrested. On the third evening, the protesters gathered on the campus of South Carolina State University. With tensions so high, things went completely awry when a highway patrolman fired his gun in the air. Other law enforcement officers began shooting into the crowd of students, with tragic results: three students were killed and another 27 were injured. This event is known as the Orangeburg Massacre. The tragedy is commemorated with a memorial plaza near the very front of the school campus.

Under the leadership of Dr. M. Maceo Nance, which spanned the late 1960s through the 1980s, the school underwent a dramatic evolution of campus facilities and academic offerings. New academic buildings were added as well as new residence halls, including Sojourner Truth Hall, which remains

Archway that once was adorned the entrance of campus.

the tallest building in Orangeburg County at 14 stories high. The university also made a unique addition with the I.P. Stanback Museum & Planetarium, the only such facility on a historically black university campus in the United States.

In 1986 Dr. Albert Smith succeeded Dr. Nance as president of the university. During Dr. Smith's tenure, the South Carolina State Assembly officially recognized the institution's university status. Dr. Smith continued to cultivate the university's academic programs, creating the Honors Program in 1988. In 1993 the university welcomed its first female president, Dr. Barbara Hatton, who, among other accomplishments, oversaw the expansion and beautification of the campus, from the plaza in front of the Student Union to the renovation of Oliver C. Dawson Bulldog Stadium, increasing the seating capacity to accommodate up to 22,000 fans. Dr. Leroy Davis began leading the university in its 100th year,

Students are hard at work in a Hodge Hall biology laboratory in the 1930s. They are working under the supervision of highly respected biologist James H. Birnie, who is standing to the left. Standing near the center in the background is T.J. Crawford, who spent nearly 70 years as a student, faculty member, and administrator at South Carolina State University.

The three young men who were killed in the Orangeburg Massacre—left to right: Delano Middleton, Samuel Hammond, and Henry Smith.

1996, and during his tenure, the school built a new Fine Arts Center.

South Carolina State University is now under the leadership of Dr. Andrew Hugine Jr., a dynamic and highly respected educator and administrator who earned his bachelor's degree in mathematics and his master's degree in higher education from SC State before pursuing his doctorate degree in philosophy at Michigan State University. In his time as a professor at SC State, he published five mathematics and pre-calculus college textbooks and was elected both Teacher of the Year and President of the Faculty Senate by his peers. Since 2003, the university has continued its evolution as a highest level academic institution under Dr. Hugine's lead.

South Carolina State University's academic curriculum is provided under three colleges and the university's School of Graduate Studies. The College of Business and Applied Professional Sciences aims to provide students practical skills as well as develop management and leadership qualities necessary to excel in the fields of business administration, accounting, agribusiness, economics, family and consumer sciences, health sciences, and military science. The College of Education, Humanities & Social Sciences is comprised of five departments that offer approximately 30 majors, many of which are offered in conjunction with

Coach Willie Jeffries, 1960s graduate, legendary football coach.

other departments of other colleges. The College of Science, Mathematics & Engineering Technology aims to foster an interdisciplinary approach to the sciences and prepare students to pursue graduate degrees in their respective fields. South Carolina State University has offered graduate studies since 1946. The very first graduate degree was a master of science in mathematics education conferred in 1948. Now the school offers 19 subjects of study under 12 degree programs.

South Carolina State University enrolls approximately 4,600 students each year, with 21 foreign countries represented among the diverse student body. Upon matriculation, students officially become SC State Bulldogs and proudly bear the school's blue and garnet colors. The school offers over 50 undergraduate and graduate majors, with unique courses of study such as undergraduate nuclear engineering and a master's program in transportation. A staff of approximately 750 contributes to the thriving academic environment at SC State, and the university's faculty is the most diverse in the state of South Carolina.

Students that have displayed high aptitude and achievement in high school or while at SC State can qualify for the university's Honor Program. GPA, advanced placement (AP) achievement, standardized test scores, and National Merit distinction are all considered for those seeking admission to this distinctive group. Increasing cognitive capabilities and critical thinking skills are priorities for Honors Program students in their first two years of undergraduate work while upperclassmen turn their focus toward in-depth studies in their major. Honors Program students can also qualify to graduate with departmental honors.

Students attend classes on a beautiful 160-acre campus. Those that live on-campus reside in modern, apartment-style housing facilities. Scholarships and financial aid are widely available to help students achieve their higher education goals. Those with good high school GPAs, class rank, and standardized test scores are eligible for full or partial scholarships. Other institutional scholarships, from the Presidential Scholarship for highly academically qualified students, as well as a host of other scholarships from ROTC and alumni groups around the region, are available to South Carolina State University students.

The university has an active athletic program, and is part of the National Collegiate Athletics Association (NCAA) Mid-Eastern Athletic Conference. Men's teams include basketball, football, track and field, cross country,

Football team of 1934.

tennis, and golf. Women's teams include basketball, bowling, cross country, golf, soccer, softball, track and field, tennis, and volleyball. The athletics department is focused on supporting the growth of student athletes, and therefore ranks academics as its number one priority for all participants. The Department of Athletics works hard to create the best sports teams and activities while nurturing the intellectual and social skills athletes will need to translate their athletic talents to leadership in their professional and personal pursuits later in life. The university believes that this is possible by building on the basics of discipline, sportsmanship, mutual respect, and fairness that sports instill.

The Army ROTC is still very active at SC State. The program has commissioned over 2,000 officers to date, and produced 13 Army generals. The detachment at South Carolina State University also has the distinction of producing the highest number of minority officers in the nation. The ROTC at SC State includes specialized organizations, such as the Advanced Course Training Club, National Society of Scabboard/Blade, and the National Society of Pershing Rifles.

Many other organizations thrive on campus as well. Student government is an important part of campus life, and SC State has an active Greek community, with four fraternities and four sororities for students to pledge and participate in. Departmental clubs and organizations also abound, giving students further opportunity to explore their areas of interest and develop ongoing personal and professional relationships that can help them in life beyond college.

Students can also get involved with advocacy organizations such as the NAACP, or make their voices heard through student-run media such as *The Collegian*, the campus newspaper, or WSSB, the school radio station, which is the most powerful college radio station in the state of South Carolina. Students can also explore artistic mediums of expression, with musical ensembles and choirs that include classical music through jazz in their repertoires. The university's Marching

Dr. Andrew Hugine, Jr., University president.

"101" Band (which actually includes approximately 300 members) is nationally known for its engaging and energetic performances at the school's sporting events and at parades and other functions. The band practices for hours on end to perfect their musical technique and intricate choreography and is very closely associated with the very identity of South Carolina State University. Their spirited performances are a

Marching 101 band.

highlight of any Bulldogs sporting event.

Beyond its service to its students, South Carolina State University seeks to always fulfill its higher purpose as a traditional land-grant institution to also provide research and outreach services to its community, the State of South Carolina, the nation, and the world. A wide variety of research projects and scientific endeavors are undertaken at the Research and Technology Center, which seeks to implement training methods for mathematical and scientific application with a special emphasis on the space sciences. The university's Research and Extension service is a multi-tiered organization that works to improve the quality of life for all people through research projects to advance agricultural techniques and technology as well as helping maximize community resources in areas of limited means across the state. There are also research facilities to examine better methods of transportation as well as the development of small businesses.

South Carolina State University has produced many notable alumni. Recently, SCSU graduate Donald W. Beatty was elected justice on the South Carolina Supreme Court, only the second black justice to be appointed since the Reconstruction era. Alumni James E. Clyburn (History, '61) is currently the Majority Whip for the United States House of Representatives, the third highest ranking member of the House, only the second African American to hold the title, and the very first South Carolinian. Pro football Hall of Famers Harry Carson of the New York Giants and Deacon Jones of the Los Angeles Rams, San Diego Chargers, and Washington Redskins are also notable graduates of SC State.

South Carolina State University meets the distinctive needs of the residents of South Carolina by providing top-notch yet affordable education that challenges students to expand their thinking and prepare them in for life in a global society, by retaining the character and traditions of a historically black institution, and introducing back to the community educated and enlightened leaders of tomorrow.

SC TECHNICAL COLLEGE SYSTEM

For more than 45 years, the SC Technical College System (the System) has been integral to South Carolina's economic development. Beginning as just a few Technical Education Centers, along with an innovative business start-up training group, the System has expanded to include 16 Technical Colleges—all of which are strategically located throughout the state to meet the identified economic needs of specific regions —and an internationally recognized customized start-up training division.

Governed by the South Carolina State Board for Technical and Comprehensive Education, the SC Technical College System offers diploma, degree, certificate and continuing education programs in hundreds of areas, ranging from allied health fields to automotive technology, paralegal training to air conditioning and refrigeration mechanics, and civil engineering technology to culinary arts.

In 1961 Governor Ernest Hollings appointed a legislative committee to create a training system that would attract new industry to the state. Soon after, the General Assembly created the South Carolina Advisory Committee for Technical Training, which included six governor-appointed members who rep-

Surgical Technology Lab, Health Sciences Building, Spartanburg Community College.

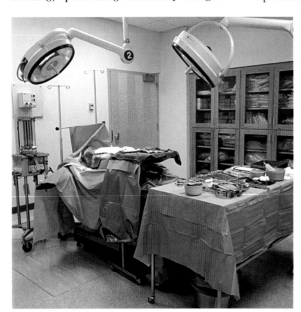

Dr. Barry Russell, SC Technical College System president.

resented each of the state's congressional districts, as well as the state Superintendent of Education and the director of the State Development Board. The first iteration of the System was established through the work of the Advisory Committee, in conjunction with the State Development Board.

The first step was the creation of the Special Schools Program, which offered start-up, short-term training for new and expanding industry in the state. In an effort to offer ongoing training to South Carolina residents interested in learning a marketable skill for immediate and future workforce needs, the Advisory Committee created a program that also included permanent technical education institutions. As part of the program, documented job needs guided training. The System was designed to include a minimum of 13 centers, with the goal of assuring that 95 percent of the state's population would be within a 25-mile radius of a center. Sponsoring counties provided land, facilities, a

portion of the operating costs, and local supervision of the centers, while the state was responsible for financial support for staff, equipment, and statewide coordination and technical support.

Within nearly 10 years of the first center's establishment, the 16-institution System was complete. Greenville Technical Education Center was the pioneer, opening in 1962. During its first year, 3,300 students enrolled. Four centers were in operation by 1963. Eleven centers were in operation by 1968 and a year later three former trade schools were merged into the System.

In 1972 the General Assembly established the State Board for Technical and Comprehensive Education as the overall governing body for the System. The State Board consists of 10 members appointed by the governor (one from each of the state's six congressional districts and four at-large), with the Secretary of Commerce and Superintendent of Education as *ex officio* members, The legislation establishing the State Board also authorized the addition of the associate in arts and associate in science degrees within the System. In 1976 the General Assembly passed legislation delegating primary responsibility for local governance and supervision of individual institutions to Area Commissions. The State Board's role in overall coordination and oversight, however, was maintained, creating the dual-governance structure that still exists today.

In 1974, in response to South Carolina's changing education needs and the expanded role of the System in meeting those needs, the State Board developed criteria for changing the names of the Technical Education Centers to Technical Colleges. One of these criteria was that the institution was required to become accredited by the Commission on Colleges of the Southern Association of Colleges and Schools. By 1980 all 16 were designated as Technical Colleges. By 1979 the System enrolled 35,000 students in degree and diploma programs in more than 150 career areas statewide (fall enrollment).

During the 1980s the emerging demand for technological expertise in the workforce prompted the System to

Technical College of the Lowcountry students get experience in reassembling a computer in a computer servicing course, one of the required courses for earning an associate degree in industrial technology.

create *Design for the '80s*. As part of the plan, resource centers were created as catalysts for economic and curriculum development as well as local points for expertise in advanced technology. The seven specialized resource centers focused on computer, robotics, advanced machine tool, microelectronics, advanced office occupations, tourism and electromechanical maintenance.

Toward the end of the 1980s 42,000 students were enrolled in credit programs at the SC Technical College System and 85,000 participated in its continuing education program.*

Combining technology and education, *Innovative Technical Training* (ITT) was developed in 1989. ITT enabled the Technical Colleges to keep pace with changes in technology, especially information technology applications, during the 1990s. New statewide two-way interactive audio/video distance education and video conferencing capa-

bilities were implemented, and Internet-based courses and the use of Internet in the classroom become more common. Currently ITT focuses on evaluating emerging technology trends, developing pilots and ongoing innovations that provide the foundation for future System-wide planning

By 1999 the System was enrolling nearly 62,000 students in credit programs and 129,000 in its continuing education program.*

In 2002 the South Carolina legislature enacted a law authorizing lottery proceeds to fund financial assistance programs for students attending the

state's colleges and universities. In 2005–06, approximately one in every three students enrolled in the System utilized Lottery Tuition Assistance (LTA).

When the South Carolina General Assembly passed the *Education and Economic Development Act* (EEDA) in 2005, the Technical Colleges responded. The purpose of EEDA is to increase high school graduation rates and help students experience a seamless transition to post-secondary education. One way the Technical Colleges are supporting EEDA implementation is by partnering with South Carolina school districts to train career development facilitators for middle and high schools. Today the Technical Colleges continue to build strong relationships with these educational institutions to close skill gaps. The System is proactively working with K–12 education institutions as part of the EEDA initiative, now renamed *Personal Pathways to Success*, to ensure that students have accurate information about careers and programs at the Colleges.

In 2003 the Special Schools Program transformed its process, marking that transformation with the adoption of a new name. The Center for Accelerated Technology Training (CATT), through its readySC™ programs, partners with individual Technical Colleges, the South Carolina Department of Commerce,

Enoree Building

local developers and regional economic development alliances to restructure and streamline the start-up workforce training delivery process for new and expanding South Carolina business and industry. Since the inception in 1961 of the System's specialized training division, it has provided customized education and training to more than 230,000 South Carolinians and more than 1,800 businesses.

The CATT/Dreamliner 787 Project, which was created in February 2005, is a good example of the overall CATT process. Vought Aircraft Industries was in need of high caliber aerospace grade employees who could produce quality materials that met Boeing and Federal Aviation Administration (FAA) requirements. To address this need, a CATT team—including personnel from one of the System's Technical Colleges—worked with Vought engineers, technicians and trainers to gain a strong understanding of the company's processes, business objectives and culture, then designed curriculum that reflected the Boeing and the FAA product requirements. This approach has proven successful, providing Vought with qualified employees, CATT and the System with a satisfied customer, and South Carolina with a strong pool of workers in a key economic cluster.

The SC Technical College System prides itself on remaining abreast of cur-

Welding at York Technical College.

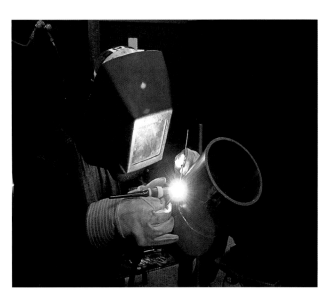

rent and future workforce needs and continues to adjust courses of study and develop projects to meet these local and state needs. Radiation protection technology, crime scene investigation and biotechnology are just a few of the recent program additions at the System. The System recently created an Allied Healthcare Initiative to address ongoing workforce shortages within the healthcare industry. The goal of the initiative is to increase the number of nursing and allied health graduates by both increasing program capacity and/or improving program retention. Initiative activities include broadening student learning experiences through innovative simulations and web-based activities, and updating the physical classroom and lab environments. At the end of the 2005–06 school year, almost one-third of the graduates from the Technical Colleges were from the Health Sciences. Similarly, two-thirds of the new associate degree programs approved for Colleges for spring and fall 2007 focused on healthcare.

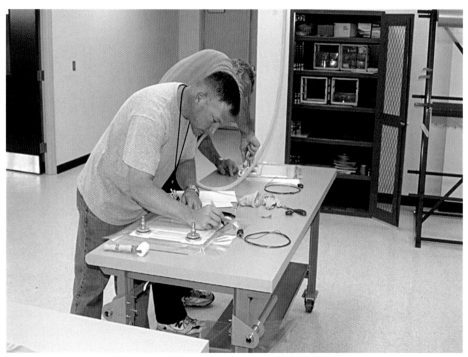

CATT Lab Training for Vought at Trident Technical College.

The SC Technical College System continues to support the appropriate use of instructional technology for course delivery. A growing number of students are completing their course-work through online instruction, taking advantage of its flexibility. Many courses have been developed as "hybrids," where some course content is delivered online and some is delivered in a lab (or classroom). Most hybrid courses require less time in the physical classroom than traditional courses.

Today the System is thriving and continues to serve as an important driver for South Carolina's economy. More than half of South Carolinians enrolled as undergraduates at a public college or university in the state attend one of the Technical Colleges. In terms of undergraduate enrollment, three of South Carolina's top five public colleges and universities in 2005–06 were part of the SC Technical College System.

Many studies have examined the future job market and the educational training needed for those jobs. Specifically, a 2001 state report indicated that approximately 65 percent of jobs of the future will require an associate degree or advanced training—exactly the type

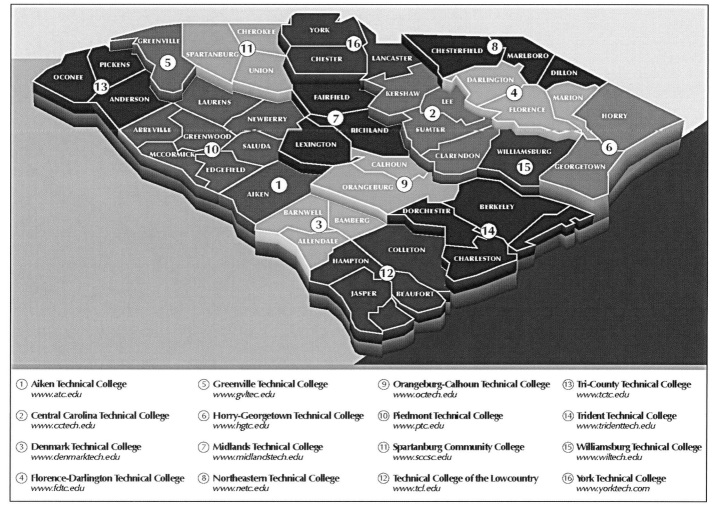

① **Aiken Technical College**
www.atc.edu

② **Central Carolina Technical College**
www.cctech.edu

③ **Denmark Technical College**
www.denmarktech.edu

④ **Florence-Darlington Technical College**
www.fdtc.edu

⑤ **Greenville Technical College**
www.gvltec.edu

⑥ **Horry-Georgetown Technical College**
www.hgtc.edu

⑦ **Midlands Technical College**
www.midlandstech.edu

⑧ **Northeastern Technical College**
www.netc.edu

⑨ **Orangeburg-Calhoun Technical College**
www.octech.edu

⑩ **Piedmont Technical College**
www.ptc.edu

⑪ **Spartanburg Community College**
www.sccsc.edu

⑫ **Technical College of the Lowcountry**
www.tcl.edu

⑬ **Tri-County Technical College**
www.tctc.edu

⑭ **Trident Technical College**
www.tridenttech.edu

⑮ **Williamsburg Technical College**
www.wiltech.edu

⑯ **York Technical College**
www.yorktech.com

of education that the SC Technical College System offers. "We're in the right place at the right time," says Dr. Barry Russell, SC Technical College System president.

The economic impact of the SC Technical College System is felt statewide as well as on a local level. The leadership at the System continuously looks at the overall opportunities and needs of the state, while also remaining in touch with businesses and employers in each community in an effort to provide education and training that meets their specific industry needs. Additionally, the Technical Colleges are collaborating with the state's research universities on ways to effectively commercialize South Carolina's innovations in South Carolina. Much of the SC Technical College System's growth can be attributed to these continued relationships on the state and local levels.

Perhaps one of the best ways to describe the impact of the Technical Colleges is through the success story of a graduate. After dropping out of high school and having a child at 16, Valerie Ramsey wanted a better life for herself and her daughter, but didn't have the resources to find it—until she discovered Tri-County Technical College, part of the System. As part of the Clerical Certificate program at Tri-County Technical College, she participated in on-the-job training at Clemson University, where she soon was hired. While working at the university, she went back to Tri-County during her lunch hour and at nights and earned her associate degree in 1988. Now celebrating more than 30 years of employment at Clemson University, Dr. Valerie Ramsey is the first alumna in the history of Tri-County Technical College to serve on its Area Commission.

The basic philosophy of the SC Technical College System has remained the

SC Technical College System Colleges and Service Areas.

same since its beginnings—to provide a variety of programs and services that promote human resource development in support of the state's economic development. This philosophy has been effective—a 2005 economic impact study showed that every dollar the state invested in the SC Technical College System in fiscal year 2004 provided a return of $12.10.

In 2005–06, the System enrolled nearly 235,000 students in its credit and continuing education programs.

Building on its past, but with an eye always to the needs of the future, the SC Technical College System is committed to fostering the expansion and success of the South Carolina economy for generations to come.

*credit numbers are derived from fall enrollment; continuing education numbers cover an entire academic year.

WOFFORD COLLEGE

Six generations of students have graduated from Spartanburg's Wofford College since it opened in the fall of 1854. Always comparatively small in size, this Methodist-related liberal arts college has played an impressively large role in terms of service to church, state, and nation. Graduates live in all 50 states and more than 25 foreign countries. Of the 14,260 living Wofford alumni in 2005, 1,148 were presidents or owners of corporations or organizations; 783 practiced medicine, dentistry or other healthcare professions; and 818 were attorneys or judges, including three of five justices of the South Carolina Supreme Court.

The college's founder, The Reverend Benjamin Wofford, was convinced by a friend to endow an institution of higher education rather than scatter his fortune among multiple charities. His bequest of $100,000 was one of the largest gifts to higher education in antebellum America. The college cornerstone was laid on July 4, 1851, and the college's early growth mirrored that of Spartanburg, which was prospering in the 1850s. Rather than prepare graduates for particular careers, the college's goal was to instill in them moral values and familiarity with the intellectual world of the mid-19th century.

Surviving the Civil War and Reconstruction solely because of the dedication of the faculty and the commitment of South Carolina Methodists to the institution, Wofford began to prosper as upstate South Carolina emerged as a railroad and textile center late in the 19th century.

Through the 1870s and 1880s, students were allowed to substitute modern languages for the classical languages

Early Wofford "Terrier" athletics teams were inspired by this mascot, Jack. The photo shows the 1909 baseball team.

required for a bachelor of arts degree, reflecting a national trend to emphasize the study of English language and literature. In 1887, seeking to improve the qualifications of entering first-year students, the board of trustees founded the Wofford Fitting School. For a number of years around 1900, a few women were admitted as commuting students and subsequently graduated. However, in the 1920s, the preparatory school was discontinued and an all-male admissions policy was reinstituted, continuing until 1971.

In 1902 Henry Nelson Snyder became president and remained in office for 40 eventful years as Wofford became established as one of the South's most respected colleges. At the height of the Great Depression, some faculty members worked without pay for seven months. Undaunted, the Wofford community focused on securing a chapter of Phi Beta Kappa, the prestigious liberal arts honor society. This goal was attained in 1941, marking the first charter granted to an independent college in South Carolina.

For a brief period in World War II, the Wofford campus was turned over to the Army Air Corps and used for cadet pre-flight training. Meanwhile, students and alumni served in the military all around the world. At least 73 of them died in the conflict. After the war, Dr. Walter K. Greene of the class of 1903 succeeded President Snyder and

Built in the Italianate style between 1851 and 1854 and still the academic hub of the campus, "Old Man" was restored inside and out in the early 2000s.

developed a new master plan for "The Wofford of Tomorrow." For example, in 1948, Wofford began its "King Teen" program, one of the first merit academic scholarship competitions in the country.

In the 1950s and 1960s, progress continued under the presidential administrations of Dr. Francis Pendleton

Leonard Auditorium, inside Main Building, spring 2007.

Named in honor of donors Jimmy and Marsha Gibbs, Wofford's beautiful football stadium is the home of each December's Shrine Bowl of the Carolinas.

Gaines Jr., Dr. Charles F. Marsh, and Paul Hardin III. It was Gaines who persuaded Spartanburg textile executive Roger Milliken to join the board of trustees, beginning a close and successful relationship that continued into the new millennium. During Marsh's presidency, the campus was transformed by the opening of new residence halls and the Milliken Science Building. A new 4-1-4 calendar, with its pioneering "Interim" term was introduced in 1967–1968. Under Hardin's leadership, there were many changes in student life, particularly in the adoption of the "Code of Students Rights and Responsibilities." The groundwork was also laid for the appointment of women to the faculty and for the admission of women as full-time students.

The year 1972 marked the beginning of the 28-year presidency of Dr. Joab M. Lesesne Jr., along with a $400,000 grant from the National Endowment for the Humanities to fund graduation requirement changes, new majors, seminar humanities courses, and reading and writing laboratories. Art and art history, music, theater and basketball, football and soccer—women's athletics as well as men's—all began to blossom at Wofford. In 1989 Wofford received a Franklin W. Olin Foundation grant of $5.5 million for a high-tech classroom building.

Jerry Richardson, owner and founder

of the NFL's Carolina Panthers, is a 1959 Wofford graduate. In 1995 Wofford became the team's summer training camp home. Since then, beautiful new athletic facilities such as Gibbs Stadium, Russell C. King Field, and the Reeves Tennis Center have made it possible for the college to compete as a member of NCAA Division I. The Terriers won Southern Conference championships in football and baseball in the early 2000s.

Wofford's tenth president, Dr. Benjamin Bernard Dunlap, took office in July 2000. He immediately challenged the faculty to update and enhance the curriculum with such innovations as "The Novel Experience." First-year students read a selected novel over the summer and then write an essay on a specific topic related to the novel. Seminar groups meet at various downtown restaurants, and the book's author visits Wofford to join in the discussions.

Wofford also has participated with 18 other colleges and universities in a National Learning Communities Project designed to strengthen innovative approaches to college teaching and learning. New facilities were added to the campus with the Roger Milliken Science Center and the beautifully renovated "Old Main."

Student housing was transformed by the development of the award-winning Wofford Village, and Wofford students have provided many hours of weekly support to Spartanburg area human service programs.

Today, Wofford offers academic majors in accounting, art history, biology, business economics, chemistry, computer science, Chinese language and culture, economics, English, finance, French, German, government, history, humanities, intercultural studies, intercultural studies for business, mathematics, philosophy, physics, psychology, religion, sociology, Spanish, and theatre. It also offers pre-professional programs in education, engineering, medical law, ministry and veterinary science.

Wofford is one of the few four-year institutions in the southeastern United States founded before the American Civil War and still operating on its original campus. Its motto, adopted in the 1850s, continues to inspire students: *Intaminatis Fulget Honoribus*—"Shining with Untarnished Honor."

A computer science class taught by Dr. Angela Shiflet.

BON SECOURS ST. FRANCIS HEALTH SYSTEM

Some things never change. It is true that the brightly lit and sparkling modern facilities of Bon Secours St. Francis today bear not the slightest resemblance to the charming, but somewhat dark halls of the Emma Booth Memorial Hospital built in 1921 in Greenville, South Carolina. It is true that the gleaming space-age technology of medicine today would flabbergast the humble Franciscan Sisters of the Poor who acquired the hospital in 1931. And the huge array of medical specialists differs dramatically from the small teams of Franciscan Sisters, nurses and doctors who cared for patients nearly a century ago.

But some things truly never change. The driving forces and core values of the Bon Secours St. Francis Health System in the 21st century remain remarkably unchanged from those of the founding leaders. Those values of utterly limitless compassion for every patient, strictest adherence to quality standards, and visionary leadership were present from the very beginning.

St. Francis began as the Emma Booth Memorial Hospital. The hospital was built in 1921, and entrusted to the Salvation Army. The core values were apparent from the start. Compassion and eagerness to care for all, quality standards, and visionary leadership are hallmarks of the Salvation Army today. But the hospital's destiny was not to be with the Salvation Army. Instead, an

The collaborative leadership style of St. Francis was pivotal in the development of Greenville County's first residential hospice house.

Diminutive in size, but not in courage and compassion, Franciscan Reverend Sisters Mary Alacoque and Aniceta, traveled to Greenville to establish St. Francis Hospital in 1932.

energetic young physician, Dr. Charles Wyatt, and the Right Reverend Bishop Walsh, the presiding Catholic Bishop of South Carolina, traveled to Cincinnati to the Franciscan Sisters of the Poor to convince the sisters to come to South Carolina to take over the hospital. It was to be. In 1932 more than 6,000 people attended the dedication of the St. Francis Hospital.

Compassion: The following decades were marked by remarkable accomplishments. Physical growth in the number of hospital beds reflected growth of the community and widening need for services from surrounding counties. Additionally, advances in the practice of medicine,

technology, and pharmaceuticals resulted in a burgeoning need for outpatient surgical, diagnostic and wellness services. Growth and change in facilities, processes, and sophistication has been relentless. But, again some things never change.

The limitless compassion that drove the decision to build the hospital continued to characterize the care both within and outside its walls. In the earliest days of 1932, a remarkable Franciscan sister, Sister Dympna, became one the earliest night supervisors. For 26 years, she quietly walked the halls of the hospital, slipping into rooms to comfort those who could not sleep or to pray for those sleeping. Her gentle touch and tender words calmed hundreds of patients over those years. Today, those values of gentle, unobtrusive caring for the needs of the whole person are addressed a little differently, but just as compassionately. Patients still receive that extra measure of attention and care at St. Francis. Patients enjoy soothing music therapy, massage, or spiritual counseling to ease minds and souls as pressing physical needs are addressed. Quiet and serene chapels at the two main hospitals provide for moments of spiritual respite, renewal and comfort for patients and families.

The extra measure of attentiveness has hard, quantifiable benefits in patient satisfaction. It is no accident that rigorous third party research shows that St. Francis consistently receives the highest levels of patient satisfaction

The rendering for the new Millennium campus looks more like a college than a hospital. Every aspect of the design, with it generous green spaces and friendly neighborhood feel, is based upon best practices research linked to quality clinical outcomes.

scores among all hospitals in the nation. Not surprisingly, the care and attentiveness of patients is equally important to physicians. St. Francis receives rankings among the best in the nation for physician perceptions of quality of care.

Walls can not contain the compassion of the St. Francis board, physicians, and staff. The caring of St. Francis has always extended well beyond the walls of the buildings into the most remote corners of the community. In 1937 the Franciscan Sisters began a tradition of gathering toys and filling stockings for dozens of children with little hope of Christmas cheer. That tradition of yesteryear has evolved into the annual Christmas tree lighting, a cherished tradition of family-oriented holiday events that benefits the St. Francis Foundation and provides cheer for thousands of Greenville families today.

The thirties, forties and early fifties were marked by the dominant textile heritage of mill villages and . . . many families without cars. It was a sense of compassion and leadership that led St. Francis to provide the first ambulance in Greenville County in 1956. That compassionate reaching out has never been stronger. But it is also ever-chang-

ing. Working closely with the United Way and needs assessment of the community, St. Francis has carefully considered its capacity along with the most pressing needs of the community in remarkably responsible stewardship. St. Francis was among the first hospitals in the state to provide a mobile "Health Express," a clinic on wheels that provided screenings throughout rural and urban corners in the county. As community and free medical clinics reduced that need, St. Francis reallocated resources to provide the first mobile dental clinic in the Upstate.

Perhaps the value of compassion has never been more apparent than the work

of St. Francis to collaborate with Greenville Technical College, Greenville Hospital System, the Hospice House Board, and hundreds of community leaders to build Greenville County's first and only residential hospice house. Some things never change. In many communities, it would have been unthinkable to have competing health systems collaborate for the greater good of the community. Not so here. St. Francis has always sought to take into consideration the needs of the community as a whole. At St. Francis, the compassion for each and every patient, and addressing needs for each person as an individual, transcends the decades.

Quality: A second value that endures is a relentless focus on quality. It was Sister Bernadine, a deceptively gentle and incredibly tough leader who clearly understood the need for a new hospital as the original building began quite literally to burst at the seams. She worked relentlessly and tirelessly from 1964 until the new hospital's dedication in 1971. Her hospital would be different from nearly all others in the Southeast. It was one of the first hospitals with all private

Compassion at St. Francis has never been contained by the walls of the hospital. The St. Francis mobile "Health Express" provides dental care throughout the upstate. To be "good help to those in need" speaks to the importance of compassion that has never been stronger.

rooms in the region. Many do not know that wards, with 2 or more beds per room, persisted in hospitals in the U.S. even in the late 1990s. Today, evidenced-based medicine has shown conclusively that private rooms lead to better clinical outcomes.

That foresight and risk-taking attitude to achieve quality of care might be attributed, in part, to the historic appreciation for individual talent and potential that bucked conventional sex, gender, and ethnicity rules of leadership.

"What I find remarkable about St. Francis is the utter and complete blindness to age, ethnicity, or gender in seeking the best and brightest for our workforce. Perhaps a factor is that our beloved Sister Bernadine, a female CEO already 65 when she arrived in Greenville in 1964, accomplished so much. That solid tradition of belief in the capacity of the individual, completely free of prejudices enables us to consistently garner top clinical and support staff that leads to the highest quality care. While we are proud of the fact that prestigious groups, AARP, South Carolina Chamber of Commerce and Martin Luther King Dream Achievers, give us top state and regional recognition for our diversity, what really counts is the quality of care for

The historic and relentless pursuit of quality is evidenced by the fact that orthopedic services at St. Francis have been recognized as number one in South Carolina for four years in a row.

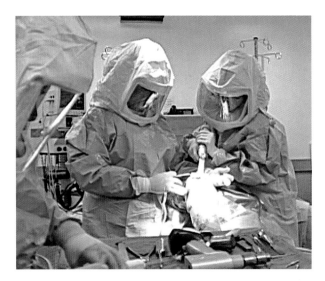

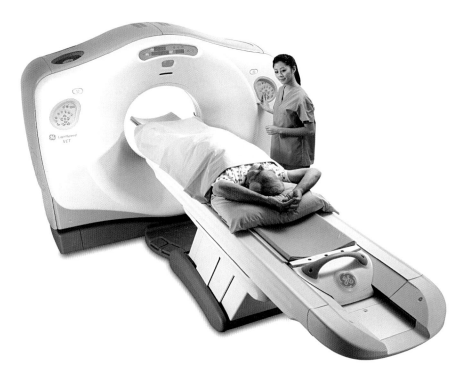

A tradition of leadership and willingness to take risks made the decision to invest in the 64 slice CT an easy one. Courtesy, Greenville News

our patients. And, I firmly believe that it is our tradition of respect for each employee and his or her contribution that enables us to deliver outstanding clinical care. Diversity is just a smart business decision." explains Marsh Collins, Board Chairman, St. Francis.

The sheer number and frequency of clinical quality awards that place St. Francis among the best hospitals in the nation for overall inpatient care and specialized areas such as heart or orthopedic care is amazing for a community hospital. The focus on quality so often recognized has deep historic tap roots. It was Sister Clarita who led the charge for St. Francis to establish the first women's hospital in South Carolina. In the 1960s, new approaches to obstetrics indicated that maternity patients had an easier time and recovered more quickly when labor, delivery and recovery took place in a single room. St. Francis was the one of the first hospitals in the state to offer this innovation.

In the last decades of the 20th century, St. Francis would continue to forge new ground with

remarkable new leadership. The Franciscan Sisters sought a perfect fit for managing all hospitals. They found a perfect match in core values of compassion, leadership and focus on quality in Bon Secours Health System, Inc. (BSHSI). This remarkable Catholic health system include 20 acute-care hospitals, one psychiatric hospital, and 6 long-term care facilities, numerous ambulatory sites, 6 assisted living facilities, 2 retirement communities, home healthcare services and hospices. These facilities are all dedicated to the Sisters' mission of providing "Good Help to Those in Need."

This new and dynamic leadership expanded care to the community by establishing home care services, a cancer care center and a heart center. Offering services has never been enough for St. Francis. Each of these new areas grew quickly to serve a growing number of patients and quickly achieve coveted third party awards for quality. Today St. Francis home health services are recognized as a "Top Elite 25," and the cancer center includes the only accredited bone marrow transplant program in Upstate South Carolina. HealthGrades recognized St. Francis heart surgery in the top 5 percent of all hospitals in the nation. Additionally, overall orthopedic services are ranked number one in South Carolina for four consecutive years in a row.

Leadership: It is impossible to consider leadership in a vacuum. The values of compassion and quality are all inexorably intertwined with leadership. The tradition of forward-thinking and risk taking associated with being the first to provide an ambulance in 1956, the first hospital to provide private rooms in 1971, and the first hospital to invest in a woman's hospital with every aspect of care dedicated to the special needs of women. It was leadership that enabled St. Francis to transfer sponsorship from the Franciscan Health Partnership to Bon Secours Health System in 2000.

Throughout the decades, St. Francis leaders continuously evidenced a tough pragmatism necessary to make the business decisions that provide foundation for excellence in patient care. That willingness and commitment to take risks in new approaches to care that enhance comfort or clinical outcomes is only possible because St. Francis

The bright smile and warm touch of a St. Francis home health nurse reassures an elderly patient.

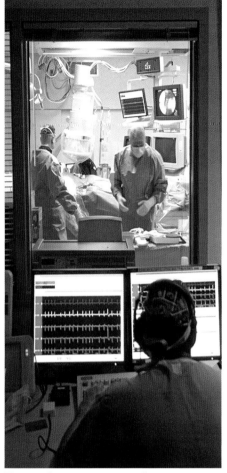

The dazzling array of technology in the cardiac cath lab would flabbergast Sisters of the early 20th century, but they would be right at home with the patient-centered care. Courtesy, Greenville News

leadership is, and always has been, visionary. Other more recent "firsts" include the first digital mammogram, rapidly becoming the gold standard for comfort and accuracy in mammogram readings. Another significant first is the 64 slice CT, a scanner that allows diagnosis in a number of areas to leap ahead of earlier technology in the precision of readings that help with precision of diagnosis and treatment.

There are books and books on leadership style. The themes in the leaders of St. Francis across all decades are themes of respect for the individual. Whether it is the patient, the attending physician, or partners in the community, St. Francis can better lead because St. Francis listens better. A second theme is collaboration. From the earliest time, St. Francis leaders showed a willingness to seek out the best thinking and greater good in collaborations. Examples abound. Collaboration with a competitor to fill the pressing need in Greenville for a residential hospice house is unique. Another great example is how St. Francis sought out a relationship with one of the top five heart centers in the entire nation to develop standards, protocols and training for cardiovascular care. The collaboration paid off with St. Francis quickly achieving outcomes that placed it among the top 5 percent of all cardiovascular hospitals in the nation.

The most recent example of bold collaborative leadership is that St. Francis sought out the most prestigious healthcare architect in the world with a special expertise in "evidence-based" design. This concept will allow St. Francis to build its new hospital on the Millennium campus with every single detail based upon greatest comfort, cost-effectiveness, and best clinical outcomes.

"The field of healthcare will continue with relentless advances in technology and clinical protocols. A century from today, we will smile at our quaint approach to medicine, but we will take great pride that our approach will still be based on compassion, quality and leadership,"—Valinda Rutledge, CEO, St. Francis Health Care System.

CARTER GOBLE LEE

In the heart of Columbia, South Carolina there is a company that is sought out by organizations from the United States and abroad for its sophisticated skills and planning savvy. In its more than 30 years advising clients worldwide on building and facilities planning, architectural design, project management, and facilities maintenance, Carter Goble Lee (CGL) has grown from a three-person operation to a multi-company presence respected the world over.

As a multi-faceted consulting firm, Carter Goble Lee brings top-of-the-line insight to its clients, guiding them from the planning phases of large-scale facilities all the way through subsequent maintenance. It is this signature ability to efficiently and systematically create order that makes governments as far away as Singapore, Ireland, and the United Arab Emirates seek out the advice of Carter Goble Lee.

While there are many consulting firms that cover any one of these areas of expertise, there aren't many, if any, that provide clients with such a full

CGL served as the planning and programming consultant for a unified communications center in the District of Columbia, establishing an operational and spatial basis for improving effectiveness and responsiveness of emergency services through co-location of critical communication functions. The UCC opened in September 2006. (Project Architect: DMJM Design)

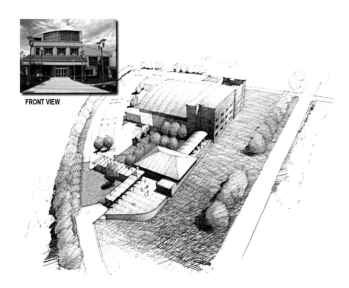

FRONT VIEW

CGL's First Program Management Project: Built in 1994, CGL served as the planning consultant, programmer, and program/construction manager for this 800-bed high-rise detention facility in downtown Arlington, Virginia. The facility is a part of the Arlington County justice complex, including court and law enforcement facilities. (Project Architect: Hansen Lind Meyer)

spectrum of services, from conceptual planning to full maintenance of a completed structure. This is where Carter Goble Lee has distinguished itself, particularly in its work with local, state, and foreign governments. Established in 1974 by Stephen Carter, who was very shortly joined by partner Robert Goble, the company initially sought to help clients interface with architects. "The client would have a need, but they wouldn't know how to define it in spatial terms, in design and function," company founder

Stephen Carter explained. As time passed and the company's experience grew, it added comprehensive services to become a turn-key operation. "We still remain planning focused," Carter continued, "But now we've expanded our services to meet our clients' needs."

Carter Goble Lee is comprised of four distinct companies with differing but interrelated focuses. *Comprehensive planning* is available to help clients uncover what their building and planning needs actually are and create a systematic plan to accomplish these goals. *Architectural design* is also available to create the blueprints to move ahead with either a new structure or renovation. *Program management* brings all of these components into play by managing the construction phase of a project, with CGL stepping in as the client's advocate and acting as the single contact source for all contractors, architects, and other players involved in putting a facility together. *Facility management* takes over once the building is up and running and maintains all security, energy systems, and other building needs in the most efficient manner possible.

When a client works with CGL, the project may be focused in one of CGL's four companies, or transverse a few or all the specialties offered. "Our business is very client focused," explains Carter, noting that one of Carter Goble Lee's six principals always works directly with the client throughout the working relationship. "This ensures that projects are being executed on time and to specification. By having a principal personally oversee each project, clients can feel confident that responsibility will be reflected from the top, down."

As the 20th century made way for the 21st, technological capabilities have opened up channels of travel and communication worldwide. While this has led to amazing innovations and changes, it has also led to more choices, options, and possibilities than ever imagined. Simple projects have now become complex problems, even before they pass the planning stages. With so many complicated components, once straightforward projects such as prisons and courthouses have now become logistical and safety conundrums. This modern reality has made the services of Carter Goble Lee all the more valuable.

"It is a complicated world," Stephen Carter agrees, "But, really, consultants love crisis. In our market area, we feel we are good at helping government make order out of chaos."

Working with various governments over the decades has given Carter Goble Lee valuable experience in this sector, along with building the company's reputation as a secure, go-to organization for all levels of government planning. Carter notes that these working relationships are some of the most challenging and rewarding, given that Carter Goble Lee is charged with strategizing how to build and maintain public facilities that will be aesthetic, secure and long-lasting while limited to a modest public budget. This is especially true with correctional facilities, one of Carter Goble Lee's fortes. Penal institutions are not generally given top priority for public spending, yet require thoughtful planning and maintenance in order to fully serve their purpose.

"Because we work largely for government, and government has limited

resources, and those resources are yours and mine, so to speak, we are very conscious that it is the taxpayers' money that we are spending," says Carter. In order to maximize these funds, it is paramount that Carter Goble Lee be the best in the field.

As a consulting firm, the company is only as valuable to its clientele as the advice it can provide. Its experts and consultants are in effect the company's "product" and are therefore a most valued asset at CGL.

A unique challenge that the company faces is finding and maintaining its talented workforce. Carter Goble Lee consultants are expected to not only know all of the relevant laws in the given jurisdiction and come up with efficient and effective solutions, often on a tight

2007 Project: Rendering of detainee annex to the central court complex in Abu Dhabi, UAE designed by Carter Goble Lee. The annex design accommodates 1,000 remand prisoners, and includes an underground tunnel system for transfer of prisoners between the two facilities.

budget, but are also away from home and on the go most of the time. "Our people spend hundreds and hundreds of hours away from home, they are constantly traveling," said Carter, pointing out that this type of jet setting, dashing from one meeting to the next, is not always glamorous. It is therefore critical that a workplace balance be struck.

"We are a consulting service," Stephen Carter reiterates. "The most valuable resource we have is going home at the end of the day. What's in their minds is our product, so we realize we must take care of our people." This means that staff integrity, happiness, and balance is vital at Carter Goble Lee. The fact that the average staff tenure is over ten years long is a point of pride.

Having earned the trust and respect of governmental clients near and far, Carter Goble Lee is poised to continue growing and advising clients around the globe. "Governments are looking for people that can help resolve conflict—how you can use limited resources and resolve a problem, getting different points of view brought together toward a common resolution," says Stephen Carter. "And that is one of the things we're quite good at."

In 1993, CGL was engaged to work with the Architect of the Capitol to develop a visionary master plan for the future of the US House Office Buildings in Washington, DC. Shown here is the 2050 Vision Plan of the South Capitol Area. (Project Architect: Wallace Roberts & Todd, LLC)

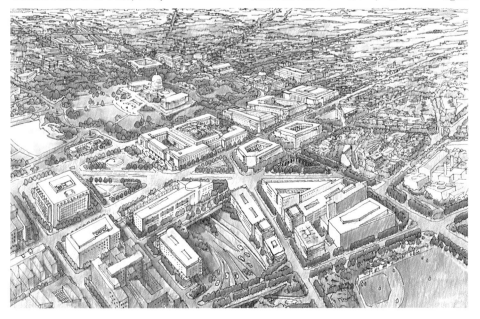

CHARLESTON METRO CHAMBER OF COMMERCE

People often think of a local chamber of commerce solely as a place to get a city map or to learn about the local weather. Having grown to more than 5,000 individual members who represent 2,300 businesses and to 40 staff members—it's clear that there's more going on at the Charleston Metro Chamber of Commerce than what most people expect. Founded on December 9, 1773, at what was Mrs. Swallows' Tavern on Broad Street, the Charleston Metro Chamber is the oldest, continually operating municipal chamber in the U.S. Among its many distinctions, it was named, by the U.S. Chamber of Commerce, a "Best Practices Model" in 2006 for its human resources management operation, one of only 29 Five Star Chambers among the almost 7,000 chambers in the country, and the "Best Overall Operation of Any Participating Chamber" in an American Chamber of Commerce Executives Association (ACCE) study of operational performance in 2006. The ACCE also named the Charleston Metro Chamber as one of three finalists for Chamber of Commerce of the Year Award in 2007.

The Charleston Metro Chamber has been making enormous strides in

Local business and military leaders annually step into the shoes of local principals to get "real-life" exposure to the challenges they face.

Opening page from one of the earliest records found for America's oldest chamber. Courtesy, South Carolina Historical Society

Charleston, South Carolina, providing a variety of services and programs for local citizens. One specific program addresses the infrastructure transportation needs of the area's growing population. In 2004 the Chamber began to raise funds and manage a campaign in support of a half-cent sales tax for Charleston County. Approved by voters that same yeat, the campaign resulted in $1.3 billion to help pay for road improvements and provide additional support for the regional mass transit system. Also, the funds help pay for green space to buy land for conservation and recreation purposes.

The Chamber's president and CEO, Charles Van Rysselberge, is one of only 200 certified chamber executives (CCE) in America, the highest professional designation one can achieve in the chamber management field. He began working in local chambers more than 35 years ago while still in college. Immediately following active military service, he began his full-time chamber career as a marketing director in Shreveport, Louisiana.

Two later chamber experiences affected him deeply. In 1988 Van Rysselberge began working for the Atlanta Chamber. During this time,

Atlanta was bidding for the 1996 Summer Olympic Games. The city began a two-and-a-half-year bidding period on marketing Atlanta internationally and was eventually awarded the 1996 Summer Games.

One of the early Chamber locations—this was home to the Chamber for a better part of the early 20th century.

In direct contrast to this experience was Van Rysselberge's unforgettable service as CEO of the Oklahoma City Chamber. He takes pride in remembering how Oklahomans came together in 1995 after experiencing the horrific bombing at the Alfred P. Murrah

Federal Building. "There was outstanding help for the victims of the bombing—every social agency offered assistance—but few," reports Van Rysselberge, "thought about the businesses that had lost personnel, or the other affected buildings."

By the time Van Rysselberge arrived at the Charleston Metro Chamber of Commerce, he had a wealth of experience under his belt. He discovered Charleston's diverse economic mix and that the city was growing while still maintaining its historic charm and cultural sophistication. Today, the region is proud of a multi-billion-dollar visitor industry, one of the Southeast's major medical hubs, an established base of national and international manufacturers, a large military presence, a leading East Coast port, as well as artistic, recreational and cultural opportunities.

One of the Charleston Metro Chamber's many accomplishments includes raising the money for and managing a military-base retention effort. In 1993, Charleston lost its Navy base, which had employed 22,000 personnel. In response to the economic impact of this closing, the Chamber began preparing for the next round of Pentagon base realignment and closure (BRAC) proceedings. In 2005 the Pentagon announced where it would close, make smaller, or realign a number of military installations. The Charleston Metro Chamber focused on retaining the regional military facilities and after a three-and-a-half-year effort, they lost only 1,100 out of 27,000 jobs at the time —both civilian and military. Due to the continued need and the economic impact of local military installations, the Chamber is already preparing its strategy for the next round of BRAC.

Around the same time frame as the BRAC decision, the Charleston area undertook a study focused on economic development. Referred to as "Forward Charleston," the study evaluated the local economy and quality of the community and found areas where the region could capitalize on existing clusters of employers to further enhance the local economy while attracting greater numbers of new jobs and invest-

The Education Foundation's award-winning brochure piece helps define its efforts in bringing the business and education communities together.

ment. As a result, several organizations involved in economic and workforce development in the region joined forces to implement a cluster philosophy concentrating on five areas outlined in the study: automotive, aerospace, bioscience, advanced security and creative/entrepreneurial. The Charleston Metro Chamber is heavily involved in ensuring the success of cluster development.

Many of the Chamber's programs and initiatives are directly tied to the economic success this approach will have in the region.

The Chamber has also been heavily involved in promoting the success and expansion of the Port of Charleston. The Port is the sixth largest cargo-container port in America. The South Carolina Ports Authority has cargo facilities in four locations, yet it's been 25 years since the last, new port terminal was built. The Chamber launched a campaign to secure statewide support for permitting a new Ports Authority Terminal on the former Charleston Naval Base and the funding of an access road to handle truck traffic. After the permit was awarded, groundbreaking for this new terminal was held in May 2007.

With the strength of the Port of Charleston and the key military installations in the region, the Chamber has developed a Homeland Security Conference to bring together key players in the advanced security arena. This event provides a unique forum for presentations and idea sharing about the latest technological advances in security— both personal and commercial.

The Charleston Metro Chamber takes great pride in helping businesses expand by responding to their needs,

Charles Van Rysselberge, president and CEO, updates the region's legislative delegation on issues impacting the Charleston region.

offering professional development opportunities, and providing counseling for small businesses. The Chamber has a Business Information Center, a library with resource materials and staff counselors who are ready to assist developing businesses. The Chamber also works to help entrepreneurs with commercially viable ideas and offers some unique programs for those with innovative technology ready for commercialization. There is a program at the Chamber called ThinkTEC® whose mission is to accelerate the growth of high-tech and knowledge-based business in the Charleston region.

As well, the Charleston Metro Chamber is home to the Center for Business Research (CBR), a resource for unbiased statistics to meet business, demographic and economic research needs. The work of the CBR has been recognized nationally through numerous awards and presentations while providing research services to organizations and institutions across the region.

In addition to working toward building a strong innovation economy with higher wages, the Chamber also has targeted programs focused on diversity, including efforts with Hispanic, African

The Port of Charleston is a multi-billion dollar economic engine for the state of South Carolina.

American and women-owned businesses. The Chamber annually schedules more than 100 events—these vary from general networking events to forums and panel discussions where members get an inside look at issues affecting the region. A majority of these events and initiatives are supported by funds raised during an annual Total Resource Campaign. This campaign involves more than 300 volunteers and 80 corporate teams who reach out to the community and secure memberships, sponsorships and donations on behalf of the Chamber.

Another initiative of the Charleston Metro Chamber is The Education Foundation, a 501(c)(3) formed by the Chamber in 1995. The Foundation focuses on the partnerships between the business community and area schools to help prepare all students for success in the workplace. As Van Rysselberge says, "We want students to see that there is hope for them—exciting things for their future. We support businesses in any effort to provide mentoring, job shadowing experiences, internships, and summer employment." The Education Foundation works in partnership with some of the largest high schools in a three-county region to implement smaller learning communities. These schools within schools are designed to create environments that are more conducive to learning, including Ninth Grade Academies which help students bridge the gap between middle and high school.

One of the more recent ventures for

Leadership Charleston participants enjoy a military session which includes a flight in a C-17 at Charleston Air Force Base.

the Chamber is the development of the Charleston Young Professionals, a group that garnered more than 500 members in its first year. This group is focused on developing and retaining the region's younger workforce by providing professional development opportunities as well as offering exposure to Charleston's established business leaders. The Chamber also has a program called Leadership Charleston, a leadership school where emerging business leaders participate in a year-long program to get an in-depth look into vital community components and learn fundamental leadership skills.

The Charleston Metro Chamber of Commerce focuses on quality of life in the area, keeping in mind the strong hospitality industry prevalent in Charleston. The Chamber worked with the Charleston Aviation Authority and the Charleston Area Convention & Visitors Bureau to attract discount air carriers. In May 2007 AirTran Airways, one of the largest low-fare airlines in the U.S., began service in the Charleston market. "This was a major step in bringing low-cost airfare to Charleston and will not only benefit the visitors to the area but will provide millions of dollars in savings for the local business community," says Van Rysselberge.

There is definitely more going on at the Charleston Metro Chamber of Commerce than what people most often look for—maps and the weather.

3V, INC.

Dr. Antonio Seccomandi is known on several continents for his leadership in the chemical industry. Seccomandi founded the 3V Group in 1956 in Mozzo, Italy. Today, the company he birthed has grown to become an integrated, multinational, force, active in the chemical, engineering and environmental fields.

3V Sigma, the chemical branch of the group, has three production sites in Italy and one in the U.S. What's more, the corporation is a strong presence in all major global markets, and has commercial offices in Switzerland, Spain, China, the United Kingdom, Germany, and France. Seccomandi built this global chemical empire with a keen focus on integrating production cycles. Indeed, this integration, combined with cutting edge research and development, has been the core of 3V's strategy over the past five decades.

Today, the company has over 50 researchers who study the synthesis of new products using the most modern research tools available. The result is

Centioni and Dr Antonio Seccomandi in 1994.

an array of 3V products that cross multiple facets of the chemical industry, including detergents, textiles, water treatment, plastic additives, cosmetics, paper, equipment, and intermediates.

Specifically, 3V supplies optical brighteners and thickeners and auxiliaries for the printing industry. The paper industry, meanwhile, depends on 3V's Optiblanc brand, recognized worldwide as a standard of excellence for optical brighteners. The company also supplies the detergent industry with additives, such as the Polygel family of rheology modifiers. These modifiers thicken products of all pH ranges, an important aspect of detergents. In the cosmetic industry, 3V supplies UV filters. In fact, 3V is among the largest producers of UV filters in the world. In the plastic and coating industry, 3V is known for its chemicals that increase the life cycle of products by protecting them from the deteriorating effect of solar radiation and heat. The firm is also one of the most important suppliers worldwide in the PVC industry with its antifouling and secondary suspending agents.

3V built a respected name brand from its headquarters in Europe and made its products well-known in the United

States before establishing a presence in North America. 3V Chemical was originally incorporated in 1978 as a distributor of specialty chemicals with offices in New Jersey. In 1980 3V Sigma executives decided to create a manufacturing structure for products already sold in the U.S., as well as other products that could generate new revenue streams,. The U.S. operations would focus on building business in its lines of fine chemicals. But company executives were first tasked with finding the right location in the United States.

That site selection process took three years and involved several technical and business trips. High level employee envoys traveled from Italy to evaluate the eastern coast of the U.S. and Canada, according to John Centioni, president of 3V, Inc. The evaluation looked for an abundant supply and easy access to the brackish water streams needed to produce its chemical-based products, as well as utilities infrastructure, land conformation, and strategic location, with close proximity to ports of entry that were capable of supporting containerized inbound supplies and outbound shipments to the European Union, South America, and Asia.

Aerial photo.

Those weren't 3V's only requirements. The company's operations also demanded access to rail spurs, a pro-business environment with low taxes, the availability of financial assistance, skilled labor, and technical resources. On top of these business-critical needs, the company also evaluated locations for quality of life concerns, such as climate conditions, recreational resources, and most of all, a warm welcome and receptive disposition to new industries from the local community. After an intensive search, 3V executives narrowed the field to Savannah, Georgia, Jacksonville, Florida, and Georgetown, South Carolina. Georgetown won the final bid. "Final selection was based on the very friendly attitude shown by local business leaders, contractors and the local community," Centioni recalls. "They were not too used to dealing with Italians, but were very open to accept our presence."

Centioni will never forget his first few trips to Georgetown. He came from his home in Italy to secure environmental permits and establish contacts with major contracting parties in April 1979. "The flowers were plentiful and blooming with beautiful colors. I saw deer and alligators, quite unexpected inhabitants of the club where I was staying," he recalls. "You have to remember, I was a guest coming fresh from Italy where deer are extinct and alligators never lived." He took that natural image home to his wife and five-year-old daughter, but the reality they found when he brought them to Georgetown five months later was quite different from the South Carolina coast he described.

"We arrived in mid-August in Myrtle Beach on a very steamy afternoon," Centioni recalls. "I had a lot to explain to my wife for several months afterwards as to why I had taken my family away from a very fashionable, cultural, and industrial northern Italian city like Bergamo to this part of the world where things are so much different."

The Georgetown facility opened with five employees the first year, focusing on its first product line of suspending agents for PVC. Through these developmental steps and ongoing hiring, the U.S. operations of the company now total more than 200 people in Georgetown. In addition to its New Jersey sales office, the company has also established sales offices in Charlotte, N.C. and Texas. 3V has become well known in Georgetown as a good corporate citizen. It has created high-paying manufacturing and contracting jobs and has helped develop the utilities infrastructure for the surrounding community so that economic development can continue to thrive in the region.

Company executives are also active participants in community-building efforts. Twice, Centioni was elected as a Georgetown Economic Ambassador for his contribution to economic development and job creation in the region. He first received the award in 1994 from Governor Carroll Campbell and again in 2000 from Governor Jim Hodges. Centioni is also a member of the University of South Carolina Industry Board for Chemical Engineering and Biochemistry Departments, as well as a Rotarian. In fact, Centioni is active in various other local development, educational, and healthcare organizations in Georgetown.

Of course, every company faces growing pains and business development challenges, despite how well the local community receives it. Stateside, Centioni admits the company has had to overcome several hurdles, not the least of which is a qualified labor force to manufacture and sell its chemical products. "From time to time there was a lack of technical personnel educated and skilled in chemical manufacturing," Centioni said, noting that the company would hire workers and train them in-house when an ample supply was not to be found in the marketplace.

3V has also had to regroup after unforeseen setbacks, such as shortages of raw materials, accidents, and unfair competition from the Far East. And, like every chemical company, 3V had to adjust to environmental regulations that become more stringent and are more closely monitored by the U.S. Environmental Protection Agency each year. Sometimes, Centioni explains, the company faced unwarranted concerns just because it is a chemical production facility. "Our Georgetown site was purposely selected to be several miles away from the coastal, recreational development of the Grand Strand, which has become a nationally recognized golf resort area of the Southeast," Centioni says. "We take pride to have not hindered quality of life and continuous commercial growth of a pristine area."

Despite the challenges, 3V's product lines have increased in number, quality, and tonnage as the company has expanded into new markets over the years. Centioni attributes 3V's success in the

3V technical building.

United States to maintaining the corporate philosophy Dr. Antonio Seccomandi instilled more than 50 years ago when he planted the seed of a global structure in Italy. That corporate philosophy is to create business and employment opportunities with full use of "inventive know-how," as well as fully integrated production cycles from conceptualization all the way through to new products. That philosophy has its strength in research and pilot testing long before industrial products, like chemicals, waste treatment technologies and process equipment, ever make their way to the market. 3V does all this with full respect to environmental and safety standards and without negatively impacting the surrounding community or the quality of life of its residents.

Most recently, 3V has seen some fortunate turns thanks to changing global chemical industry conditions. For example, Centioni says, consolidations

of multinational companies bring manufacturing structures outside the U.S. territory and leave more market shares for small producers like 3V. This, he explains, offers advantages to domestic chemical manufacturers like 3V. Indeed, the industry is also taking steps to thwart unfair competition for Asia, such as mandating adequate process improvements and employment prequalification.

3V's new corporate initiatives are a vision of continuing its strengths in technological advancement, innovation, and global concern, to improve the quality of global citizen's daily lives. These initiatives are founded on 30 years of leadership, the highest quality achievements and dedicated contributions of our employees in the chemical and engineering fields worldwide.

Today, Centioni proudly points to three children all grown, multi-lingual and college educated . . . and. . . a wife not too fond of spending vacations in Italy. Of all of his accomplishments, Centioni is most proud of the fact that 3V has created more than 200 jobs. When asked what the future of the organization holds, he answered, "Hopefully more jobs will be created, more business opportunities will come our way, and we can improve the quality of existing community in Georgetown."

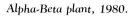
Alpha-Beta plant, 1980.

EAGLE AVIATION, INC.

In Columbia, South Carolina Eagle Aviation, Inc. recently celebrated its fortieth year in business, providing high quality service to the aviation industry. Occupying more than 36 acres at the Columbia Metro Airport, the company has spent time and effort in building an international reputation for excellence. Eagle has greatly expanded all aspects of the fixed-base operator business and today remains one of a few truly full-service FBOs in the country.

Eagle was started by its current chairman, Michael Laughlin, in Aiken in June of 1967. Laughlin had returned to live in Aiken in 1966 after graduating from the University of Virginia. While at Virginia he had become an investor in Horizon Aviation, which would later become a part of Eagle. With experience from his work with Horizon, he worked with the City of Aiken and its city manager Roland Windham to improve the local airport. This resulted in Laughlin becoming the fixed-base operator, which led to the establishment of Eagle Aviation.

While working on the airport project, Laughlin saw that the area had many needs and felt that they could be better addressed if he were to attempt to handle them from a political office. He ran for

Grand opening photo (ribbon cutting) are from left to right: Senator Michael Laughlin, Congressman William Jennings Bryan Dorn. Senator Strom Thurmond, Mayor H. Odell Weeks of Aiken.

the State Senate and was elected as one of its youngest members, despite being under the minimum age of twenty-four. The Senate waived the age restriction and Laughlin served two terms. After his terms in the Senate he went on to serve as an Aeronautical Commissioner.

Eagle expanded by buying Brannon Aviation in Greenville and acquiring all of Horizon Aviation in Virginia and then in 1970 bought VIP Aviation in Columbia, which was the start of the Columbia base, and later that year

bought Hall Aviation. These two operations make up the nucleus of the present facilities at the Columbia Metropolitan Airport.

With the acquisition of VIP Aviation, the company got its first general manager and vice president, William F. Quimby, and vice president of maintenance, William Holecek. Holecek was the founder of H&H Aviation, VIP's predecessor. Over the years, the smaller operations were sold—the last was Aiken in 1977. Eagle Aviation's main focus became the FBO at the Columbia Metropolitan Airport. T. H. Dorsey followed Quimby as president and David Lipski, the current president, succeeded him.

Over the past 40 years, Eagle has greatly expanded its facilities, continually adding more hangar and workspace to accommodate the company's ever-growing business. Eagle now has more than 38,000 square feet totally dedicated toward aircraft maintenance and is presently in the process of adding more hangar space to accommodate its customers.

Eagle maintenance department.

Owens field facility.

Eagle now employs more than 260 people in its varied business sectors, ranging from aircraft sales, maintenance, avionics, completions, and line service to charter, flight training, and contract services. An aircraft sales department was established in 1971 with the addition of both Royal "Zipper" Robins and a Mitsubishi turboprop distributorship, followed by a Cessna dealership in 1976. In 1978 Eagle became a Cessna full line and Conquest turboprop dealer, then the leading worldwide Conquest dealer, averaging more than $100,000,000 in aircraft sales annually. Eagle presently concentrates on selling used Cessna Citation jet aircraft around the world, as well as Cessna piston and turboprop aircraft in the local market.

The aircraft maintenance department continues to expand its capabilities to handle increasingly sophisticated jet, turboprop, and piston aircraft. The maintenance department is an autho-

rized service center for Cessna, Cirrus, Twin Commander, and many other aircraft manufacturers. A parts department supports the company's service efforts with more than $1,000,000 in parts inventory. An integral part of the service process is the avionics shop, which handles both repairs and installations of the latest in avionics technology for all the leading avionics manufacturers.

To further increase their capabilities, Eagle opened a completions center that provides customers with a full paint,

Eagle's Citation V charter aircraft.

Eagle Terminal in Columbia.

interior, and cabinet shop capable of handling all sizes of aircraft through midsize corporate jets. With the completions center, Eagle is one of the few FBOs capable of handling all of an aircraft owner's requirements.

In addition to sales and service, Eagle offers flying lessons, utilizing the Cessna Pilot Center program. Eagle also offers aircraft management and provides charter service with one of the company's two Citation V jet aircraft. "Anywhere, Anytime" is the charter department's slogan.

With a modern facility that never closes, and all possible corporate amenities, customers are privy to a first-class gateway to the city of Columbia. Also provided are fueling services to all airlines servicing Columbia, the military, and all of the freight carriers. In support of UPS, the line service department also provides freight loading and unloading in Greenville, South Carolina, and Greensboro, North Carolina.

In 2006 the operation at Columbia's downtown airport, Owens Field, became available and Eagle took over the operation from Jim Hamilton. Eagle Aviation quickly improved the line service and maintenance capabilities available at Owens and plan to offer additional services. Eagle is actively exploring other possible acquisitions in the Southeast that fit the company's business plan. Eagle remains committed to continuing the expansion of its services in Columbia and beyond, one day becoming the largest FBO operation in the Carolinas.

GMK ASSOCIATES, INC.

In 1966 William Geiger, Don McElveen, and Robert Kennedy struck out on their own and started GMK. They had a vision for a firm that would provide professional services in the design and construction marketplace, one that has stood the test of time. Today, GMK Associates specializes in planning, design, and construction in the education, healthcare, and retirement markets. The firm employs more than 120 individuals with backgrounds in architecture, engineering, interior design, design-build, and construction management services. To better understand how GMK evolved into the firm it is today, it's best to go back to the beginning.

In the early years, Bill Geiger was what Robert Kennedy calls "The Rainmaker." He would go out into the community, meet with prospective clients, and bring business back to the firm. Don McElveen was involved primarily with the construction side of the business. And Robert Kennedy, an architect, was the principal designer for all early projects, primarily K-12 schools. Kennedy was influenced by architectural heavyweights such as Mies Van der Rohe (believing "less is more") and Robert Stern (a "modern traditionalist"). Evidence of their influence appears in his designs.

The team's first project was Dillon High School. According to Mr. Kennedy, "We hadn't designed a school before, so the Dillon Superintendent took us on faith." GMK went on to

Ira and Nancy Koger Center of the Arts, University of South Carolina, Columbia, South Carolina.

design and oversee the building of many public schools, each different from the other. Says Kennedy, "School administrators liked the idea of standardizing plans—believing they could save money." In theory, it makes sense. Unfortunately, standardizing rarely works. Each school always has special needs leading to different design solutions.

Through the 1970s and 1980s, South Carolina's school boards undertook large building projects and GMK was a big part of that era of school-building projects. Two award-winning projects of note include the Darla Moore School of Business at the University of South Carolina and the Ira and Nancy Koger Center for the Arts, a 2,400-seat performing arts center that enjoys notoriety for its concerts, ballet performances, graduations and traveling shows that come through town.

Other clients GMK has had the privilege of working with include Benedict College, Central Carolina Technical College, College of Charleston, Clemson University, Francis Marion University, Medical University of South Carolina, Midlands Technical College, SCE&G Summer Nuclear Training Facility, University of South Carolina, University of South Carolina–Aiken, University of

South Carolina–Upstate, Voorhees College, and Winthrop University.

Another market segment that had started a period of tremendous growth in the state was healthcare. This led to a dramatic shift in the type of work the firm did and became known for. GMK's founders saw a need for expertise in the design of healthcare facilities and found an answer in Val Satko, AIA, and Bob Heilman, a businessman with a wealth of experience in hospital equipment planning. Together they brought the experience and expertise that allowed GMK to develop into a leader in the design of healthcare facilities. Today, 90 percent of GMK's projects are healthcare oriented.

In 2006 GMK's design-build division completed 150,000 square feet of healthcare-related facilities including hospital additions and renovations, surgery centers, medical office buildings and tenant upfits, ranking them the seventh largest healthcare design-build firm in the country. GMK currently has more than $250 million in healthcare projects in design and under construction.

GMK has had the opportunity to work with 13 of the hospitals across the state, including; Abbeville Area Medical Center, Aiken Regional Medical Center, Beaufort Memorial Hospital, Kershaw County Medical Center,

Abbeville Area Medical Center, Abbeville, South Carolina.

Laurens County Healthcare System, Lexington Medical Center, Loris Healthcare System, McLeod Health, Newberry County Memorial Hospital, Palmetto Health, Providence Hospital, Self Regional Healthcare, Seacoast Medical Center, and The Regional Medical Center of Orangeburg and Calhoun Counties. This experience allows new clients to tap into the expertise as it pertains to their projects.

Another segment that has had tremendous growth over the years is ambulatory surgery centers. Because of hospital concerns such as declining reimbursement and rising operational costs, freestanding surgery centers have become overwhelmingly popular. GMK has responded to the needs of many different types of facilities including those for cardiology, gastroenterology, ophthalmology, orthopaedics, internal medicine, sports medicine, and urology. Mary Elkins, practice administrator at Carolina Orthopaedic Surgery Associates in Rock Hill, states, "For our ASC project, we selected GMK because of their experience with similar projects and their understanding of our needs and all aspects of the project." Today, GMK has designed more than half of the Ambulatory Surgery Centers in the state of South Carolina. Their designs help improve staff efficiency and are easily accessible. The goal is always to create environments that are comfortable for patients, staff and visitors that, at the same time, offer quality care.

Another unique market segment includes hospice facilities, which are becoming more and more widespread because of the aging population. These facilities create a homelike environment, with such elements as private patient rooms, handicap accessible areas, chapels, family areas and separate staff areas for breaks and meetings. Bernardin Hospice House, completed in 2000, was the first Hospice house that GMK designed. GMK then went on to design Hospice House at Hospice Care of the Piedmont, which was completed in 2005. Nancy Corley, executive director, states "GMK has an impressive record of hospice projects around the region. We felt their past experience

GMK Associates, Inc., Columbia, South Carolina.

spoke for itself." Since then GMK has been planning for and designing three other hospice facilities in South Carolina and seven others in North Carolina. GMK strives to understand the needs of the individuals and their families during their difficult time, by creating warm, peaceful environments.

GMK's Interior Design group is also involved in designing retirement communities. GMK Interiors work encompasses all phases of design, including space planning, specification of furniture, preparation of color and furniture boards, furniture layouts, accessorizing, procurement and installation of furniture. One of their long-standing retirement clients, for more than ten years, has been Bishop Gadsden Retirement Community. GMK won the International Gold Key Award for this project in 1998. Executive Director Bill Trawick states, "Our long-term relationship with GMK has been very rewarding for our staff and residents. They have literally become a part of the Bishop Gadsden family and are true team players." Other clients representative of their interiors include Bailey Manor, Carter May Retirement, Savannah Lakes Retirement Village, Still Hopes Retirement Community, The Cascades at Verdae, Wesley Commons Retirement Community, and Westminster Towers.

All of GMK's divisions have continuously changed with the times and have adapted to the needs of each individual client request. GMK takes pride in its four-decade history and will continue to do work for the education, healthcare and retirement markets as it moves forward. The company's mission, for more than 40 years, has been to meet client needs first and provide high-quality solutions for all building projects.

Seacoast Medical Center, North Myrtle Beach, South Carolina.

JESSE FRANK HAWKINS NURSING HOME

The Jesse Frank Hawkins Nursing Home is a nonprofit care facility that initially opened in 1965 to provide for the aging residents of Newberry County. The idea for the home started with state legislator, Jesse Frank Hawkins. When the citizens began requesting the need for a rest home, Hawkins took their sentiments to the county council. The council, together with a nursing home board, prepared a budget and decided what they needed to get the project underway. Later, both Hawkins and his wife became residents of the new rest home.

The Jesse Frank Hawkins Nursing Home is located in the town of Newberry, South Carolina just two blocks off Main Street (which becomes Highway 219) and is close to the main bypass, Highway 76 which runs into Interstate 26, making it easily accessible to county and state residents.

The original nursing home began as a 36-bed unit and by January 22, 1981 a second unit of 42 beds was constructed. Soon after, the community felt there was a need for a chapel. Otis Whittaker and his wife, both Newberry residents, rallied around the cause to make this possible. By the late 1990s Hawkins added a third unit of 20 beds for dementia patients.

As the years went on, Newberry County contained the largest number of senior citizens in all of South Carolina and Hawkins responded once again to this need by building the retirement center, Springfield Place in 1997. Springfield is a county-owned independent living facility with 4 cottages, 15 patio homes, 50 assisted-living beds, 34 apartment units, and an additional 20 nursing home beds. Located a block from the Hawkins Home, Springfield provides a natural transition for residents as they move into more dependent living at the facilities of the Hawkins Nursing Home.

When Hawkins opened, it was run by about 15 staff, including cooks, nurses, and aides. Its superintendent was a most notable woman named, Evelyn Hayes R.N. According to those who knew and worked with her, she operated a top notch facility and many of the standards

NURSING HOME WEEK PROCLAIMED: Newberry Mayor C. A. Shealy is shown signing a proclamation proclaiming Nursing Home Week in Newberry. Looking on are, left to right—Newberry County Representative D. P. Folk, Mrs. Evelyn Hayes, Administrator at the J. F. Hawkins Nursing Home in Newberry; and Hubert Bedenbaugh, chairman of the Nursing Home's Board of Directors. —Observer Photo.

Nursing Home Week Being Observed At Hawkins Home

The J. F. Hawkins Nursing Home is participating in National Nursing Home Week which began on Mothers' Day, May 13-19 sponsored by the American Nursing Home Association.

Mrs. Evelyn H. Hayes said the theme for Nursing Home Week is "Nursing Home: For the Better Life" and reflects the new program to provide a better life for the nation's elderly and the convalescent and chronically ill of all ages who are patients in long term care facilities.

"We are joining with the 7,200 member homes of the national association in a massive nationwide effort to see that a

not a single patient is missed during the Mother's Day visitation program," quoted Mrs. Hayes.

Today's modern nursing home provides more than just medical, nursing and personal care. It provides for the rehabilitation, recreational, spiritual and diversional needs of the patient. But our efforts alone to provide for a fuller life for those from your garden for example, crippled with age and disease are not enough. It is for this reason that we are calling for community cooperation to provide a renewed and more sensible link between our patients and the community of which so many of them have been a part.

Many of the patients are alert, with keen interest in current events and in the great world outside their "home". The goal of Nursing Home Week is to assure that every patient in nursing homes will be visited on Mother's Day or throughout the week.

It would be nice to bring along a token gift, of a flower or really brighten the day for some one.

Mother's Day was chosen to begin the observance of Nursing Home Week because two out of three patients in nursing homes are women.

Share in this program of giving—by giving of yourself.

Newberry Mayor C. A. Shealy (seated) signing a proclamation proclaiming Nursing Home Week in Newberry. Looking on are Left to right: D.P. Folk, Mrs. Evelyn Hayes, administrator at J. F. Hawkins Nursing Home and Hubert Bedenbaugh, chairman of the Nursing Home's board of directors. Courtesy, The Newberry Observer

of care she set into motion are still followed today.

One woman who remembers Hayes fondly, is Esther Penny, an employee of Hawkins for 32 years. "When Hayes first started I was working as a nurse's assistant. She was one of my role models. If they were short in the kitchen, laundry, or housekeeping, Miss Hayes would help out. She would do anything. If a nurse was out sick, she would work the floor for her," says Penny, who now serves as activities director.

Martha Bursinger, Hawkins administrator since 2005, states that Hayes was adamant about keeping a home-like atmosphere and strict hospital sanitary standards. She made sure that residents' needs were not overlooked or undervalued. She believed residents' rooms should be kept tidy, they should be given good quality food, be kept very clean and dry, and turned regularly in order to avoid pressure areas. Hayes was responsible for training a number of nursing assistants at the home.

"She stood for a high level of care that is congruent with my own standard," says Bursinger, who was director of nursing from 1991–2000. "While much has changed at Hawkins over the past 40 years in administration and nursing, Mrs. Hayes standards are still intact

The dedication of Jesse Frank Hawkins Rest Home in Newberry. Senator Hawkins (middle) is congratulated by Senator Thurmond. Courtesy, The Newberry Observer

here. I adopted a philosophy from Hayes that if you can't do it right the first time, when will you ever have time to do it again. So, let's do it right the first time." Because of their reputation for quality care, Hawkins operates at capacity most of the time and maintains a waiting list from those within the county and around the state.

The Hawkins Nursing Home has not been without its struggles, some of which have centered around the goal to keep the home locally owned. "At one time there was some question as to whether the county needed to continue to be in the nursing home business. However, the residents wanted to keep Hawkins locally owned and not be handed over to a corporation," says Bursinger. "I applaud the county council for continuing to support the old county home concept and securing a place for their county residents to live. There has always been community support to keep this a county facility." This has been proven over the years as generations of families choose Hawkins for their grandparents and then, their own parents.

Jesse Frank Hawkins Nursing Home.

Living room at Jesse Frank Hawkins Nursing Home.

Another set of challenges for Hawkins, like most long-term care facilities, is increasing regulations and scarce resources. Running a top notch nursing home can become a strain, but Hawkins remains focused on their high standards of quality care. "When a resident goes to a nursing home, they have a sense they are losing a lot of control and it can be very stressful for them," says Bursinger. "We try to give them something back for what they've lost. That something is compassion and caring."

Hawkins encourages visitors and activities programs for residents. Good tasting and nutritious food is a priority, much like it was in the beginning, notes Bursinger. "And we believe in the Golden Rule here. We realize that patient you are caring for could one day be you. I learned the Golden Rule in second grade and now that same second grade teacher is a resident at Hawkins. Every time I see her, I remember the Golden Rule."

A key part to maintaining this philosophy is having the right people on staff and keeping them happy. With a community hospital and a corporate nursing home nearby, Hawkins often competes for skilled nurses. Not surprisingly, they have found the same

philosophy that draws residents to Hawkins, also draws nurses. "We have employees who have left and then come back and want to work here again," says Bursinger. "It goes back to our overall concept that our community wants good quality of care and a place that treats people the right way."

Personal assistance is part of the Jesse Frank Hawkins Nursing Home experience.

JOSEPH WALKER & COMPANY, INC.

Joseph Walker Clarke refers to a quote from his favorite book, *Red Hills and Cotton*, "Cotton is a state of mind with us—a philosophy. We continue to plant it and sell it despite the fact that we have not made money on cotton more than once in about ten or twenty years."

Walker claims that the beauty of the cotton business is that it is based on relationships, between the merchant and the farmer, and between the merchant and the spinning mill customer. These relationships have formed a strong bond among cotton people. For decades this cotton community has been responsible for the delivery and consumption of cotton across the U.S. and it is now responsible for delivering cotton around the world.

When Joseph Walker & Co., Inc. first opened its firm as a U.S. cotton merchant, the company was charged with bidding on bales of raw cotton, purchasing the bales, warehousing the commodity, sampling the cotton to determine its grade, and delivering bales to spinning mills for consumption. There is still bidding, purchasing, warehousing, and sampling of cotton today, but technology has dramatically altered these steps. Bales are rapidly moved into warehouses, samples are drawn from each bale, the USDA classifies these bale samples while the grade information is offered for bids. The USDA cotton classing offices run each sample over a High Volume Instrument (HVI)

Joseph Walker Clarke and Nick Earlam met playing golf.

to determine the bale's grade, leaf, micronaire (coarseness), color, trash content, staple (length of fiber), grams per tek (breaking strength), uniformity and other characteristics. Each of these characteristics can determine the premium or discount the bale may bring in the marketplace based on a market or "futures" price established in New York's cotton exchange, now called the New York Board of Trade.

There is much to know about cotton and the industry that surrounds it. One can learn much of the cotton industry from Joseph Walker & Company, Inc., a fourth-generation cotton-merchandising firm headquartered in Columbia, South Carolina. In 1901 Joseph Walker started working in the cotton business in Columbia. He was born in a small village called Yorkville, now called York, South Carolina. He received his early education at the Kings Military Academy, a school no longer in existence. As a boy, he worked for a local cotton merchant, Latta Brothers. At the age of 17, Joseph Walker made the decision to move from his family farm in York to Columbia to support his family. In Columbia, he applied to work for another cotton merchant, holding only a letter from Latta Brothers that reads: "Yorkville, SC, Sept 25th, 1901. The bearer of this letter, Joseph Walker, has been with us

Joseph Walker at his first desk, 1923, upon the formation of Joseph Walker and Co.

the past two seasons and we have found him thoroughly honest and reliable and not afraid of work. We consider him an exceptional good young man and believe he would be faithful to any position entrusted to him."

As a confirmation of what Joseph Walker stood for and what he started with during the tough times of the 1900s, his grandson, Joseph Walker Clarke, still has a framed copy of this handwritten letter on his office wall today. Walker Clarke confirms that this was the philosophy Joseph Walker & Company was born with and continues to live and operate by today. Longevity and success in the cotton business continues to be rooted in hard work, strong relationships, and reliability of quality and service.

Joseph Walker was initially hired by W.E. Smith Cotton Company, which was based in Columbia. M.C. Heath and Company then hired the young Joseph to work where he was soon promoted to partner with Mr. M. C. Heath. After 14 years of service, Joseph departed to form a new firm, Hollowell and Walker, which later merged with American Products Export and Import Company. In 1923 Walker formed his own cotton company, Joseph Walker & Company, partnering with his younger brothers, Robert Bratton Walker and Cosmo Lowry Walker (who came to work with their brother after WWI ended), as well

Joseph O. Walker in the center and his six sons around him. To his right is Joseph, next to oldest, to his left is Felix, above is Deleon, below is Cosmo, above Felix is Claude and below Felix is Robert (Bob).

Joseph Walker, his five sons: Joseph Jr., Robert C., Claude M., Felix Deleon, John S. and son-in-law Sam Clarke.

as with friend, Jay Earle Davis. Upon the brothers' return, they discovered that Joseph had started expanding their business into Spartanburg, Anderson and Sumter, South Carolina.

Joseph Walker, known as Mr. Joe, married Claudia Moore Sadler, of Rock Hill, South Carolina. The young couple had seven children—two daughters and five sons. Daughter Minnie Lowry Walker died at age two. Marion Walker Clarke married Samuel Laffitte Clarke of Estill, South Carolina. One son, Felix Deleon "Jack" Walker, became a cotton farmer. The other brothers—Joseph Walker, Jr., Robert Cosmo Walker,

Early photo from cotton warehouse "The Standard Warehouse Co."

Claude Moore Walker and John Sadler Walker—all went to work for their father's cotton merchandising firm. Additional partners during this time were brother-in-law Samuel L. Clarke, cousin Robert Bratton Walker, Jr., Sam A. MacPherson, Blake Edmunds and John B. Edmunds. During this time, the company bought J. B. Hubbard and Co. of Dallas, Texas, which they operated for several years in the late '60s, early '70s.

While Mrs. Joseph Walker lived to be 91 years of age, Mr. Joseph Walker Sr. lived to be only a few months short of his 100th birthday, in 1984. He had seen his company start, establish and grow within the cotton industry. He had started a cotton firm during some of the toughest times our country had ever endured, sent five sons and one nephew to Europe to fight in World War II (John S. Walker received the Bronze Star and two purple hearts; Joseph Walker Jr. and Robert C. Walker received the Bronze Star) and lived to see the second and third generations lead his firm into the future.

The first of the firm's many leaders after Joseph Walker was his eldest son, Joseph Walker, Jr. Joseph Jr. was known for his keen business acumen and his market savvy. Joe, Jr. was responsible for much of the expansion of the business during this period. He became chairman of the board of The Standard Corporation, leading and developing the warehouse business. Robert C. Walker then led the company, commanded the greatest respect from his peers and is considered by many as one of the grand men of the industry. Claude M. Walker was the company's chief financial officer

and became known for his diligent and precise manner in managing company finances. John S. Walker always had an excellent feel for the cotton market and was recognized as one of the best salesmen the company ever had. Robert B. Walker was known for his strong will, wisdom, and clear business decisions. Samuel L. Clarke was a dedicated partner, a magnificent salesman and an ambassador for the cotton business, continually creating new accounts for the firm.

Each of the brothers became the managing partner of Joseph Walker and Co. Two of these second-generation

Joseph Walker Sr., with governor of South Carolina Richard Manning, early 1900s.

Early photo of Walker family. Left to right: Claude Walker, "Jack" Felix Walker, John Walker, Joe Walker, Jr., Robert C. Walker, Claudia "Mammy" Walker, Sam Clarke, Jr. in arms of Joseph Walker and Marion Walker Clarke.

partners of Joseph Walker & Company, Robert C. Walker and Robert B. Walker Jr., also served as presidents of the Atlantic Cotton Association, further enhancing the respect the firm had within its industry.

This second generation established Joseph Walker and Company as a most respected name in the cotton industry, serving farmers and mills throughout the entire southeastern United States. Not enough can be said of this group of men as they all led the company through the 1950s, 1960s, 1970s and 1980s. They were charged with leading a family business through some of the most difficult times our country has ever seen. Depressions, wars, changing government programs and U.S. farm bills were all handled with commitment, love and patriotism. With the coming of another generation came many changes in the cotton business.

Grandsons Joseph Walker Clarke and his older brother Samuel Laffitte Clarke Jr. became the first of the third generation to enter the cotton business. After both completed college and Army service in the early-1960s, "Walker" (Joseph Walker Clarke) and Sam started

working with the firm in the cotton "sample room" by sweeping up lint and preparing cotton samples for classification and shipping. Sam Clarke was eventually designated to learn the cotton warehousing business as brother Walker Clarke pursued purchasing and sales of raw bales.

The partners of Joseph Walker and Co. bought an old cotton warehousing company, The Standard Warehouse Co. Sam was placed in charge of that aspect of the business to add a new dimension, warehousing, to the family firm. Sam saw an opportunity in the warehousing business, turning cotton warehouses into

something more than cotton storage. He began replacing the old wooden warehouse structures with modern steel buildings to warehouse general and miscellaneous merchandise. The warehouse company soon became The Standard Corporation. Claude M. Walker, Jr. and James H. Walker, sons of the second-generation partners, teamed with Sam Clarke in building the successful Standard Corporation. This leg of the family business grew into a large national warehouse business that has since been successfully sold to a larger logistic organization, UTi Worldwide, Inc.

Following Walker and Sam Clarke as third-generation members in the family cotton business were the sons of Claude M. Walker, Sr., Joseph Walker II and Frank E. Walker. One of John S. Walker's daughters, Amanda Walker, also joined the firm for a short period of time before marrying Joe E. Taylor, Jr., South Carolina's current secretary of commerce.

Walker Clarke, Joseph Walker II, and Frank Walker have all served as

Joseph Walker receiving the Rotary Paul Harris Fellow Award. Back row left to right: Sam L. Clarke, John S. Walker, Felix D. Walker, Claude M. Walker, Robert C. Walker, Sam Clarke Jr. Front row left to right: Joseph Walker II, Marion Walker Clarke, Joseph Walker, Joseph Walker Jr. amd Joseph Walker Clarke.

president of the Atlantic Cotton Association. Both Walker Clarke and Joseph Walker II have also served as president of The American Cotton Shippers Association and vice president of the National Cotton Council.

This third generation of Joseph Walker & Company tripled the volume of cotton handled by the firm. It also handled cotton through some of the more difficult years of the business as new government programs arrived and disappeared while participating in historic volatile market moves. During this generation's tenure, cotton prices reached historic highs of $1.17 per pound as well as matching Civil War lows in the 30 cent range. The U.S. also grew more cotton as U.S. mills used more than they ever had before.

As the fourth generation—the generation currently running the company—came into the business, the cotton industry was again undergoing radical change. To meet altering market conditions, the company incorporated and entered the global marketplace.

When Walker Clarke first entered the cotton business, cotton was still mainly being picked by hand in the U.S. His first job was to travel to each of the regional cotton gins in South Carolina, North Carolina, and Georgia. Once in a gin yard, he would use a knife to cut into a bale of cotton, pull out a sample and examine it. He would manually classify the fresh sample according to its color, trash or leaf content, lint preparation, and then "staple" the bale—the art of pulling the fibers out in an even matt—to determine the fiber's length.

Visiting these gin yards engages a person in meeting people from all backgrounds who work with cotton. As Walker has said, cotton folks are "some of the finest people you'll ever want to meet." Whereas he used to travel up to 100 miles to cotton gins and cotton spinning mills in the Southeast region of the U.S., the fourth generation now flies thousands of miles to visit the entire U. S. cotton-growing region and new cotton spinning mills around the globe.

"It still boils down to relationships," the third generation Walker Clarke maintains. "We've always had strong

relationships." Today, Walker Clarke is retired but remains chairman of the board of directors of the firm. Forester Adams, Walker's son-in-law, serves as president and Edward Clarke, one of Walker's sons, serves as senior vice president as well as vice president of the Atlantic Cotton Association. Joe Pearson, another fourth generation member of the firm, is a grandson of the late Robert C. Walker and is a vice president and the firm's office manager. Joseph Walker Clarke, Jr., Walker's elder son, is president of Palmetto Cotton Warehouse, in Lake City, South Carolina, and serves as project manager and point man for new business ventures for the firm.

Joseph Walker Clarke "stapling" a bale to determine its quality.

Joseph Walker Clarke and Samuel Clarke, Jr. (The Standard Corporation).

Before warehousing cotton, this warehouse was owned by the family of Walker's wife, Jane Bowen Clarke, which the family used to hold tobacco for storage and auction. As tobacco auction lines became obsolete, so did the warehouses that held the tobacco. "We had this family warehouse, which is about 225,000 square feet," says Walker. "Our cotton company decided to buy it from the Bowen family and turn it into a cotton facility that would enable them to provide a more rapid response to customers in this current world market."

In 1874 the first American cotton was unloaded in Liverpool, England. There were only eight bags of cotton on that boat. Less than forty years later, half a million bales were arriving every year from America. With growing trade, other countries also supplied cotton to Liverpool, including Brazil, Egypt and India. By 1850 cotton accounted for almost half of the city's trade—more than 1.5 million bales of imported cotton.

Cotton may not grow in Britain, but for 150 years most of the world's raw cotton came through Liverpool, on its way to Lancashire's textile mills.

Liverpool was the center of the raw cotton trade. Millions of bales were unloaded on the city's quaysides and many people were involved in moving, storing, buying and selling cotton. Today, approximately 60 percent of the world's cotton is still traded under rules developed in Liverpool.

In 2003 Joseph Walker & Co. joined with Plexus Cotton Limited, a world-wide cotton company based in Liverpool. Nicholas Peter Francis "Nick" Earlam, the CEO of Plexus, "started his own company, like my grandfather did," says Walker Clarke. "His organization is very service-oriented, as we are. Plexus operates with the same business ethics as Joseph Walker & Company." Nick has served twice as president of the Liverpool Cotton Association, now known as the International Cotton Association, and he has earned a reputation for being a premiere international cotton merchant. Nick and Walker became friends through cotton conventions, meetings, and committee discussions. "We became friends while playing golf," Walker says. "We always talked about doing business together. He was in the export business, and I was doing business solely in the U.S. When the U.S. mills started to fail and go out of business, I was looking for somewhere to sell U.S. cotton abroad and Nick was looking for a source of U.S.

Family gathering photo featured in a story "The Tie That Binds."

Walker Clarke with the fourth generation.

cotton. I heard about this and called him up. He said I'll be in your office tomorrow, and he came to Columbia. Later, we both attended a cotton meeting in Boca Raton, Florida, and had breakfast. On the back of a napkin at breakfast, we worked out a plan and put our businesses together. His company was much larger than we were, but we saw an opportunity for both our firms and made it happen."

Joseph Walker & Company, Inc. is part of The Cotton Alliance formed by Nick Earlam. The Alliance consists of companies and partnerships around the world building a network to benefit all those who participate within the group. Nick Earlam has built companies in Singapore, Germany, Australia, Africa and Brazil as well as working with Joseph Walker & Company in the U.S. As Walker Clarke says, "Being part of the Plexus family of businesses we have the globe surrounded. We feed information into our central office and have marketing meetings with everyone. We help each other in our decision-making but operate as an entirely separate outfit in the U.S."

"Plexus is now a majority shareholder in what has become Joseph Walker & Co., Inc. The union that we have between our firms in Columbia, South Carolina, and Liverpool, England, is the result of a remarkable journey," says Walker Clarke. "Just to look at my business and see where it was at one time, my grandfather shipping cotton out of the Port of Charleston for delivery to Liverpool, and now here we are partnering with a Liverpool company, shipping cotton all over the world. It is gratifying to see how this relationship has developed new life in our business."

Like any other business, Joseph Walker & Company has seen its share of obstacles. Between 1920 and 1922, the boll weevil invaded the United States, destroying cotton fields as it swept north and east from Texas. Cotton's only natural enemy, the boll weevil destroyed 70 percent of South Carolina's cotton crop in two years, terrorizing cotton farmers, until an eradication program took hold in the mid–1970s. Today, with only a bare minimum of boll weevil found in South Carolina, the state is considered weevil-free.

Joseph Walker & Company has endured extreme movements in the market, increased volume to match demand and has entered new markets around the world—all this in order to be a more viable business to those the company serves. There are few cotton mills left in the U.S. today. Having produced more than 20 million bales of cotton, the U.S. now consumes only an

Samuel Sumpter Clarke and Forester Bailey Adams, Jr. in Jack Walker's cotton field at Cedar Creek Farms, Hopkins, South Carolina. The fifth generation?

estimated 4.5 million of those bales—the balance serving the export market.

What does the future hold for Joseph Walker & Company, Inc. after a century-old history? The company has a niche in the U.S. market. It is capable of buying cotton from California to South Carolina. A healthy American organization, it is part of Plexus, one of the finest international cotton companies in the world. Its owners and operators have excellent relations with their supplier, the cotton farmer. Its name has developed over several generations and its reputation has remained

Edward Clarke, Matthew Earlam and Forester Adams: the fourth generation.

strong due to its integrity, honesty and fair dealing.

The future is global, we are in that global market now, and we are making friends around the world," says Walker. "We're beginning to develop a handshake that reaches around the world, and we attribute this to our relationship with Plexus." The company will handle cotton in the same way it always has, as fairly as it knows how, and will continue to participate in the global marketplace. "We're blessed with very talented people," he says. "Our men, along with Nick Earlam, his brother Jo Earlam, and now Nick's son Matthew, who is the newest family addition, comprise what I think encompasses the link to the future success of the business. We were blessed to have Matthew intern at Joseph Walker & Company. He is quite

a "fine young man," to quote an old letter.

As the generations pass, Joseph Walker & Company has always been driven to be an industry leader, to provide a market for the U.S. cotton farmers, and to service cotton spinning mills. "We are a service industry, in that we provide a market for cotton, we create markets for cotton, and we are a conduit for the farmers to the world market," concludes Walker. And ideally, Joseph Walker & Company will be for generations to come.

The Palmetto Cotton Warehouse, Inc., Lake City, South Carolina.

SOUTH CAROLINA CHAMBER OF COMMERCE

The mission of the South Carolina Chamber of Commerce is to achieve global competitiveness by growing individual wealth through increased productivity. Since its beginning, the South Carolina Chamber has established ambitious goals to improve life for all South Carolinians.

After organizing a series of meetings and study committees, a group of South Carolina business leaders met in 1940 under the name Organized Business Inc. of South Carolina. Organized by C&S National Bank Vice President C. Norwood Hastie of Charleston, the group's first board meeting was held September 30, 1941. Hastie stressed the importance of this inaugural meeting to its attendees, saying many people were expecting the group to die out like other organizations had.

"Many hesitate to join us because they have seen this happen and don't realize that no other organization was ever backed by so many of the best men in the state," he said.

During these early years, Hastie, who was elected the organization's first president, served a membership of 142 directors from around the state. During this time, the organization dealt with many

Early leaders of the South Carolina Chamber meet to make plans to improve the state's business community.

Gov. Mark Sanford addresses attendees at the South Carolina Chamber's 2006 Business Speaks at the State House in Columbia.

issues that are still focused on today, including the state's economy, education funding, and the introduction of legislation.

In 1948 the organization's name was changed to the South Carolina State Chamber of Commerce. Then in the 1950s, the Chamber became more heavily involved with legislation through the leadership of General Manager John Floyd.

When Greenwood attorney, Howard L. Burns, became president in 1961, the Chamber was dealing with preserving the state's right-to-work laws, states' rights, and trade balance. When Joseph P. Riley Sr. of Charleston became president in 1963, his staff worked with Governor

Ernest F. Hollings and Congressman L. Mendel Rivers to open doors in Washington.

The fourth decade saw John H. Lumpkin, then chairman and chief executive officer of South Carolina National Bank, serve as president. Lumpkin and his staff worked hard to get top company executives involved, a practice that still exists today.

In the 1970s, the organization dropped "State" from its name and became the South Carolina Chamber of Commerce. John Riddick succeeded Floyd as executive director, and the title was changed to executive vice president. The 1970s also saw the organization more involved with programs dealing with industrial relations, tourism, occupational safety and health, economic education, human relations, and environmental control.

The Chamber's human relations work led to the development of the Carolina Human Relations Council. Its educational efforts established the South Carolina Council on Economic Education. The Chamber also worked with the South Carolina Department of Parks, Recreation, and Tourism to form the Council on Tourism.

The 1980s started with a two-year term for Chamber President John G. Wellman. Wellman's leadership launched Leadership South Carolina, a highly respected program that is now independent from the Chamber. In addition, Wellman worked to align the South Carolina Chamber with local chambers, forging partnerships that still exist today.

Lowell Reese became the executive vice president after Riddick. Reese moved the Chamber from its location at the corner of Park and Calhoun streets to an office at 1301 Gervais Street in downtown Columbia. The Chamber later moved to its current location across the street from the State House in the prestigious Capitol Center skyscraper in 1989.

Perhaps one of Reese's greatest accomplishments was establishing the *South Carolina Business Journal* and *South Carolina Business* magazine. The *South*

Carolina Business Journal enjoyed a successful run until it was discontinued in October 2006. In the *Journal's* place, *South Carolina Business* was expanded from its previous annual format to a monthly magazine the following January. *South Carolina Business* currently reports on issues impacting the regional, domestic, and international competitiveness of businesses across the Palmetto State.

The magazine was the brainchild of Mat Self, president of the Chamber in 1985. Thomas L. Gregory, president of Gregory Electric Company Inc., of Columbia, and executive vice president Ken Oilschlager led the Chamber into the early '90s. S. Hunter Howard Jr. became president and chief executive officer in 1992 and remains president today.

The Chamber has remained the unified voice of business throughout the years. The Chamber's Public Policy department, led by chief operating officer Otis Rawl, maintains a constant presence at the State House. The Chamber's annual legislative priority list, or Competitiveness Agenda, which began in 1994 as the Chamber became more proactive, is based on feedback from Chamber members throughout the state during a series of nine annual grassroots meetings.

"Our members' concerns are our concerns," said Rawl. "We take note of the issues that are impacting their businesses in order to determine a plan of action to keep South Carolina's business community competitive."

Numerous pieces of business-friendly legislation have passed over the years as a result of the Chamber's efforts.

"In recent years, we have worked to get passage of pro-business legislation, including tort reform, comprehensive workers' compensation reform, and the Education and Economic Development Act. This work allows us to improve South Carolina's business competitiveness and make life better for South Carolina's 4 million citizens," said Howard.

The Chamber is the state's largest statewide broad-based business association representing more than 5,000 mem-

ber companies and more than 500,000 member employees, with 89 percent of membership comprised of small businesses. According to Barbara Beckham, vice president of member relations, members are the driving force of all the Chamber does.

"We offer seminars, programs, publications, and events that are beneficial to business operations and their bottom line, and our members can take part in these opportunities at discounted rates," said Beckham.

The Chamber offers a variety of functions throughout the year, including the annual Business Speaks at the State House and the annual Washington Night in South Carolina, both designed to engage legislators in panel discussions and provide networking opportunities for members. During the summer, high school students from across the state attend South Carolina Business Week, an annual business education program that introduces students to principles of leadership, teamwork, and the U.S. free enterprise system. In addition, the Chamber hosts membership and legislative receptions, an Annual Summit, HR conferences, awards dinners, an annual golf tournament, and numerous other events and seminars.

Under Howard's leadership, the South Carolina Chamber was recog-

S. Hunter Howard Jr. (left, foreground) and members of the South Carolina Chamber of Commerce staff receive the "Accreditation, with Distinction" plaque from Moore Hallmark (right, foreground), executive director of the U.S. Chamber's Southeastern Office.

nized in 2006 by the U.S. Chamber of Commerce as an Accredited State Chamber, with Distinction, for its effective organizational procedures and outstanding contribution to positive change in South Carolina. The South Carolina Chamber was the first chamber of commerce in the country to achieve this status.

"This was a great achievement for our staff and board of directors. It really demonstrates how important governance, government affairs, and technology are to the Chamber," said Howard.

If the South Carolina Chamber's accomplishments over the years are any indication, the Chamber will help to improve the state's business climate for years to come.

"The South Carolina Chamber has made many strides for the business community throughout the years, and steps will continue to be taken to further grow our state's per capita income so that South Carolinians can enjoy a better quality of life," said Howard.

VENDORS SUPPLY, INC.

In 2006, the state of South Carolina, in association with the South Carolina Chamber of Commerce, held its 22nd ranking of the state's top 100 privately owned companies. The group ranked Vendors Supply, Inc. 30th out of those 100. How did James and Greta Sikes' company land in the top third of the state's largest private organizations? With God's help, hard work, an eye for innovation, and a strong business ethic.

To get a sense of the company's accomplishment, it's important to understand its beginnings. James Sikes was born and lived in Georgia until age 15, when his family moved to Winnsboro, South Carolina. There he finished school and studied at the University of South Carolina. After serving as a Marine in the Armed Forces, he worked from 1953 to 1963 for Southern Bakeries and then for another bakery as a sales representative. He worked twelve-hour days selling pastry snacks to food vending companies.

While working with these bakeries, Sikes recognized the need for a distribution company that could consolidate the various food lines and better enable these vending companies to meet the needs of the customer. Through discussions with J. Sponseller, owner of the Canteen franchise for the state of South Carolina, he realized the problems vending companies were having. They needed to receive their products between 4:00 and 6:00 a.m., and the bakeries could not consistently accommodate them.

An innovative thinker, Sikes spotted an opportunity to meet a need in the marketplace, better serve the vending companies, and go into business for himself. He left the bakery, sold his car, and purchased a half-ton pickup truck. He installed high side panels in the bed of the truck and purchased a canvas tarp to secure the pastries he would then deliver to the vending companies on a timely basis. He made his deliveries on Sunday night so the pastries would be available early Monday morning. In the meantime, Sponseller contacted other vending companies to recommend Sikes' new delivery service. Vendors Supply, Inc. was off and running.

Jim and Greta Sikes.

Says Sikes, "I decided to join the industry as a vend product distributor in 1964. I worked during the day and with my wife, Greta, delivered pastry products in the early mornings to vending operators. My warehouse was my garage and my transportation was an old pickup truck." His first impression of the vending industry was that it had great potential to grow. There were limited products available to operators at the time, but he sensed that the industry would change. He made a decision to play a part in that change.

Ads that promote vending as a career claim a vendor's cash flow begins on day one, as soon as vending machines are in place. Was this true for Vendors Supply, Inc.? Sikes' first week of sales, in June 1964, totaled $1,350. At year end, his new business showed a net profit of $1,353. In the first week of March 1965, his largest customer went bankrupt and Sikes lost all but three dollars of the profits that the company had generated in the first six months. In hindsight, he says, "If I were starting my business in today's environment, I would make sure that I had a fair amount of solid financial resources."

By 1970 the vending industry was creating a business profile of its own, apart from those of the amusement and bottling industries. A new marketing approach was developed that better informed a customer of what vending was and what it provided the consumer. Sikes enjoyed being part of the surge in meeting the need of a new marketplace, despite the challenge in assuring customers of the freshness of the products they were receiving.

Rallying from the company's initial loss, Vendors Supply, Inc. is today a multi-million dollar distribution organization with seven distribution centers. In 1972 the entrepreneurial owner expanded into North Carolina by establishing a branch in Salisbury. In 1978 he expanded again into Tennessee with a branch in Knoxville and into Georgia with a branch in Atlanta. Branches in Petersburg, Virginia and in Cincinnati, Ohio followed in 1986 and 1992 respectively. The company's customer service area now includes Alabama, Georgia, Florida, Indiana, Kentucky, North Carolina, Ohio, Pennsylvania, South Carolina, Tennessee, Virginia, and West Virginia and includes over 200,000 square feet of warehouse space. Sikes

North Carolina office.

credits much of the company's success to God, his loyal employees and excellent customer service.

National vending companies play a smaller part today than they did when Sikes started in business more than 40 years ago. "When I began," he says, "most of them were selling a few pastry products and crackers. There is much more diversity now and a lot more people utilize vending machines."

One of his best selling products, he admits, is sausage biscuits. He explains the reason by asking a question:

South Carolina office of Vendors Supply, Inc.

"Have you noticed what people eat for breakfast these days? I was telling my wife that no one cooks breakfast anymore. People used to wake up and cook a good breakfast. These days, nobody does, so we sell a lot of sausage biscuits, Danish, and other breakfast items. The most amazing part of the business," he says, "is that 82 percent of the products we distribute are sold before 2:00 p.m.," proving his point that many busy people today get their breakfasts from vending machines.

The vending industry has evolved over time. Changes began with glass-front vending machines, which have more slots and versatile pricing mechanisms. Refrigerated machines have also come a long way since their inception. In 2000 Vendors Supply, Inc. took a big step in its development by purchasing a frozen food warehouse facility in Winston-Salem, North Carolina. Refrigerated tractor-trailer trucks have replaced that original pickup truck which allow for the freshest delivery of juices, candy, and sandwiches. "In comparison to fast food or chain stores, the general public now views the vending industry as a provider of a varied selection of products at a very competitive price," says Sikes.

Today, James and Greta Sikes own V. S. Inc., the parent company of

Vendors Supply, Inc. V. S. Inc. has annual sales of between $125 and $140 million and is the second largest food vending distributor in the United Sates. Vendors Supply, Inc. employs 150 full-time workers and approximately 25 part-time workers. James Sikes says he likes to keep a low profile in this "person-to-person" business. He says that in today's market, the greatest challenge is educating employees to best meet the needs of customers. Says Sikes, "I'm not a person who is adverse to change; however, one thing I miss in this industry from the old days is the commitment to a job. Overall in our society today, people aren't as committed to their jobs as they once were." Proud of his company, he says, "In all of these years, I've never laid off one employee."

Jim Sikes is continually aware of the ways the vending industry has changed over time.

"I was plant manager of a bakery when I started," says Sikes. "We used to have wholesale bakeries by the dozens, but not anymore. The problem," he passionately complains, "is that when you do away with availability, prices go up. If more people are selling a certain item, everyone gets a better price. There also used to be a lot of well- known manu-

Ohio location.

facturers, such as Nabisco and General Foods," Sikes explains, "but they have been absorbed by much larger companies. That's another reason prices go up."

Other changes that Sikes has seen include the fact that vending machines have replaced the indoor snack bars that used to be a part of larger companies. Also, when he first started selling pastries, they had to be sold within seven to ten days to ensure freshness. At the time, pastry was packaged in waxed paper. With today's technology in packaging and ingredients, bakery products are good for up to 30 days.

Another factor that has affected the vending marketplace is the country's focus on nutrition. "We used to sell large quantities of fried pies," Sikes says. "Do you remember those? We don't sell many of those anymore because consumers are more health conscious."

Vendors Supply, Inc. is doing extremely well, but like most companies and individuals, the organization is challenged by high gas prices and the cost of insurance. The company's 28 tractor-trailers average six miles per gallon. As for insurance, the cost for 150 full-time employees has become one of the company's greater challenges. But, Vendors Supply, Inc. has a good plan and takes care of its employees.

Always fighting to stay on top and deliver their best, Vendors Supply, Inc. keeps tabs on everything it sells. Keeping track of 180 different manufacturers, their products, and the product sales, allows them to order products as needed and to know how well each product is selling.

In 1996 James Sikes received the prestigious Ernst & Young "Entrepreneur of the Year" award and in 1997 was asked to serve as a "Distinguished Judge" to help select that year's recipient of the same award. Vendors Supply's placement as number 30 among 100 of South

Virginia office.

Carolina's top privately owned companies has, no doubt, served the company well.

James has been married to Greta Sikes for more than 50 years. Their eldest son, Randy, a University of South Carolina graduate who started in the business driving a truck, is now executive vice president. Son-in-law, Ronnie Stokes, who is married to their daughter, Debbie, a school teacher, is vice president of finance. The Sikes' youngest son, Jaye, worked with the company until 1998 as director of sales, and now lives and works in Florida. James and Greta have five grandchildren.

A member of Park Street Baptist Church, where he teaches and is an active participant, Jim Sikes is continually involved in philanthropic causes. For him, the future looks promising. "With your faith in God and good people, good things happen," he says. "The key to success is that you are only as good as your employees."

Tennessee location.

Georgia location.

WILBUR SMITH ASSOCIATES

For more than 50 years, Wilbur Smith Associates (WSA) has been recognized as a leader in transportation and infrastructure engineering and planning services. With approximately 1,100 employees in 60 offices worldwide, this award-winning global consulting firm provides professional services for the development of airports, interstate highways, toll road systems, railways and more. Although its practice has a global reach, WSA has its roots in Columbia, South Carolina, where it is headquartered.

In 1952 Wilbur S. Smith, a South Carolina native who was educated at the University of South Carolina and Harvard University, founded the firm in order to provide transportation planning and traffic engineering services. A visionary in the field of transportation, Wilbur recognized that the rapidly growing popularity of the automobile and the increasing development of suburban areas would lead to an increase in the need for transportation and infrastructure consulting services. Wilbur enlisted the assistance of his brother James M. Smith, a lawyer and FBI agent, to help run the newly founded company.

Initially, Wilbur operated an office based in New Haven, Connecticut, where he was teaching at the Yale Bureau of Highway Traffic. At the same time James established an office in their hometown of Columbia, South Caro-

Wilbur S. Smith

lina. During those early years, Wilbur and James made some creative hiring decisions. They enlisted the help of their wives for typing and clerical services, and Wilbur recruited his students and fellow faculty members to assist him with the firm's first projects. Those initial projects were focused on traffic consulting and roadway planning in the northeastern and southeastern states. To complete the projects, WSA pioneered many processes, procedures and techniques that have since become the standard in transportation planning today.

WSA soon extended its services across the U.S. and branched out into roadway and bridge design services. Although WSA was growing rapidly,

Wilbur wasn't content to remain a regional or even a national firm. From the beginning, Wilbur envisioned that WSA would become a global force in the transportation planning industry. By 1961 that dream became a reality with WSA's first international projects. A transportation plan for the island nation of Ceylon (now Sri Lanka) and the London Transport Study earned international acclaim and led to numerous other projects in major cities around the world.

Through key acquisitions and diversification, WSA moved in several new directions throughout the 1960s and 1970s. The firm expanded its capabilities in aviation, railways, ports and waterways. During this time, WSA also added new services, including municipal engineering, land development, urban and regional planning, economics, environmental planning, architecture, and building systems.

During the 1970s and 1980s WSA underwent a series of organizational and leadership changes. Wilbur took on the roles of chairman and CEO while James was elected president in 1976. In 1981 the firm became a subsidiary of Armco, Inc. of Middletown, Ohio. Just a few years later in 1983 Wilbur retired and James took over as chairman and CEO. By 1986 WSA's leadership determined that the firm could achieve greater success on its own and undertook an initiative to reacquire the firm from Armco through an Employee Stock Option Plan (ESOP).

Although Wilbur retired, his legacy as an innovator and his commitment to providing the highest quality services remained the foundation of the company. James continued to uphold Wilbur's business philosophy until his own retirement in 1985. Today, James's son—and Wilbur's nephew—Stevenson Smith carries on the family legacy. A graduate of the University of South Carolina, Steve joined the family firm in 1973 as an entry-level civil engineer. He held numerous positions with increasing responsibilities within the company before earning the leadership role as Chairman and CEO in 2004. Another family member, Steve's cousin

James Island Expressway

Ken Smith, operates the North Carolina region of WSA. He also graduated with an engineering degree from the University of South Carolina and has been with WSA over 35 years.

Since assuming the leadership role, Steve has continued to build upon WSA's global presence. WSA has been involved with thousands of projects on six continents in more than 120 countries. Among its most noteworthy international projects, WSA provided finance and revenue projections for the Euro Tunnel between France and England. Another award-winning international study was the Hong Kong Electric Road Pricing Feasibility Study. On this project, WSA worked with the Hong Kong Transport Department to evaluate and test electronic road pricing options. For the award-winning Latin America Trade and Transportation Study, WSA was retained by 13 southeastern states and Puerto Rico to evaluate the potential for increased trade with Latin America.

The firm continues to expand its international reach and currently maintains offices in China, India, Saudi Arabia, the United Arab Emirates (UAE), Bangladesh, and Thailand. The UAE office in Dubai counts as one of the firm's fastest-growing locations. Increased development activity in that region has created a high demand for infrastructure consulting. To satisfy those needs, the Dubai office, which currently boasts about 100 employees, is expected to quadruple in size in the coming years.

Although its international presence is growing rapidly, WSA continues to have a major impact in the U.S. and in the local region as well. Noteworthy U.S. projects include the redesign of 2.5 miles of I-40 through urban Knoxville, known as the SmartFix 40, one of the most dangerous stretches of interstate in the country. Other high profile projects include converting the Minneapolis I-394's HOV lanes to express toll lanes, and a light rail transit project in Salt Lake City linking the city with the West Valley community.

Among its many projects that have served to improve transportation and

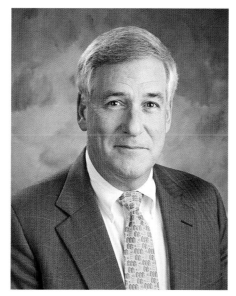

M. Stevenson Smith

traffic conditions in its home state of South Carolina are the James Island Expressway bridge in Charleston and improvements to I-85, one of the heaviest traveled routes in the state of South Carolina, which includes upgrades to the Greenville/Spartanburg Airport and a new directional interchange to serve the BMW manufacturing plant in Spartanburg County. The firm is also currently conducting an environmental

and corridor study for the South Carolina segment of the Michigan to SC I-73 corridor, a new interstate that will serve the north coast of South Carolina with access to I-95 and continuing into North Carolina and Virginia.

WSA's impact on the local community goes far beyond its transportation services. Striving to be a good corporate citizen, WSA has consistently made donations to local and national charitable organizations. The firm enhanced its corporate giving by creating its "Our Family Helping Families" program. This program allows employees in WSA offices around the nation to help determine which local charities will receive theirs and company contributions.

Just as WSA's charitable contributions expand, so do its contributions to the transportation and infrastructure engineering and planning sector. As the region, the nation, and the world continue to move forward with expanded development activity, WSA moves with them to meet their growing needs. As demand for its services increases, WSA is expected to keep pace by doubling in size within the next five years.

Hong Kong Electric Road Pricing

In 1954 Frank Selvy playing for Furman
University in Textile Hall in Greenville
scored 100 points in a game against
Newberry College. After graduation from
Furman, he played professional basketball
before returning to coach at his alma mater.
Courtesy, Furman University

Founded in 1797, downtown Greenville is
the center of one of the major metropolitan
areas in the state. Since the 1970s Main
Street and the West End have been
revitalized and become a center for the arts,
entertainment, and dining. Courtesy,
Square D Photographers

Celebration on Hilton Head Island.
Residential development began on the
island shortly after World War II.
Photo by McKenzie and Dickerson

At a Tuberculosis International Conference
in Paris in 1887, Summerville was cited as a
healthful place for sufferers of lung disorders.
Shortly thereafter Captain F.W. Wagener
and other businessmen built this plush
resort hotel, the Pine Forest Inn, there.
Courtesy, Library of Congress

A TIMELINE OF SOUTH CAROLINA HISTORY

1521
Lucas Vasquez de Allyon's expedition reached the coast, perhaps Winyah Bay. **1525** Settlement established at San Miguel, once thought to be on Winyah Bay, more likely on the Georgia coast.
1540
Hernando de Soto crossed the Savannah River at Silver Bluff and visited a Native American settlement on the Wateree River.
1562
Jean Ribaut established a French settlement, Charlesfort, on Parris Island.
1566
Pedro Menendez de Aviles established Santa Elena on Parris Island as the capital of Spanish Florida. The Spanish abandoned it in 1587.
1629
Charles I of England granted Sir Robert Heath a patent for Carolana. No permanent settlement resulted.
1663
Charles II granted a charter for Carolina to eight Lords Proprietors. Planters from Barbados sent William Hilton to explore the Carolina coast. A second charter in 1665 expanded the original grant.

Modern reconstruction of the palisade surrounding the original site of Charles Town in 1670. Courtesy, A. V. Huff, Jr

1669
Under the leadership of Anthony Ashley Cooper, the proprietors launched an expedition to settle the new colony. Enslaved Africans were among the first settlers.
1670
First permanent settlement on the Ashley River named Charles Town. In 1680 Charles Town relocated to Oyster Point between the Ashley and Cooper rivers.
1685
In France Louis XIV revoked the Edict of Nantes, and Huguenots began to

Allyon's expedition reached the South Carolina coast in 1521, perhaps at Winyah Bay near Georgetown. Courtesy, A. V. Huff, Jr

settle in Carolina. That same year a rice crop was first planted.
1702
Carolinians attacked the Spanish in St. Augustine, followed by a Spanish attack on Charles Town in 1706.
1708
Enslaved Africans outnumbered European settlers for the first time.
1712
Carolinians attacked the Tuscarora Indians in present-day North Carolina. In 1715 the Yemassees threatened the colony.
1718
Colonel William Rhett captured the pirate Stede Bonnet.
1719
Revolt against the proprietors.
1729
South Carolina became a royal province.
1730
Governor Robert Johnson proposed the creation of a series of townships to attract more settlers and protect coastal plantations from attack, known as Governor Robert Johnson's township scheme.

245

1739
Stono Rebellion followed by passage of the Negro Act of 1740.
1741
First indigo crop grown by Eliza Lucas Pinckney.
1753
Construction of Fort Prince George
1754
Scotch-Irish began moving into the Back Country
1759–1761
Cherokee War.
1762
Gadsden Election Controversy.
1767
Regulator Movement began; Circuit Court Act passed in 1768.
1765
Protests against the Stamp Act in Charles Town; South Carolina sent delegates to the Stamp Act Congress in New York.
1769
Commons House voted to support the Wilkes Fund.
1773
General Meeting in Charles Town to protest the Tea Act.
1774
South Carolina sent delegates to the First Continental Congress in Philadelphia.
1775
First Provincial Congress met; Royal governor William Campbell fled.
1776
Second Provincial Congress met and drew up the Constitution of 1776; British fleet attacked Fort Moultrie; South Carolina delegates voted for independence in Philadelphia.
1780
British took Charles Town; partisan militia formed to defend the state; British defeated the Americans at Camden; American militia defeated Loyalists at Kings Mountain.
1781
American forces won the battle of Cowpens.
1782
South Carolina legislature met at Jacksonborough; British evacuated Charles Town.
1787
South Carolina delegates attended the

The monument at Purrysburg on the Savannah River marks the site of the town laid out as part of Governor Robert Johnson's township scheme of 1730. Courtesy, A. V. Huff, Jr

Constitutional Convention; the state ratified the Constitution in 1788.
1786
Columbia became the state capital.
1790
State convention adopted the Constitution of 1790.
1791
President Washington visited South Carolina.
1800
South Carolina support for Jefferson

tipped the election to the Republicans.
1793
Eli Whitney's invention of the cotton gin made short-staple cotton a major crop in South Carolina.
1801
South Carolina College chartered by the state legislature.
1808
The Compromise of 1808 provided the upcountry with greater political power in the state legislature.
1819
The economic Panic of 1819 saw the rapid fall of agricultural prices in South Carolina; many planters and farmers moved to the new states of the south-

west; the legislature approved a program of internal improvements—canal and road-building.

1822
The threatened Denmark Vesey slave insurrection forced the legislature to tighten laws governing free blacks as well as slaves.

1824
Native son John C. Calhoun was elected vice president; in 1828 South Carolina native Andrew Jackson became president.

1828–1832
The Tariff of 1828 prompted the state's leaders to threaten and then adopt nullification as a way to assert the state's right of opposing a federal law it disapproved.

1830
South Carolina Railroad made its first run.

1845
William Gregg championed southern textile mills; he opened Graniteville Mill as a model.

1856
In the debates over expanding slavery into the western territories, Congressman Preston Brooks caned Senator

---

The invention of the cotton gin by Eli Whitney in 1793 made possible the cultivation of short-staple cotton across much of South Carolina. This cotton gin is on exhibit at the South Carolina State Museum. Courtesy, A. V. Huff, Jr

Charles Sumner of Massachusetts.

1860
After the election of Abraham Lincoln, South Carolina was the first state to secede from the Union.

1861
Confederate forces fired on Fort Sumter in Charleston Harbor, thus beginning the Civil War.

1865
General William T. Sherman's Union army invaded South Carolina; Columbia was burned; the Confederate armies surrendered; and the war was over. The Thirteenth Amendment ended slavery.

1866
Dexter E. Converse opened the Converse textile mill at Glendale, beginning the era of cotton textile manufacturing in South Carolina.

1867
Congressional Reconstruction began in the Southern states; South Carolina was put under military rule.

1868
The Reconstruction state government enacted the progressive Constitution of 1868.

Colleges for black students opened during Reconstruction—Claflin, Benedict, Allen.

1876
In a disputed election former Confederate general Wade Hampton III became governor with the support of Republican president Rutherford B. Hayes.

The Great Hall of the Exchange Building in Charleston was the site of many meetings leading up to and during the American Revolution. Courtesy, A. V. Huff, Jr

The Civil War began in Charleston Harbor on April 12, 1861 when Confederate batteries opened fire on Fort Sumter. Courtesy, A. V. Huff, Jr

The Confederate flag flying over the State House in Columbia was removed to the Confederate Monument in 2000. Courtesy, A. V. Huff, Jr

1885
Benjamin R. Tillman began the Farmers Movement with a speech in Bennettsville.
1889
Clemson Agricultural and Mechanical College chartered by the legislature.
1890
Tillman was elected governor.

Bright leaf tobacco introduced into the state by Frank M. Rogers
1895
The state constitution adopted which discriminated against African American voters and legally established racial segregation.
1896
S.C. State College opened in Orangeburg.
1914
Richard I. Manning elected governor.
1917–1918
Over 64,000 South Carolinians served in World War I.

The boll weevil entered the state.
1920s
Agricultural depression began in South Carolina.

Reappearance of the Ku Klux Klan.
1924
"Pay As You Go" Highway Act 6-0-1 Act.
1933
Franklin D. Roosevelt became president. The New Deal began.
1941–1945

One hundred and seventy thousand South Carolinians served in World War II.

James F. Byrnes became known as "Assistant President."
1947
Federal judge J. Waites Waring ordered the end of the white primary in South Carolina.
1948
Governor Strom Thurmond ran for president as a Dixiecrat.
1950
Clarendon County parents filed a federal suit challenging school segregation in *Briggs v. Elliott*. The case went to the U. S. Supreme Court as part of *Brown v. Board of Education*.
1962
Technical Education Act.
1964
South Carolina voted for a Republican, Barry Goldwater, for president for the first time since Reconstruction.
1968
Orangeburg Massacre.
1970
Public schools totally integrated by court order.

John West defeated Albert Watson for governor.
1971
Revision of the 1895 state constitution began.
1974
James B. Edwards elected first Republican governor since Reconstruction.
1979
Nancy Stevenson elected first women lieutenant governor.

1983
African American I. D. Newman elected to the state Senate.
1984
Education Improvement Act.
1989
Operation Lost Trust.

Hurricane Hugo ravaged the coast from Charleston to Myrtle Beach and inland as far north as Rock Hill.
1993
Government Reorganization Act.
1994
Ernest A. Finney, Jr. elected first African American chief justice of the State Supreme Court.

Republicans won control of the House of Representatives; David Wilkins elected speaker.
2000
Compromise over the Confederate flag adopted.

Jean H. Toal elected first woman chief justice of the State Supreme Court.

Republicans won control of the Senate.
2003
Congress created Congaree National Park, the only national park in South Carolina. Originally a national monument (1967), it contains the largest stand of old-growth, bottomland hardwood in the United States.
2006
Governor Mark Sanford elected to a second term.

Looking North on Main Street, Post Office at right, Sumter, South Carolina.

BIBLIOGRAPHY

In limiting these selections we have tried to give the reader a brief but fair sample of literature on the state's history. Some are brief and light; some are primarily pictorial and of a local nature; some are memoirs of South Carolinians; some are detailed works of scholarship; however, all are commendable for their ring of authenticity.

Ackerman, Robert C. *Wade Hampton III.* Columbia, SC: University of South Carolina Press, 2007

Ashmore, Nancy V. *Greenville, Woven from the Past: An Illustrated History.* Sun Valley, Cal.: American Historical Press.

Badders, Hurley E. *Anderson County: A Pictorial History.* Norfolk: The Donning Company, 1983.

Ball, William Watts. *The State That Forgot: South Carolina's Surrender to Democracy.* Indianapolis: Bobbs-Merrill Company, 1932.

Bass, Jack. *Porgy Comes Home: South Carolina . . . After 300 Years.* Columbia: R.L. Bryan Company, 1972.

Bass, Robert D. *Gamecock: The Life and Campaigns of General Thomas Sumter.* New York: Holt, Rinehart and Winston, 1961.

———. *Swamp Fox: The Life and Campaigns of General Francis Marion.* New York: Henry Holt and Company, 1959.

Bleser, Carol, ed. *The Hammonds of Redcliffe.* New York: Oxford University Press, 1981.

Brown, Richard Maxwell. *The South Carolina Regulators.* Cambridge, Mass.: Belknap Press, 1963.

Byrnes, James F. *All in One Lifetime.* New York: Harper and Brothers, 1958.

Capers, Gerald D. *John C. Calhoun—Opportunist: A Reappraisal.* Gainesville: University of Florida Press, 1960.

Carlton, David L. *Mill and Town in South Carolina, 1880–1920.* Baton Rouge: Louisiana State University Press, 1982.

Channing, Steven. *Crisis of Fear: Secession in South Carolina.* New York: Simon and Schuster, 1970.

Clark, E. Culpepper. *Francis Warrington Dawson and the Politics of Restora-tion: South Carolina, 1874–1889.* University, Ala.: University of Alabama Press, 1980.

Clowse, Converse D. *Economic Beginnings in Colonial South Carolina, 1670–1730.* Columbia: University of South Carolina Press, 1971.

Coit, Margaret L. *John C. Calhoun: American Portrait.* Boston: Houghton Mifflin Company, 1950.

Cooper, William J., Jr. *The Conservative Regime: South Carolina, 1877–1890.* Baltimore, Md.: The Johns Hopkins Press, 1968.

Davidson, Chalmers G. *The Last Foray: The South Carolina Planters of 1860: A Sociological Study.* Columbia: University of South Carolina Press, 1971.

Edgar, Walter B. *South Carolina: A History.* Columbia, SC: University of South Carolina Press, 1998

Edgar, Walter B., editor. *South Carolina Encyclopedia.* Columbia, SC: University of South Carolina Press, 2006

Eleazer, J.M. *A Dutch Fork Farm Boy.* Columbia: University of South Carolina Press, 1952.

Faust, Drew. *James Henry Hammond and the Old South: A Design for Mastery.* Baton Rouge: Louisiana State University Press, 1982.

Fields, Mamie Garvin, with Karen Fields. *Lemon Swamp and Other Places: A Carolina Memoir.* New York: Free Press, 1983.

Fite, Gilbert C. *Cotton Fields No More: Southern Agriculture, 1865–1980.* Lexington: University Press of Kentucky, 1984.

Freehling, William W. *Prelude to Civil War: The Nullification Controversy in South Carolina, 1816–1836.* New York: Harper and Row, 1965.

Graydon, Nell S. *Tales of Beaufort.* Beaufort, S.C.: Beaufort Book Shop, 1963.

———. *Tales of Columbia.* Columbia, S.C.: R.L. Bryan Company, 1964.

———. *Tales of Edisto.* Atlanta, Ga.: Tupper and Love, 1960.

Heyward, Duncan C. *Seed from Madaga-car.* Chapel Hill: University of North Carolina Press, 1937.

Hollis, Daniel W. *University of South Carolina.* 2 vols. Columbia: University of South Carolina Press, 1951, 1956.

Holt, Thomas. *Black Over White: Negro Political Leadership in South Carolina During Reconstruction.* Urbana: University of Illinois Press, 1977.

Jarrell, Hampton M. *Wade Hampton and the Negro: The Road Not Taken.* Columbia: University of South Carolina Press, 1949.

Johnson, Michael, and James L. Roark. *Black Masters: A Free Family of Color in the Old South.* New York: W.W. Norton and Company, 1984.

Joyner, Charles. *Down by the Riverside: A South Carolina Slave Community.* Urbana: University of Illinois Press, 1984.

Julien, Carl, and James M. Dabbs. *Pee Dee Panorama.* Columbia: University of South Carolina Press, 1951.

Julien, Carl, and C.R. Martin. *Sea Islands to Sand Hills.* Columbia: University of South Carolina Press, 1955.

Julien, Carl, and C j. Milling. *Beneath So Kind a Sky: The Scene and Architectural Beauty of South Carolina.* Columbia: University of South Carolina Press, 1947.

Julien, Carl, and H.L. Watson. *Ninety Six: Landmarks of South Carolina's Last Frontier Region.* Columbia: University of South Carolina Press, 1950.

Kibler, Lillian A. *Benjamin F. Perry, South Carolina Unionist.* Durham, N.C.: Duke University Press, 1946.

Kohn, August. *The Cotton Mills of South Carolina.* Columbia: State Department of Agriculture, 1907.

Lambert, Robert S. *South Carolina Loyalists in the American Revolution.* Columbia: University of South Carolina Press, 1987.

Lander, Ernest M., Jr. *The Calhoun Family and Thomas Green Clemson: The Decline of a Southern Patriarchy.* Columbia: University of South Carolina Press, 1983.

———. *A History of South Carolina,*

1865–1960. 2nd edition. Columbia: University of South Carolina Press, 1970.

———. *Reluctant Imperialists: Calhoun, the South Carolinians, and the Mexican War*. Baton Rouge: Louisiana State University Press, 1980.

———. *The Textile Industry in Antebellum South Carolina*. Baton Rouge: Louisiana State University Press, 1969.

Lane, Mills. *Architecture of the Old South: South Carolina*. Savannah, Ga.: Beehive Press, 1984.

Lippy, Charles H., editor. *Religion in South Carolina*. Columbia, SC: University of South Carolina Press, 1993

Lumpkin, Henry. *From Savannah to Yorktown: The American Revolution in the South*. Columbia: University of South Carolina Press, 1981.

Maxey, Russell. *South Carolina's Historic Columbia, Yesterday and Today in Photographs*. Columbia: RL. Bryan Company, 1980.

McCoin, Choice. *Greenville County: A Pictorial History*. Norfolk, Va.: The Donning Company, 1983.

McGee, Charles M., Jr., and Ernest M. Lander, Jr. *A Rebel Came Home: The (Civil War) Diary of Floride Clemson, 1863–1866*. Columbia: University of South Carolina Press, 1961.

McMillan, Lewis K. *Negro Higher Education in the State of South Carolina*. Privately published, 1952.

Newby, Idus A. *Black Carolinians: A History of Blacks in South Carolina from 1895 to 1968*. Columbia: University of South Carolina Press, 1973.

Racine, Philip N. *Spartanburg County: A Pictorial History*. Virginia Beach, Va.: The Donning Company, 1980.

Rankin, Hugh F. *Francis Marion: The Swamp Fox*. New York: Crowell, 1973.

Rice, John A. *I Came Out of the Eighteenth Century*. New York: Harper and Brothers, 1942.

Robertson, Ben. *Red Hills and Cotton: An Upcountry Memory*. Columbia: University of South Carolina Press, 1960.

Rogers, George C. *Charleston in the Age of the Pinckneys*. Columbia: University of South Carolina Press, 1980.

Rogers, George C., Jr. and C. James Taylor, *A South Carolina Chronology, 1497–1992*. 2nd edition. Columbia, SC: University of South Carolina Press, 1994.

Savage, Henry, Jr. *River of the Carolinas: The Santee*. New York: Rinehart and Company, 1956.

Schaper, William A. *Sectionalism and Representation in South Carolina*. Reprint edition. New York: DaCapo Press, 1968.

Simkins, Francis B. *Pitchfork Ben Tillman, South Carolinian*. Baton Rouge: Louisiana State University Press, 1944.

Simkins, Francis B., and Robert H. Woody. *South Carolina During Reconstruction*. Chapel Hill: University of North Carolina Press, 1932.

Simians, M. Eugene. *Colonial South Carolina: A Political History, 1663–1763*. Chapel Hill: University of North Carolina Press, 1966.

Smith, Alfred G. *Economic Readjustment of an Old Cotton State: South Carolina, 1820–1860*. Columbia: University of South Carolina Press, 1958.

Stokes, Thomas L. *The Savannah*. New York: Rinehart and Company, 1951.

Stoney, Samuel G. *Plantations of the Carolina Low County*. Charleston, S.C.: Carolina Art Association, 1938.

Taylor, Rosser H. *Antebellum South Carolina: A Social and Cultural History*. Chapel Hill: University of North Carolina Press, 1942.

Tindall, George B. *South Carolina Negroes, 1877–1900*. Columbia: University of South Carolina Press, 1952.

VerSteeg, Clarence L. *Origins of a Southern Mosaic: Studies of Early Carolina and Georgia*. Athens: University of Georgia Press, 1975.

Wallace, David D. *South Carolina: A Short History, 1520–1948*. Columbia: University of South Carolina Press, 1961.

Weir, Robert M. *Colonial South Carolina: A History*. Millwood, N.Y.: KTO Press, 1983.

Whitelaw, Robert N.S., and Alice F. Levikoff. *Charleston: Come Hell or High Water*. Columbia, S.C.: R.L. Bryan Company, 1975.

Wikramanayake, Marina. *A World of Shadow: The Free Black in Antebellum South Carolina*. Columbia: University of South Carolina Press, 1973.

Williamson, Joel. *After Slavery: The Negro in South Carolina During Reconstruction*. Chapel Hill: University of North Carolina Press, 1965.

Wood, Peter. *Black Majority: Negroes in Colonial South Carolina from 1670 Through the Stono Rebellion*. New York: Alfred A. Knopf, 1974.

Workman, William D., Jr. *The Bishop from Barnwell: **The** Political Life and Times of Edgar A. Brown*. Privately published, 1963.

Zahniser, Marvin R. *Charles Cotesworth Pinckney, Founding Father*. Chapel Hill: University of North Carolina Press, 1967.

INDEX